OWNER'S RE[PAIR GUIDE]
MITSU[BISHI]
SPACE W[AGON]

1.8 LITRE PETROL ENGINE
1.8 LITRE TURBO DIESEL ENGINE
ALL MODELS — FROM 1985 TO 1989

GW00722359

COVERING:

BY PETER RUSSEK

Published by
Peter Russek Publications Ltd.
Little Stone House, High Street,
Marlow, Bucks.
Tel.: High Wycombe (0494) 440829

ISBN NO.   0 - 907779 - 81-6

WITH FAULT FINDING SECTION
AT END OF MANUAL

The publisher would like to thank the Colt Car Company Limited for their co-operation in producing this manual.

Printed in England

PREFACE

Small though this Workshop Manual is in size, it lacks no detail in covering the whole of the servicing and repair of the Mitsubishi Space Wagon since introduction, both with 1.8 litre petrol and turbo diesel engine. Brief, easy-to-follow instructions are given, free from all necessary complication and repetition, yet containing all the required technical detail and information, and many diagrams and illustrations.

Compiled and illustrated by experts, this manual provides a concise source of helpful information, all of which has been cross-checked for accuracy to the manufacturer's official service and repair procedures, but many instructions have derived from actual practice to facilitate your work. Where special tools are required, these are identified in the text if absolutely necessary and we do not hesitate to advise you if we feel that the operation cannot be properly undertaken without the use of such tools.

The readers own judgement must ultimately decide just what work he will feel able to undertake, but there is no doubt, that with this manual to assist him, there will be many more occasions where the delay, inconvenience and the cost of having the car off the road can be avoided or minimised.

The manual is called "Owner's Repair Guide" with the aim that it should be kept in the vehicle whilst you are travelling. Many garage mechanics themselves use these publications in their work and if you have the manual with you in the car you will have an invaluable source of reference which will quickly repay its modest initial cost.

A fault finding (trouble shooting) section is included at the end of the manual and all items listed are taken from actual experience, together with the necessary remedies to correct faults and malfunctioning of certain parts.

0.   GENERAL INFORMATION

0.0.   Introduction

The models covered in this publication is the Mitsubishi Space Wagon, fitted with a 1800 c.c. petrol or turbo diesel engine. The petrol engine is of the type 4G37, similar to the "G3" series engines fitted to other Mitsubishi vehicles. A "4G65" diesel engine with turbo charger is used in the other version.

The Space Wagon is a conventional front-wheel drive vehicle, with a transversely fitted engine.

Both engine types are fitted with an overhead camshaft, driven by a toothed belt from the crankshaft. The oil pump is fitted to the front housing and is driven from the engine timing belt. The cylinder head is made of aluminium alloy and has semi- spherical combustion chambers. Solid-skirt pistons of alloy material and a five-bearing crankshaft are fitted.

The engine is fitted with two balance shafts to obtain a vibration-free running.

The transmission is fitted below the engine. Either a five-speed transmission or a three-speed automatic transmission can be fitted to both variants.

The front suspension consists of McPherson struts with integral hydraulic shock absorbers, coil springs, reaction rods and a stabiliser bar, also known as anti-roll bar. Coil springs and hydraulic shock absorbers are also used for the rear suspension. The rear suspension arms are attached at their outer ends to a centre axle tube.

A rack and pinion steering is fitted. Disc brakes at the front and self-adjusting drum brakes at the rear, together with a dual-line braking system and a brake servo make up the brake system.

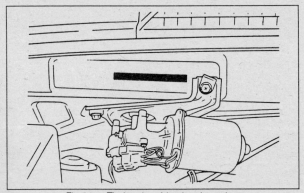

Fig. 0.1. — The location of the chassis number.

0.1   Vehicle Identification

A vehicle can be identified by the following type identification plates:

Chassis Number: The chassis number is stamped into the centre of the engine compartment bulk head, as shown in Fig. 0.1. Vehicle model, engine type, transmission type and model year are contained in this type identification plate. The fifth letter indicates that the vehicle is a Space Wagon (D), followed by either "05" (petrol engine) or "08" (diesel engine). The letter "W" (wagon) is next, followed by the code letter for the model year (for example "G" for 1986). The type of transmission fitted is shown by either the letter "N" (five-speed transmission) or "K" (automatic transmission). The following numbers are the actual chassis number.

Vehicle Information Code Plate: This plate is riveted to the front end of the L.H. wheel house inner panel. The plate shows the model code, engine type, transmission type and the body colour code.

Engine Number: The engine number of a petrol engine is stamped into the R.H. front side on the top edge of the cylinder block, visible from above and its location is shown in Fig. 0.3. Fig. 0.4 shows where the number of a diesel engine is located.

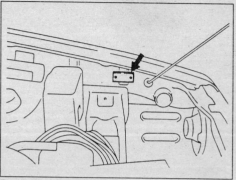

The serial number always commenced with the engine type.

Further identification numbers are stamped into the upper part of the transmission. The transmission serial number returns from 99999 to 00101 and the letter changes in their alphabetical order.

These numbers and codes are important when ordering replacement

Fig. 0.2. The location of the vehicle information code plate. The plate is on the R.H. side on models other than for Europe.

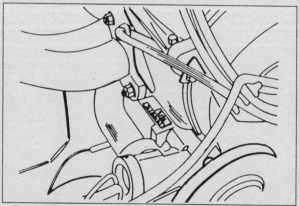

Fig. 0.3. — The location of the engine number when a petrol engine is fitted.

parts and should always be quoted. Your Dealer will only be in a position to supply you with the correct part if he is able to identify your particular model.

0.2.   Dimensions and Weights

Overall Length: . . . . 4295 mm (169.1 in.)
Overall Width: . . . . 1640 mm (64.6 in.)

5

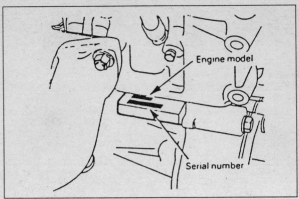

Fig. 0.4. — The location of the engine number of the diesel engine.

Overall height: . . . . 1525 mm (60.0 in.)

Wheelbase: . . . . 2625 mm (103.3 in.)

Front Track: . . . . 1410 mm (55.5 in.)
Rear Track: . . . . 1375 mm (54.1 in.)
Ground clearance: . . . . 150 mm (5.9 in.)

Weights
Kerb weight:
   Petrol model . . . . 1095 - 1145 kg (2414 - 2524 lbs.)
   Diesel model: . . . . 1170 - 1220 kg (2579 - 2690 lbs.)
Max. gross vehicle weight:
   Petrol model: . . . . 1690 kg (3726 lbs.)
   Diesel model: . . . . 1745 kg (3847 lbs.)

0.3.　　Capacities

Fuel Tank: . . . . 50 litres (11 Imp. galls.)
Cooling system: . . . . 6.0 litre (10.7 Imp. pts.)
   Expansion tank: . . . . 0.65 litre (approx. 1 pint)
   Engine oil cooler: . . . . 0.25 litres (approx. 0.5 pints)
   Oil cooler for automatic transmission: . . . . 0.5 litre (approx. 1 pint)
Engine oil — Petrol Engine:
   After engine overhaul: . . . . 4.2 litres (7.5 Imp. pts.)
   Oil change with filter: . . . . 4.0 litres (7.14 Imp. pts.), 3.9 litres from 1989 model
   Oil change without filter: . . . . 3.5 litres (6.25 Imp. pts.)
Engine Oil — Turbo Diesel:
   After engine overhaul: . . . . 5.6 litres (9.8 Imp. pts.), 6.0 litre (10.6 Imp. pts.) from 1989 model
   Oil change with filter: . . . . 5.6 litres (9.8 Imp. pts.), 6.0 litres (10.6 Imp. pts.) from 1989 model
   Oil change without filter: . . . . 5.0 litres (8.8 Imp. pts.), 5.2 litres (9.2 Imp. pts.) from 1989 model
   Oil filter capacity: . . . . 0.8 litres (approx. 1 ¼ Imp. pts.)
Manual transmission:
   Petrol model: . . . . 2.1 litres (3.6 Imp. pts.)
   Diesel model: . . . . 2.3 litres (4.1 Imp. pts.)
   Petrol and diesel models from 1988: . . . . 2.5 litres (4.4 Imp. pts.)
Automatic transmission: . . . . 5.8 litres (10.2 Imp. pts.)
Power assisted steering: . . . . 975 c.c. (1.8 Imp. pts.)

0.4.   General Servicing Notes

The servicing and overhaul instructions in this Workshop Manual are laid out in an easy-to-follow step-by-step fashion and no difficulty should be encountered if the text and diagrams are followed carefully and methodically. The "Technical Data" sections form an important part of the repair procedures and should always be referred to during work on the vehicle.

In order that we can include as much data as possible, you will find that we do not generally repeat in the text the values already given under the technical data headings. Again, to make the best use of the space available, we do not repeat at each operation the more obvious steps necessary — we feel it to be far more helpful to concentrate on the difficult or awkward procedures in greater detail. However, we summarise below a few of the more important procedures and draw your attention to various points of general interest that apply to all operations.

Always use the torque settings given in the end of most of the sections.

Bolts and nuts should be assembled in a clean and very lightly oiled condition and faces and threads should always be inspected to make sure that they are free from damage, burrs or scoring. DO NOT degrease bolts or nuts.

All joint washers, gaskets, tabs and lock washers, split pins and "O" rings must be replaced on assembly. Oil seals will, in all cases, also need to be replaced, if the shaft and seal have been separated. Always lubricate the lip of the seal before assembly and take care that the seal lip is facing the correct direction.

References to the left-hand and right-hand sides are always to be taken as if the observer is at the rear of the car, facing forwards, unless otherwise stated.

Always make sure that the vehicle is adequately supported, and on firm ground, before commencing any work on the underside of the car. A small jack or a make shift prop can be highly dangerous and proper axle stands are an essential requirement for your own safety.

Dirt, grease and mineral oil will rapidly destroy the seals of the hydraulic system and even the smallest amounts must be prevented from entering the system or coming into contact with the components. Use clean brake fluid or one of the proprietory cleaners to wash the hydraulic system parts. An acceptable alternative cleaner is methylated spirit, but if this is used, it should not be allowed to remain in contact with the rubber parts for longer than necessary. It is also important that all traces of the fluid should be removed from the system before final assembly.

Always use genuine manufacturer's spares and replacements for the best results.

Since the manufacturer uses metric units when building the cars it is recommended that these are used for all precise units. Inch conversions are given in most cases but these are not necessarily precise conversions, being rounded off for the unimportant values.

Removal and installation instructions, in this Workshop Manual, cover the steps to take away or put back the unit or part in question. Other instructions, usually headed "Servicing", will cover the dismantling and repair of the unit once it has been stripped from the vehicle. It is pointed out that the major instructions cover a complete overhaul of all parts but, obviously, this will not always be either necessary and should not be carried out needlessly.

There are a number of variations in unit parts on the range of vehicles covered in this Workshop Manual. We strongly recommend that you take care to identify the precise model, and the year of manufacture, before obtaining any spares or replacement parts.

The following abbreviations are sometimes used in the text and should be noted:

Std.:	To indicate sizes and limits of components as supplied by the manufacturer. Also to indicate the production tolerances of new unused parts.
O/S U/S:	Parts supplied as Oversize or Undersize, or recommended limits for such parts, to enable them to be used with worn or re-machined mating parts. O/S indicates a part that is larger than Std. size. U/S may indicate a bore of a bushing or female part that is smaller than Std.

Max.:	Where given against a clearance or dimension indicates the maximum allowable. If in excess of the value given it is recommended that the appropriate part is fitted.
TIR:	Indicates the Total Indicator Reading as shown by a dial indicator (dial gauge).
HT:	High Tension (ignition) wiring or terminals.
TDC:	Top Dead Centre (No. 1 piston on firing stroke).
MP:	Multi-Purpose grease.

0.5.   Jacking up the Vehicle

Due to the construction of the vehicle, a jack and/or chassis stands should only be placed under the vehicle at certain position. These are shown in Fig. 0.5.

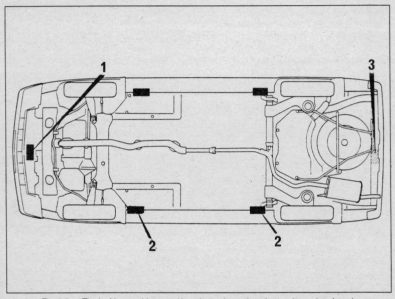

Fig. 0.5. — The jacking positions and locations where chassis stands can be placed.
1. Jacking position at front   2. Jacking position at side or chassis stands   3. Jacking position at rear

To jack up the front of the vehicle, place a mobile jack underneath the front suspension crossmember, as shown by "1" in the illustration. A piece of rubber or other soft material should be inserted between crossmember and jack head to prevent damage. Apply the handbrake or chock the rear wheels to add safety to the operation.

To jack up the rear end of the vehicle, place the jack underneath the position "3" in the illustration. Again use a piece of soft material between jack head and the jack location. The front wheels should be chocked (for example a brick) or a gear engaged to prevent the vehicle from rolling off the jack.

Always use secure chassis stands when working underneath the vehicle. Fig. 0.5 shows with "2" where chassis stands can be located.

Before any jacking operation, check the condition of the ground to make sure the jack or the chassis stands cannot "sink" into the ground.

1. PETROL ENGINE

1.0. Main Features

NOTE: The Turbo Diesel Engine is covered separately at the end of the manual (Section 15).

Engine Identification: 4G37
Number and arrangement of cylinders: . . . . 4, in-line
Arrangement of camshaft: . . . . In cylinder head (OHC)
Camshaft drive: . . . . Toothed timing belt

Engine Capacity: . . . . 1755 ccm

Cylinder Bore: . . . . 80.6 mm (3.17 in.)
Piston stroke: . . . . 86.0 mm (3.39 in.)
Compression ratio: . . . . 9.5 : 1

Max. Performance: . . . . 89.9 HP at 5500 rpm
Max. Torque: . . . . 13.7 kgm (98.5 ft.lb.) at 3500 rpm

Compression Pressures at 250 rpm: . . . . 13.5 kg/sq. cm. (192 psi.)
Min. compression pressure at 250 rpm: . . . . 12.0 kg/sq.cm. (171 psi.)

Firing order: . . . . 1 — 3 — 4 — 2

Valve Clearances (engine warm):
  Inlet valves: . . . . 0.15 mm (0.006 in.)
  Exhaust valves: . . . . 0.25 mm (0.010 in.)
Valve Clearances (cold):
  Inlet valves: . . . . 0.07 mm (0.003 in.)
  Exhaust valves: . . . . 0.18 mm (0.007 in.)

Ignition timing: . . . . 13° before T.D.C. at idling speed

Oil pump type: . . . . Gear-type pump
Oil sump capacity: . . . . See Section 0.3
Carburettor: . . . . Two-stage downdraught carburettor
Ignition distributor: . . . . With electronic ignition

1.1 Engine — Removal and Installation

The engine is removed together with the transmission. Read section 0.5 before jacking up the front of the vehicle for operations to be carried out from underneath.

- Open the bonnet. Mark the outline of the bonnet panel (using a pencil) and unscrew the bonnet from the hinges. This will give greater freedom of movement and will prevent damage to the bonnet paint work. Lift off the bonnet and store it in a safe place.
- Drain the cooling system. A drain plug is fitted to the bottom of the radiator. A further plug is fitted into the R.H. side at the rear of the cylinder block.
- Disconnect the battery and complete remove the battery. Also remove the battery carrier. One bolt is fitted from the top, one from the side.
- Drain the fluid from the power steering system as described in the relevant section.
- Disconnect the inlet and the outlet hoses for the heating system at the engine side after slackening of the hose clamps. Tight hoses can be removed by turning them to and fro — not by pulling them off.
- Remove the air cleaner and lift off the engine. Immediately cover the opening of the carburettor opening to prevent entry of foreign matter.

- Disconnect the vacuum hose from the brake servo unit connection.
- If an automatic transmission is fitted, disconnect the hoses from the oil cooler. Mark the hoses in suitable manner to prevent mistakes during installation. Be careful not to spill any of the oil or fluid out of the hoses. Arrange the hose ends with the open sides upwards and tie them in position.
- Remove the cooling system expansion tank and the windscreen washer reservoir.
- Disconnect the hoses from the upper and lower radiator connections after slackening the hose clamps (Fig. 1.1), remove the radiator mounting bolts and lift out the radiator.

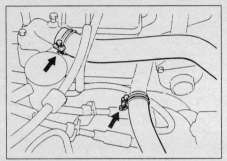

Fig. 1.1.—The arrows show the connections of the two hoses on the radiator.

- If a manual transmission is fitted, disconnect the clutch cable from the side of the transmission; if an automatic transmission is fitted, disconnect the control cable at the side of the transmission.
- Unscrew the knurled nut securing the speedometer drive cable at the transmission end and withdraw the cable.
- Disconnect the accelerator cable from the carburettor. Push the cable out of the way.
- Disconnect the engine earth cable from the bulkhead.

- Disconnect the power steering pump hoses at the pump side. Collect dripping fluid and close off open hose ends.
- Withdraw the centre cable out of the ignition coil and disconnect the disconnect the two thin cables from the ignition coil terminals.
- Disconnect the connectors for the alternator harness and the oil pressure gauge unit.
- Disconnect the cable from the temperature sender unit from the cylinder head.
- Disconnect the fuel return hose

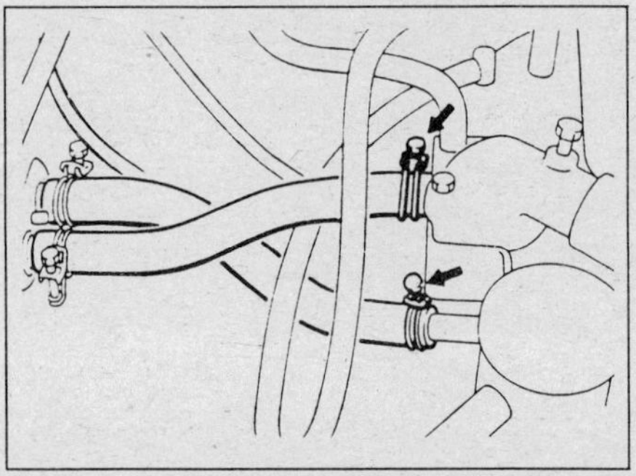

Fig. 1.2. — The arrows show the connections of the two heater hoses at the engine side.

from the carburettor and the main return hose from the fuel pipe. Plug the ends of the open connections to prevent entry of foreign matter.
- Refer to Fig. 1.3 and remove the selector control valve for the transmission from the transmission mounting.
- Jack up the front end of the vehicle (refer to Section 0.5) and carry out the following operations from underneath the vehicle:
- If a manual transmission is fitted, remove the extension rod for the gearchange mechanism from the side of the transmission (one bolt). Remove the lockwire from the bolt securing the gearchange rod, remove the bolt and disconnect the rod.
- If an automatic transmission is fitted, refer to Fig. 1.4 and remove the split pin from the bottom of the trunnion for the gearchange cable, remove the washers and remove the trunnion. Unscrew the nut from the end of the gearchange cable and withdraw the cable. Also on these models disconnect the electrical cable from the starter inhibitor switch.

- On models with manual transmission, disconnect the electrical leads from the reversing light switch.
- Disconnect the battery negative cable from the side of the engine.
- Disconnect the starter motor cables and push them out of the way.
- Disconnect the cable for the fuel cut-off solenoid from the carburettor.
- Disconnect the front exhaust pipe from the exhaust manifold. Use a piece of wire to suspend the exhaust system from the bottom of the vehicle.
- Disconnect the drive shafts from the L.H. and R.H. sides of the vehicle as described in Section 10 under the relevant heading. The strut bar and stabiliser bar connections on the two suspension arms must be removed in order to withdraw the drive shafts. The two snap rings on the shaft ends can be removed immediately as they must be replaced. Cover the openings in the transmission by placing a piece of plastic over them and taping it in position. This will prevent dirt from entering the transmission.
- Suspend the engine and transmission on a chain or rope and slightly lift the unit until just under tension. Remove the engine and transmission mountings as follows, referring to Section 1.1.2 for detailed information:

  — Remove the nut securing the L.H. engine mounting without removing the bolt.
  — Remove the front tie rod upper mounting bolt on the side of the crossmember.
  — Remove the bolt securing the rear tie rod mounting.
  — Remove the nuts securing the L.H. engine mounting from the wing.
  — Remove the covering inside the R.H. wing apron and unscrew the bolts securing the transmission mounting. Remove the bolts securing the transmission mounting to the mounting bracket. Remove the mounting bracket.

- Slowly lift the power unit until the weight of the engine and transmission is no longer resting on the mountings and then hold it in that position. Fully remove the bolts securing the rear engine tie rod and the L.H. mounting bracket. Fig. 1.5 shows details of the L.H. mounting bracket.
- Push the transmission downwards and at the same time lift the assembly out of the engine compartment. Continuously check that none of the connections, cables, etc. can get caught in the engine compartment or are still connected.

To install the power unit, lift the assembly into the vehicle and attach all power unit mountings and the two tie rods finger-tight. Fully lower the power unit and tighten all nuts and bolts to the tightening torques given in Section 1.6.

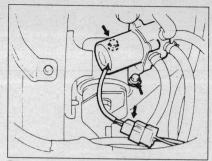

Fig. 1.3. — The arrows show where the selector control valve is secured to the transmission mounting.

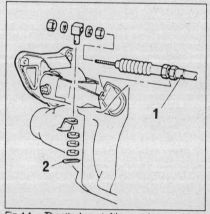

Fig. 1.4. — The attachment of the gearchange cable (1) for the automatic transmission. Remove the split pin (2) to remove the trunnion.

Fig. 1.5. — The arrows show the mounting bolts for the L.H. engine mounting (L.H. view) and the mounting bolt for the transmission mounting (R.H. view).

All other operations are carried out in reverse order to the removal procedure. Fill the transmission with the correct quantity and type of oil. Fill the cooling system with anti-freeze. Check the operation of the gearchange mechanism after connecting the gearchange rod and extension rod (manual transmission) or the gear selector cable (automatic transmission).

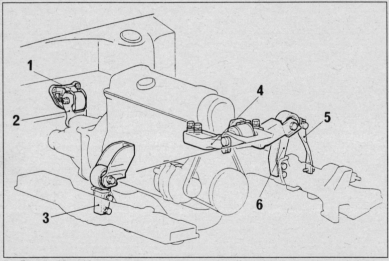

Fig. 1.6. — View of the transmission and engine mountings of a model with manual transmission.

1 Transmission mounting	3 Front roll bracket	5 Rear roll stopper stay
2 Transmission mount bracket	4 L.H. mount bracket	6 Rear roll stopper bracket

1.1.1   Removal and Installation of Engine Mountings

Fig. 1.6. shows a view of the front and rear engine mountings of a model with manual transmission. The mountings on a model with automatic transmission are slightly different.

The rear tie rod stopper stay is omitted and the transmission mounting bracket (2) is different. Engine and transmission mountings can be replaced with the engine and transmission fitted to the vehicle:

Engine Mounting (L.H. side):

- Attach a rope or chain to the engine lifting hooks and lift the engine out of the mountings until they are no longer under tension.
- Remove the bolts from the L.H. engine mounting and remove the mounting bracket from the engine. Fig. 1.5 shows the attachment of the engine mountings.

Installation is a reversal of the removal procedure. Tighten the bolts and nuts to the torque given in Section 1.6.

Transmission Mounting (R.H. side)

Remove the transmission mounting bracket bolts shown in Fig. 1.4. The selector control valve must be removed, if a manual transmission is fitted, or the gear change cable, if an automatic transmission is fitted. Remove the covering panel inside the R.H. front wing and remove the three bolts securing the mounting bracket from the transmission.

The installation is a reversal of the removal procedure. The tightening torques of nuts and bolts are given in Section 1.6.

Front Roll Stopper Bracket (Petrol Engine)

This is item (3) in Fig. 1.6. To remove the bracket, remove the bolts securing it to the engine and to the centre engine carrier. The bracket can then be removed.

The installation is a reversal of the removal procedure. The rubber mounting of the front roll bracket can be replaced. Use a suitable mandrel to press out the old bush. Driving out the bush will be difficult. Note that different bushes are used for models with manual transmission and automatic transmission when a new one is purchased. Fig. 1.7 shows the difference. Tighten the bolts and nuts to the torque values given in Section 1.6.

Rear Roll Stopper Bracket

This is item (5) in Fig. 1.6. To replace the bracket, remove the bolt securing the rear roll stopper bracket to the engine and remove the bolts securing the bracket to the crossmem-

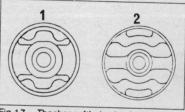

Fig. 1.7. — The shape of the bushes for the front roll stopper bracket for manual transmission (1) and automatic transmission (2).

member. As in the case of the front roll stopper bracket, the bush in the bracket is different for models with manual transmission and automatic transmission. Fig. 1.8. shows the shape and installation direction of the bush. Use a suitable mandrel and a press to replace the bush. The installation of the bracket is

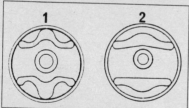

Fig. 1.8. — The shape of the bushes for the rear roll stopper bracket for manual transmission (1) and automatic transmission (2).

a reversal of the removal procedure. Tighten the nuts and bolts as specified in Section 1.6.

Engine Damper Assembly (Diesel Engine)

The damper takes the place of the front roll stopper bracket on a petrol engine. Remove the bolt and nut securing the upper end of the damper, followed by the lower nut and bolt. Remove the damper from the engine. If the damper bracket must be removed, unscrew the two bolts securing the bracket to the engine mounting carrier.

The installation of the damper is a reversal of the removal procedure. Tighten the bolts and nuts to 4.5-6.0 kgm (33-43 ft.lb.).

1.2. Dismantling the Engine

Before commencing dismantling of the engine, all exterior surfaces should be cleaned as far as possible, to remove dirt or grease. Plug the engine openings with clean cloth first to prevent any foreign matter entering the cavities and openings. Detailed information on engine dismantling and assembly is given in the section dealing with servicing and overhaul and these should be followed for each of the sub-assemblies or units to be dealt with.

Dismantling must be carried out in an orderly fashion to ensure that parts, such as valves, pistons, bearing caps, shells and so on, are replaced in the same position as they occupied originally. Mark them clearly, but take care not to scratch or stamp on any rotating or bearing surface. A good way to keep the valves in order is by piercing them through an upside-down cardboard box and writing the number against each valve.

It is of advantage if a dismantling stand can be used. Otherwise it will be useful to make up wooden support blocks to allow access to both the top and bottom faces of the engine. The cylinder head, once removed from the block, should be supported by a metal strap, screwed to the manifold face and secured by two nuts onto the manifold studs.

1.2.1. Basic Dismantling

The normal order of removal or parts for a complete engine strip-down is given below but this may, of course, be modified if only partial dismantling is required. Proceed as follows:

● Remove all engine ancilliary parts. If in doubt, refer to specific sections for removal details of a certain component.

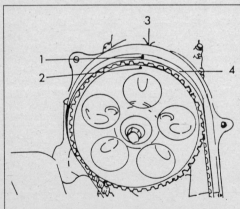

Fig. 1.9. — View of the timing marks.

1 Mark line in timing belt   3 Mark in rear guard panel
2 Mark in camshaft wheel   4 Timing belt

● Remove the clutch. To do this, counterhold the flywheel ring gear by means of a strong screwdriver. Mark the relation of the clutch to the flywheel with a centre punch (punch at opposite points into clutch and flywheel) and evenly and slowly unscrew the clutch securing bolts.

● Slacken the alternator securing bolts and take off the drive belt. The alternator can now be removed completely. Also remove the tensioning link from the cylinder block.

● Unscrew the upper timing belt cover.

● Rotate the engine until the piston of the No. 1 cylinder is at T.D.C. position. Check that the timing mark at the rear of the inner timing belt guard ("3", Fig. 1.9) and the timing mark (2) in the front face of the camshaft timing gear are in line. Using a felt pen or chalk, mark a line (1) across the timing belt to identify its fitted position.

- Remove the camshaft wheel securing bolt and withdraw the wheel together with the timing belt from the camshaft and rest the wheel onto the support below the timing wheel. If the gap is excessive, insert some kind of spacer between timing wheel and support, as shown in Fig. 1.10. Crankshaft and camshaft must not be rotated after the camshaft timing wheel has been removed.

- Remove the spacer ring from the front of the camshaft.

- Unscrew the rear timing belt guard panel (3 bolts) and take off the panel.

- Unscrew the cylinder head cover and remove. Make a note where the various retaining clips are located to facilitate the installation. Remove the gasket.

- Unscrew the camshaft bearing cap bolts and lift off the rocker shaft assembly.

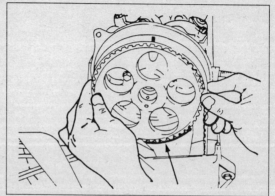

Fig. 1.10. — A spacer must be placed as shown by the arrow to prevent the timing belt from disengaging.

- Remove the camshaft oil seal from its location and withdraw the distributor drive gear from the camshaft.

- Lift out the camshaft without damaging the bearing journals or cams.

- Counterhold the flywheel ring gear with a strong screwdriver and remove the crankshaft pulley bolt. Use two tyre levers, inserted under the pulley at opposite points, and push the pulley off the crankshaft.

- Referring to Fig. 1.11 remove the cylinder head bolts in the order of the numbered sequence shown. A special Allen key (Part No. MD 998360) with an 8 mm hexagon must be used to undo the bolts.

- The cylinder head is located by two dowels and must be lifted straight up. Use a rubber or plastic mallet to free a sticking head. Never attempt to wedge the blade of a screwdriver between the sealing faces in order to separate the head. Take off the cylinder head gasket and immediately clean all gasket faces.

Front

| 3 | 5 | 10 | 8 | 2 |
| 1 | 7 | 9 | 6 | 4 |

Fig. 1.11. — Sequence for removal of the cylinder head bolts.

- Referring to Fig. 1.12, slacken the nut (5) securing the timing belt tensioner (2) and push the tensioner into the direction shown by the arrow. Re-tighten the nut in the new tensioner position. Check that the tensioner cannot return under its own spring tension and lift off the timing belt.

15

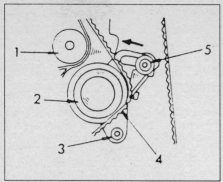

Fig. 1.12. — Removal of the timing belt.

1 Water pump   4 Timing belt
2 Belt tensioner   5 Securing nut
3 Securing bolt

- Remove the crankshaft timing gearwheel. A timing wheel with a heavy fit can be removed by means of special tool MD 998311 (puller).
- Unscrew the timing belt tensioner.
- Remove the oil sump and unscrew the oil suction strainer.
- Remove the oil pump together with the front housing. A screwdriver can be inserted into the notch at the side of the housing to prise off the assembly. Take care not to damage the sealing faces.
- Turn the cylinder block so that the bottom end is at the top or, on a bench, rest the block on the cylinder head face.

- Rotate the crankshaft until two of the connecting rods are at bottom dead centre. Unscrew the two big end bearing cap nuts and carefully tap the cap with a hammer until it can be removed. Take off the bearing shell and immediately insert it into the removed cap.
- Using a hammer handle push the connecting rod with the piston towards the top of the cylinder bore. If a carbon ring has formed at the top of the bore, preventing an easy removal, use a scraper and remove the carbon without damaging the bore. A number is stamped into the side of the connecting rod and this should always face towards the crankshaft pulley side. Mark the connecting rod and the piston with the cylinder No.

- Attach the removed bearing cap and the shell to the connecting rod and remove the other connecting rod and piston.
- Rotate the crankshaft until the other two big end bearing caps are at bottom dead centre and remove the two connecting rod and piston assemblies as described above. Make sure that each assembly is marked with the cylinder number.
- Block the flywheel by inserting a strong screwdriver into the teeth of the ring gear and remove the flywheel bolts. Remove the flywheel, using a rubber or plastic mallet if necessary. Take care not to drop the flywheel.
- Remove the rear engine intermediate plate.

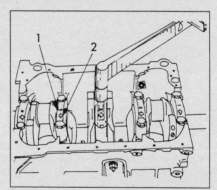

Fig. 1.13. — Removal of the crankshaft main bearing caps. The bearing number (1) and an arrow (2) are cast in- to each bearing cap.

- Remove the rear oil seal retainer from the cylinder block and unscrew the rear oil seal flange. Take off the gasket. Remove the oil seal from the flange with a suitable drift.
- Slacken the crankshaft main bearing cap bolts, commencing at the outsides and working towards the centre. Remove the caps one after the other, using a rubber mallet if they stick to the block. The caps are numbered and each cap has an arrow, facing towards the front of the engine (Fig. 1.13). The bearing shells must be kept with the caps.
- Carefully lift out the crankshaft. Remove the remaining main bearing shells from the

crankcase and keep them together with the other shell and bearing cap of each bearing.

1.2.2.2   Pistons and Connecting Rods — Dismantling

The piston pin has a floating fit in the piston and a press-fit in the connecting rod small end. For this reason it is essential that the piston pin is only removed under a press with a special extractor, available under Part No. MD 998300.

Remove the piston rings with a pair of piston ring pliers (Fig. 1.14). Take care not to break the rings if any other tool is used.

Support the piston from underneath when pressing out the pin. Fig. 1.15 shows how the pin is pressed out of the piston and connecting rod.

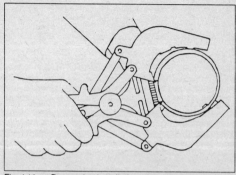

Fig. 1.14. — Removal or installation of the piston rings with a pair of piston ring pliers.

1.2.2.3.   Valves and Rocker shafts — Dismantling

The removal of the valves requires the use of a valve spring compressor. Compress the valve spring until the two valve cotter halves can be removed with a pair of pointed pliers from around the valve stem.

Remove the parts from each valve and keep each valve in its correct order of installation. Also keep the parts of each valve in a small cardboard box or plastic bag.

Fig. 1.17 shows a sectional view of the cylinder head. Fig. 1.16 shows the cylinder head in exploded condition.

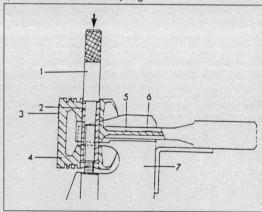

Fig. 1.15. — Removal of a piston pin.

1 Press mandrel	5 Connecting rod
2 Piston pin	6 "Front" mark
3 Arrow mark	7 Tool support
4 Piston	

1.3.   Assembling the Engine

Refer to the sections commencing at 1.4. for details of the assembly procedure for individual parts and units. Follow the general instructions below at all times. In general proceed in

17

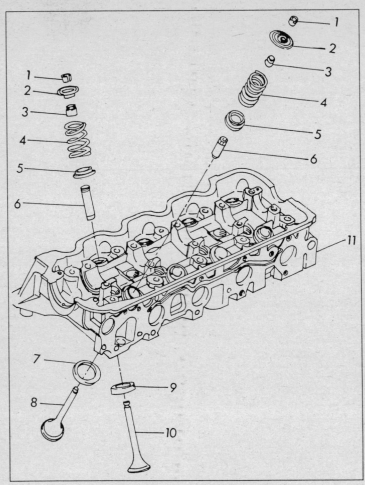

Fig. 1.16. — Exploded view of the cylinder head.

1	Valve cotter halves	7	Inlet valve insert
2	Valve spring cup	8	Inlet valve
3	Valve stem seal	9	Exhaust valve seat insert
4	Valve spring	10	Exhaust valve
5	Valve spring seat	11	Cylinder head
6	Valve guide		

reverse order to the dismantling procedure, but note the points given below:

- Take care that parts are only assembled in a clean condition.
- Keep tools, benches and hands free from dirt and swarf. Use only lint-free rags to wipe over the parts.
- Apply a film of clean engine oil to all parts that slide or rotate. Do this **before** the parts are assembled so that the lubricant is actually on the bearing surfaces. It will **not** do to apply the

18

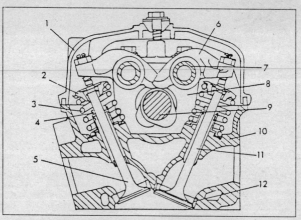

Fig. 1.17.—Sectional view of the cylinder head.

1 Cylinder head cover	7 Rocker shaft
2 Valve spring cup	8 Camshaft bearing cap
3 Valve spring	9 Camshaft
4 Valve stem oil seal	10 Cylinder head
5 Exhaust valve	11 Inlet valve
6 Rocker lever	12 Valve seat insert

oil to the completed assembly.

● Make sure that all parts have been properly inspected for wear and damage before fitting. Renew any parts that are not up to standard.

● Obtain all spares and replacement parts from an authorised dealer, quoting the vehicle chassis number and the engine number. The manufacturers adopt a policy of continuous up-dating and improvements and only their official representatives are in a position to advise you of the latest component improvements and their application to your particular engine.

● Follow all tightening torques at the end of this manual.

1.4 Overhaul of the Engine

1.4.0. Cylinder Head

1.4.0.0. Technical Data

Cylinder head material: .... Light-alloy with pressed in valve guides and valve seat inserts

Max. distortion of cylinder head surface: ...... Less than 0.10 mm (0.008 in.)

Valves

Valve seat angle:..45°, all valves

Correction angles: ....30° and 65°, all valves

Valve Stem Diameters: ....8.05 - 8.55 mm (0.3169 - 0.3366 in.)

Valve Seat Width:

Inlet and exhaust valves: ....0.9 - 1.3 mm (0.035 - 0.051 in.)

19

Valve Stem Running Clearance in Guides:
Inlet valves: . . . . 0.03-0.06 mm (0.0012-0.0024 in.)
    Wear limit: . . . . 0.10 mm (0.004 in.)
Exhaust valves: . . . . 0.05-0.09 mm (0.002-0.0035 in.)
    Wear limit: . . . . 0.15 mm (0.006 in.)

Thickness of Valve Head Edge:
Inlet valves: . . . . 1.2 mm (0.047 in.)
Exhaust valves: . . . . 1.5 mm (0.06 in.)
    Wear limit — Inlet valves: . . . . 0.7 mm (0.028 in.)
               — Exhaust valves: . . . . 1.0 mm (0.04 in.)

Valve Guides
Length of Valve Guides:
Inlet valve guides: . . . . 44.0 mm (1.7323 in.)
Exhaust valve guides: . . . . 48.0 mm (1.8889 in.)
Valve Guide Outer Diameters: . . . . 13.06-13.07 mm (0.5142-0.5146 in.)
Oversizes: . . . . 0.05, 0.25, 0.50 mm
Valve guide inner diameter: . . . . 8.00-8.018 mm (0.3150-0.3157 in.)

Valve Springs
Free length:
Red or green identification colour: . . . . 45.9 mm (1.807 in.)
Blue identification colour: . . . . 49.2 mm (1.937 in.)
Length under load:
Red or green identification colour: . . . . 37.3 mm at 28 kg (1.4685 in. at 62 lbs.)
Blue identifaction colour: . . . . 37.3 mm at 31.7 kg (1.4685 in. at 68 lbs.)
Max. distortion of valve spring at upper end,
    spring placed vertical oon surface plate: . . . . 1.6 mm (0.06 in.)
Valve spring identification: . . . . Both valves have identical valve springs
Valve identification colour spot: . . . . Red or green or blue
Arrangement during installation: . . . . Colour code must be at the top

Valve Clearances
Engine Hot:
Inlet valves: . . . . 0.15 mm (0.006 in.)
Exhaust valves: . . . . 0.25 mm (0.10 in.)

Engine Cold:
Inlet valves: . . . . 0.07 mm (0.0028 in.)
Exhaust valves: . . . . 0.17 mm (0.0067 in.)

Camshaft
Camshaft end float: . . . . 0.05-0.15 mm (0.002-0.006 in.)
Cam Height — Camshaft Identification Number 1:
Inlet cams: . . . . 36.36 mm (1.4315 in.)
Exhaust cams: . . . . 36.41 mm (1.4335 in.)
Cam Height — Camshaft Identification Number 6:
Inlet valves: . . . . 36.52 mm (1.4378 in.)
Exhaust valves: . . . . 36.57 mm (1.4398 in.)
    Wear limit: . . . . 0.5 mm (0.02 in.) less
Bearing journal diameter: . . . . 33.935-33.950 mm (1.33602-1.33661 in.)
Bearing running clearance: . . . . 0.05-0.09 mm (0.002-0.0035 in.)
Max. run-out of shaft: . . . . 0.10 mm (0.004 in.)
Camshaft identification in end face: . . . . 1 or 6

Rocker Shafts
Rocker shaft diameter: . . . . 18.885-18.928 mm (0.7435-0.7440 in.)
Running clearance of shaft: . . . . 0.01-0.04 mm (0.0004-0.0016 in.)
Rocker Shaft Length:
Inlet valve shaft: . . . . 356.5 mm (14.035 in.)
Exhaust valve shaft: . . . . 350.0 mm (13.780 in.)

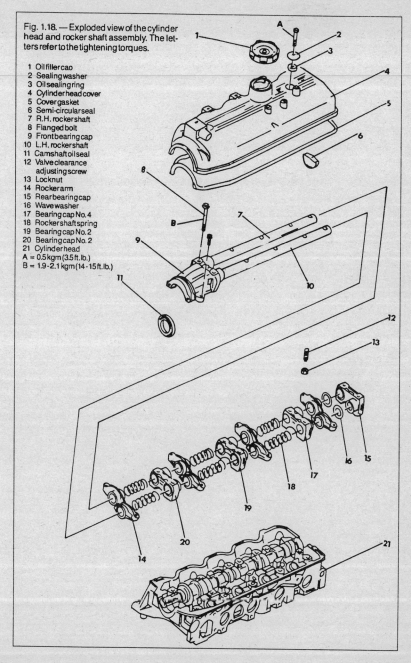

Fig. 1.18. — Exploded view of the cylinder head and rocker shaft assembly. The letters refer to the tightening torques.

1 Oil filler cao
2 Sealing washer
3 Oil sealing ring
4 Cylinder head cover
5 Cover gasket
6 Semi-circular seal
7 R.H. rocker shaft
8 Flanged bolt
9 Front bearing cap
10 L.H. rocker shaft
11 Camshaft oil seal
12 Valve clearance
    adjusting screw
13 Locknut
14 Rocker arm
15 Rear bearing cap
16 Wave washer
17 Bearing cap No. 4
18 Rocker shaft spring
19 Bearing cap No. 2
20 Bearing cap No. 2
21 Cylinder head
A = 0.5 kgm (3.5 ft. lb.)
B = 1.9 - 2.1 kgm (14 - 15 ft. lb.)

The cylinder head is made of light-alloy. Valve guides and valve seat inserts are pressed into the cylinder head. The arrangements of the inlet valves, exhaust valves and rocker levers are shown in Figs. 1.17 and 1.18.

The individual components of the valve and timing mechanisms should be checked for wear or damage and parts must be repaired or overhauled as necessary. The engine has an overhead camshaft, located by removable camshaft bearing caps and is fitted with two rocker shaft assemblies.

1.4.0.1. Valve Springs

Check the valve springs for free length and load. Replace springs which do not conform to the values given in Section 1.4.0.0 (Technical Data).

Springs can only be properly checked if a spring tester is available. Otherwise compare the old springs with new springs. Slide the originally fitted spring and a new spring together over a long bolt (with large washers under bolt head and nut) and screw a nut on the end of the bolt. Clamp the bolt head into a vice and tighten the nut. If the coils of the original spring close before the coils of the new spring, replace the spring as a set, as the other springs will have similar defects.

Place the springs one after the other onto an even surface and place a steel square next to the spring. Check that the gap between the spring and the steel square at the top is not larger than 1.6 mm (0.06 in.). If this is the case, replace the spring.

Valve springs are identified by a colour spot at one end and when fitting the springs, this spot must always be at the top, with the close coiled end to the head. The colour spot on the valve springs has a special significance, as only springs with a red or green spot or a blue spot, depending which type of springs is fitted, must be used.

1.4.0.2. Valve Guides

Remove the valve stem seals, fitted over each valve guide, with a pair of pliers as shown in Fig. 1.19 and throw away the seals.

Valve guides and valve stems should first be inspected for visible wear. Clean the inside of the valve guides with a rag moistened in petrol, inserting the rag into the guides and move it to and fro to clean the inside bore. Valve stems are best cleaned by clamping them into an electric drill and using a wire brush to clean off the carbon deposits.

Valve guides can be checked for wear with a dial gauge, suitably clamped to the cylinder head. Check as follows:

- Lift the valve in question from its guide until the distance between the cylinder head face and the face of the valve head is approx. 30 mm (1 ⅛ in.).

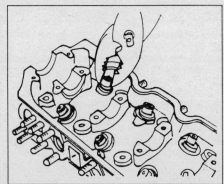

Fig. 1.19. — Removal of the valve stem oil seals with a pair of pliers. The seals are pushed over the valve guides.

- Push the valve to one side and set the dial gauge to zero. Move the valve to the opposite side and read the indication on the dial gauge.
- The max. permissible reading is 0.20 mm (0.008 in.). If this value is exceeded, either the valves or the valve guides, or both, must be replaced.

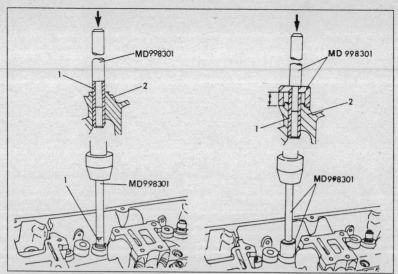

Fig. 1.20. — Replacing the valve guides (1) in the cylinder head (2). Shown are the special tools. The dimension is the protrusion of the guide and must be as given in the text.

To replace the valve guides, press out the old guides from the rocker shaft side as shown in Fig. 1.20, using the mandrel shown or any mandrel that will fit inside the guide bore. The cylinder head must be heated to 250° C to press out the guides.

Before pressing out the guides measure the height of the guide above the cylinder head face with a depth gauge. Press the new guides into the cylinder head from the upper face, until the dimension previously measured has been obtained. This dimension must be between 13.7-14.3 mm (0.539 - 0.563 in.). Fig. 1.20 (right) shows the installation of a valve guide with the special tools.

Valve guides are available in three oversizes, i.e. 0.05, 0.25 and 0.50 mm (0.001, 0.01 and 0.02 in.) and are marked with "5", "25" and "50" to identify them. The locating bores in the cylinder head must be reamed out to take the new guides.

Inlet valve guides and exhaust valve guides are of different length. Exhaust valve guides are longer and care must be taken to press the correct guides into the cylinder head.

NOTE: Valve guides to be removed and replaced at room temperature of 60° C. Valve seats must be re-ground, irrespective of their condition, if the valve guides have been replaced.

1.4.0.3.   Valve Seats

Check the valve seats for signs of wear or pitting. Slight blemishes can be removed with a 45° cutter as shown in Fig. 1.21. Extended wear can only be rectified by fitting new valve seat inserts. In this case the cylinder head should be taken to a dealer to have the new seat inserts fitted. New valve seat inserts are available in oversizes of 0.3 or 0.6 mm (0.012 and 0.024 in.) and the cylinder head locating bores must be machined to the size in question to take the new inserts. Only precision machinery can carry out this operation.

A re-cut valve seat must be lapped. Use a suction tool to grind-in the new valve. Use fine lapping compound and work the seat until an uninterrupted ring is visible around the face of the valve.

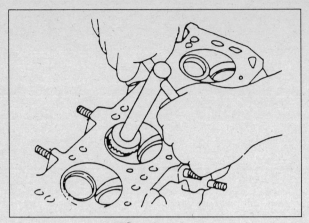

1.21. — Re-cutting a valve seat.

After grinding-in the valve, clean the cylinder head, and even more important the inside of the valve guide bores thoroughly. Any lapping paste left inside the cylinder head will accelerate the wear of the new parts.

Measure the width of the valve seats with a caliper. The width of inlet and exhaust valve seats is the same (0.9 - 1.3 mm/0.035 - 0.05 in.).

Fig. 1.22 shows the cutter angles used to re-cut the valve seats and also shows where the seat width is measured.

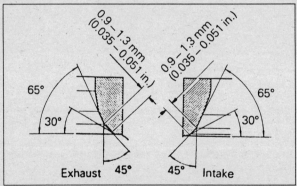

Fig. 1.22. — The valve seat width is to be measured between the arrows.

After installation of the valve measure the height of the fitted valve spring as shown in Fig. 1.23. If the dimension is more than 37.3 mm (1.469 in.), with a maximimum tolerance of 1.0 mm (0.04 in.), the valve seat inserts must be replaced, as the seat is cut too deep into the cylinder head.

1.4.0.4. Valves

Valves with bent or pitted stems should be replaced. Grinding or straightening of the valve stems is not permissible. A maximum of 0.5 mm (0.02 in.), however, can be taken off

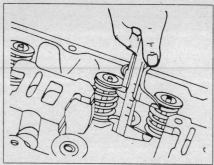

Fig. 1.23. — Measuring a valve spring height after installation.

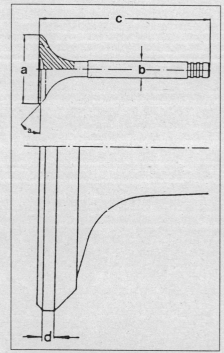

Fig. 1.24. — The principle valve dimensions are measured at the positions shown. The valve head thickness or edge "d" must have a min. thickness of 0.7 mm (0.028 in.) for the inlet valves or 1.5 mm (0.06 in.) for the exhaust valves after a valve has been re-ground in a valve grinding machine.

  a. Valve head diameter
  b. Valve stem diameter
  c. Valve length
  d. Valve head thickness

the ends of valve stems if the contacting area for the rocker levers needs attention. This should be carried out in a grinding machine with a proper chuck to ensure a straight face at the end of the stem. If stems ends are badly worn, check the rocker levers as described in the next section as these may also have suffered.

Slight blemishes on the valve head faces can be removed by grinding-in the valves as described in Section 1.4.0.3. Deeper grooves or other damage can be rectified in a valve grinding machine. The valve head thickness must not be smaller than 0.7 mm (0.028 in.) in the case of the inlet valves or 1.5 mm (0.06 in.) in the case of the exhaust valves, after grinding a valve to its original seat angle. Also measure the stem diameter and compare the results with the "Technical Data" in Section 1.4.0.0. Reject any valves which do not conform to the minimum values.

Check the running clearance of each valve stem in the valve guide bores as described in Section 1.4.0.2. and decide if it is necessary to replace the guides before any further inspection work is carried out on the valves.

1.4.0.5   Rocker Shafts and Rocker Levers

Check the rocker shafts and rocker levers for wear, pitting and other visible damage. Measure the outside diameter of each rocker shaft and the inside diameter of the rocker levers. The difference between the two dimensions should not exceed 0.02 - 0.05 mm (0.008 - 0.002 in.) and is the running clearance for rocker levers.

If the running clearance is exceeded it is not always certain that shafts and rocker levers must be replaced. Check the shafts for grooves at the areas where the rocker levers are operating. Deep grooves at these areas indicate wear of the shaft. If on the other hand the shaft has no visible ridges it may only be the rocker lever that needs replacing.

A maximum of 0.5 mm (0.02 in.) can be ground of the rocker lever ends where they contact the valve stems.

25

Badly pitted rocker lever ends make the adjustment of the valves difficult and only a smooth surface should be visible. If after grinding to the thickness given there is no improvement, replace the rocker lever in question.

The following points should be noted when dealing with the rocker shaft assembly:

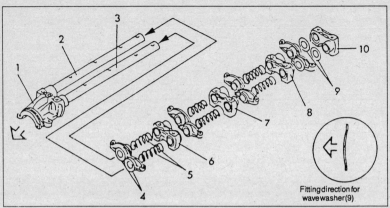

Fig. 1.25.—Exploded view of the rocker shaft assembly.

1 Front bearing cap	6 Bearing cap No. 2
2 R.H. rocker shaft	7 Bearing cap No. 3
3 L.H. rocker shaft	8 Bearing cap No. 4
4 Rocker lever	9 Wave washer
5 Spring	10 Rear bearing cap

● The right-hand rocker shaft has eight oil holes; the left-hand rocker shaft has four oil holes. The oil holes must be facing towards the bottom when the shafts are fitted.

● The rocker levers on the left-hand and right-hand shafts are identical, but should be fitted to their respective shafts if they are to be re-used.

● The springs between the rocker levers are of the same length. The free length of each spring is 53.3 mm (2.098 in.). Replace any springs which are shorter.

● The wave washers are located at the rear rocker shaft bearing cap and must be fitted in the direction shown in Fig. 1.25.

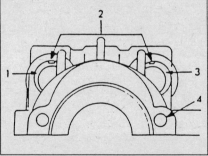

Fig. 1.26.—The arrows (2) point to the cut-outs in the rocker shafts which must be in the positions shown.

1 R.H. rocker shaft	3 L.H. rocker shaft
2 Cut-outs in shafts	4 Front bearing cap

Assemble and refit the rocker shaft assembly as follows:

● Referring to Fig. 1.25. insert the R.H. shaft (2) and the L.H. shaft (3) into the front bearing cap (1). Fit the bolts to secure the shafts in position.

● Check that the cut-out of each shaft is exactly centred at the top, as shown in Fig. 1.26.

● Slide the rocker levers, springs and bearing caps over the two rocker shafts in the order shown in Fig. 1.25. Fit a wave washer to each shaft end in the direction shown.

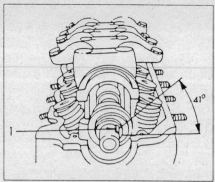

Fig. 1.27. — Rotate the camshaft until the key (1) has the indicated angle in relation to the cylinder head top face.

Fig. 1.28. — Fitting the spacer over the front end of the camshaft. The dowel pin must be on the outside.

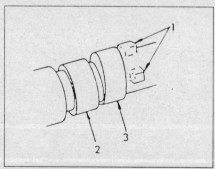

Fig. 1.30. — Minor rotations of the camshaft can be accomplished by tapping against either lug with a screwdriver.

1 No. 2 bearing journal   3 No. 2 exhaust cam
2 No. 2 inlet cam   4 Lugs

- Fit the rear bearing cap over the shafts and secure with the two screws.

- Place the assembled rocker shaft over the cylinder head. The camshaft must be rotated until in the position shown in Fig. 1.27.

- Fit all bearing cap bolts and tighten them gradually and evenly to a torque reading of 1.0 kgm (7.2 ft.lb.). Commence with the centre cap, then No. 2 and No. 4, then the front cap and finally the rear cap. In the same order tighten all bearing caps to 1.7 - 2.0 kgm (12 - 15 ft.lb.).

- Grease the inside of a new camshaft oil seal and drive the seal in position. A special tool is normally used for this operation and care must be taken not to damage the seal.

- Fit the rear timing belt guard panel.

- Oil the outside of the camshaft spacer and slide it over the camshaft end (Fig. 1.28).

- Assumed that the timing wheel and the timing belt are still in position, as shown in Figs. 1.9 and 1.10, lift the assembly off the support (remove the packing underneath, if used) and push the timing wheel over the camshaft. If the dowel pin in the end of the spacer does not engage immediately with the hole in the timing wheel, use a screwdriver and carefully tap against the lugs shown in Fig. 1.30 to slightly rotate the shaft.

- Ensure that the timing marks shown in Fig. 1.9 are aligned, fit the camshaft timing wheel bolt and tighten the bolt to 6.0 - 7.8 kgm (49 - 56 ft.l.b).

- All other operations are carried out in reverse order to the removal procedure. Adjust the valve clearances as described in Section 1.4.0.8. As valves must be adjusted in hot condition, fit the cylinder head cover provisionally only. Start the engine and run it warm. Adjust the valves as described.

- After the valve adjustment apply sealing compound to the cylinder head as shown in Fig. 1.31. Fit the cylinder head cover with a new gasket and tighten the screws to 0.5 - 0.6 kgm (3 - 4 ft.lb.).

27

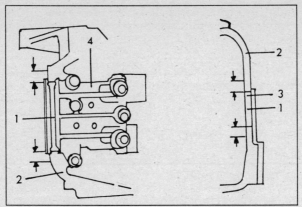

Fig. 1.31. — Application of sealing compound on the cylinder head. The sealing compound between the arrows must be applied in a width of 10 mm (0.4 in.).

1	Apply sealing compound	3	Half-round oil seal
2	Cylinder head	4	Front bearing cap

1.4.0.6. Cylinder Head

Thoroughly clean the cylinder head face of old gasket material and check the surface for distortion. To do this, place a steel ruler over the cylinder head face in the directions shown in Fig. 1.32 and with a feeler gauge measure the gap between the ruler and the head surface. The cylinder head must be re-ground, or in severe cases replaced, if the gap is more than 0.10 mm (0.004 in.) at any of the points.

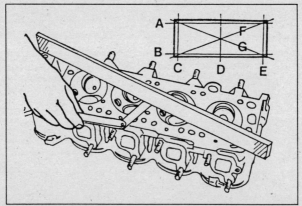

Fig. 1.32. — Checking the cylinder head gasket surface for distortion. Measure along the different directions shown.

NOTE: The max. regrind value for the cylinder head is 0.25 mm (0.010 in.). If it is possible to re-use the cylinder head, take it to an engine repair shop to have the face re-ground. Cylinder head gaskets are available in one thickness only.

1.4.0.7. Cylinder Head — Assembly and Installation

Refer to Fig. 1.16 when assembling the cylinder head:

- Place the valve spring seats over the valve guides.
- Fit the valve stem oil seals. To avoid oil leaks, a special tool, as shown in Fig. 1.33 should be used for this operation. Place the seals over each guide and carefully tap down with the hollow tool. Never attempt to use the old valve stem seals.

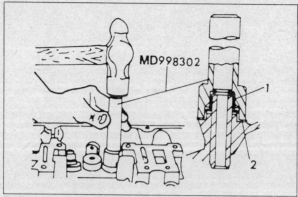

Fig. 1.33. — Driving a valve stem seal in position, using the special tool.

1. Valve stem seal   2. Valve spring seat

- Coat the valve stems with thin engine oil and insert into the correct valve guide. Take care not to damage the valve stem seal when the valve is inserted. Make absolutely sure that the valve is inserted into the guide where it has been lapped into the valve seat.
- Fit the valve springs (correct side up), place the upper spring retainer (cup) over the valve and using a valve compressor, as shown in Fig. 1.34 compress the valves springs until the two valve cotter halves can be inserted into the groove of the valve stem. Remove the valve compressor and check that the cotters have engaged in their groove by tapping the ends of the valve stems slightly with a hammer. Place a rag over each valve stem end to prevent the cotter halves from flying out.

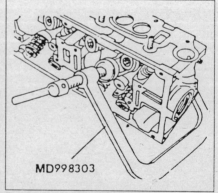

Fig. 1.34. — Compressing the valve springs with a typical, special valve spring compressor. Any other compressor with the same working principle can also be used.

The installation of the cylinder head is carried out as follows:

- Thoroughly clean the sealing faces of cylinder head and cylinder block and place a new cylinder head gasket in dry condition over the cylinder block. Under no circumstances use sealing compound. Gaskets for this engine are marked with "37". Fig. 1.39 shows where the identification number is located. Make sure to use the correct gasket.

- Tighten the cylinder head bolts in the order shown in Fig. 1.36 in several stages to a tightening torque of 7.0 - 7.5 kgm (50 - 54 ft.lb.). with the special cylinder head wrench (8 mm Allen key — No. MD 998361). These values apply to a cold engine. The cylinder head bolts of a warm engine are tightened to 8.0 - 8.5 kgm (58 - 61 ft.l.b).

- Place a new exhaust manifold gasket in position on the left-hand side. Before fitting the gasket, coat the shaded area in Fig. 1.37 (for the water passage) on both sides of the gasket with sealing compound.

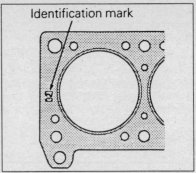

Fig. 1.35. — The location of the identification number on the cylinder head gasket.

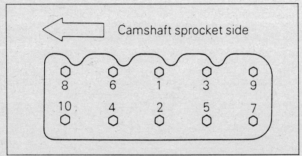

Fig. 1.36. — Tightening sequence for the cylinder head bolts.

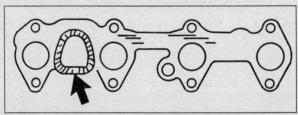

Fig. 1.37. — Coat the shaded area of the inlet manifold gasket on both sides with sealing compound.

- Fit the inlet manifold together with the carburettors and tighten the nuts to 1.5 - 2.0 kgm.
- Fit a new exhaust manifold gasket, place the manifold in position and tighten the manifold nuts to 1.5 - 2.0 kgm (11 - 15 ft.lb.).
- All other operations are carried out in reverse order to the removal procedures.

1.4.0.8.   Adjusting the Valve Clearances

Valve clearances can be adjusted with the engine hot or cold, but the final check, however,

30

must be carried out on a hot engine. The cold values are 0.07 mm (0.003 in.) for the inlet valves and 0.17 mm (0.007 in.) for the exhaust valves. On a warm engine, adjust the inlet valves to 0.15 mm (0.006 in.) and the exhaust valves 0.25 mm (0.010 in.). The engine must have the coolant at its operating temperature, i.e. the temperature gauge must indicate "Normal".

The valves should only be adjusted on a cold engine after the cylinder head gasket has been replaced or the engine has been overhauled. Otherwise adjust the valves to the "hot" values when the engine has its operating temperature.

The clearances are adjusted as shown in Fig. 1.38, using a ring spanner and a screwdriver. Check each clearance in the order given below with a feeler gauge. Insert the gauge of correct thickness between the end of the valve stem and the adjusting screw. The other end of the rocker lever must be resting against the heel of the cam, i.e. the valve must be fully closed. To check if the correct valve is being dealt with, grip the end of the lever with thumb and forefinger and check if a small clearance can be felt.

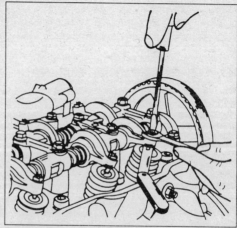

Fig. 1.38. — Adjusting the valve clearances with feeler gauge, screwdriver and open-ended spanner.

Adjust the clearances as follows:

- Rotate the engine until both valves of the No. 1 cylinder are closed, i.e. both rocker levers must have a slight play as described above. The notch in the crankshaft pulley must be in line with the "T" on the ignition timing scale (top dead centre).

- Adjust these two valves and in the same engine position all other valves marked "A" in Fig. 1.39.

Fig. 1.39. — Adjusting sequence for the valve clearances. The upper row of valves shows the exhaust valves.

- Slacken the locknut for the valve adjusting screw with a ring spanner and turn the adjusting screw with a screwdriver. Turn the screw in a clockwise direction to reduce the valve clearance or in an anti-clockwise direction to increase the clearance.

- Tighten the locknut without rotating the adjusting screw. Re-check the clearance as before after the locknut is tight.

- Rotate the engine by one complete turn and check that both valves of No. 4 cylinder are closed. In this position adjust all valves marked with "B" in Fig. 1.39 as described above.

1.4.0.9. Checking the Cylinder Compression

Compression loss can be due to a valve not closing properly, a broken or worn piston ring, worn pistons or other faults in the cylinder. To check which of the cylinders is at fault, a compression check should be carried out. The engine must be at operating temperature to avoid incorrect readings.

- Unscrew the spark plugs.
- Fully depress the throttle pedal and make sure that the choke valve is fully open.
- Place the compression tester into the first spark plug hole and have the starter motor operated by a second person, with the throttle pedal fully to the floor.
- Crank the engine until the highest reading is indicated on the compression tester chart.
- Check the remaining cylinders in the same manner. At the end there will be four graphs showing the compression of each cylinder.

None of the cylinders must have a compression of less than 80% of the best cylinder. A low, irregular compression could be caused by worn piston rings, which is also shown by excessive oil consumption. Section 1.0 gives the standard values and the min. value for the comnpression.

1.4.1.   PISTONS AND CONNECTING RODS

1.4.1.1.   Technical Data

Pistons
Material and construction: . . . . Special alloy, solid skirt
Arrangement of Piston Pin:
   Fit in connecting rod: . . . . Press-fit
   Fit in piston: . . . . Floating

Piston Diameter: . . . . 80.57 - 80.60 mm (3.1720 - 3.1732 in.)
Max. ovality of bores: . . . . Less than 0.02 mm (0.0008 in.)
Max. taper of bores: . . . . 0.02 mm (0.0008 in.)
Piston running clearance: . . . . 0.01 - 0.03 mm (0.0004 - 0.0012 in.)
Oversize pistons available: . . . . 0.25, 0.50, 0.75 and 1.0 mm

Side Clearance of Rings in Grooves:
   No. 1 ring: . . . . 0.03 - 0.07 mm (0.0012 - 0.0028 in.)
      Wear limit: . . . . 0.15 mm (0.006 in.)
   No. 2 ring: . . . . 0.02 - 0.06 mm (0.0008 - 0.0024 in.)
      Wear limit: . . . . 0.12 mm (0.003 in.)

Piston Ring Gaps:
   No. 1 rings: . . . . 0.30 - 0.45 mm (0.012 - 0.018 in.)
      Wear limit: . . . . 0.8 mm (0.03 in.)
   No. 2 rings: . . . . 0.20 - 0.35 mm (0.008 - 0.014 in.)
      Wear limit: . . . . 0.8 mm (0.03 in.)
   Oil control rings: . . . . 0.20 - 0.70 mm (0.008 - 0.028 in.)
      Wear limit: . . . . 1.0 mm (0.04 in.)

Piston Pins:
   Outer diameter: . . . . 19.001 - 19.007 mm (0.7481 - 0.7483 in.)
   Press-in load: . . . . 500 - 1500 kg (1100 - 3300 lb.)
   Press-in temperature: . . . . Room temperature

Connecting Rods:
Rod Identification: . . . . No. ''37'' in shaft
Length, centre to centre: . . . . 153.6 - 153.7 mm (6.047 - 6.051 in.)
Max. bend of connecting rods: . . . . 0.05 mm (0.002 in.) per 100 mm (3.94 in.) of length
Max. twist of connecting rods: . . . . 0.10 mm (0.004 in.) per 100 mm (3.94 in.) of length
Big end end float: . . . . 0.10 - 0.25 mm (0.004 - 0.001 in.)
   Wear limit: . . . . 0.40 mm (0.016 in.)

1.4.1.0. General

The pistons and connecting rods are pushed out from the top of the block after removing the bearing caps and lower shells. Before carrying out these operations, note the following:

- Mark each of the pistons and connecting rods to the cylinder bore from which it is removed. This can be carried out by numbering the piston crowns with the numbers 1, 2, 3 and 4, as shown in Fig. 1.40 and with an arrow each, which should be facing towards the crankshaft pulley. Remember that the arrow marked into the piston crown cannot be seen due to the carbon deposits.

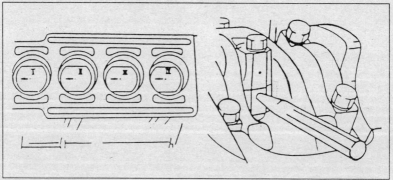

Fig. 1.40. — The L.H. view shows the piston identification. The top of the pistons should be marked with their cylinder number and arrows. The R.H. view shows how a connecting rod and bearing cap can be marked.

- Before removing the connecting rod bearing caps, mark each of the con rods and its cap with a centre punch to ensure assembly in the same position (Fig. 1.40).
- Mark the bearing shells and the rod to which they belong and mark the **upper** and the **lower** shells as soon as they have been removed.

Remove the bearing caps and shells to take out the piston assemblies, making sure that there is no ridge of carbon in the bore that might prevent removal.

- Push out the piston pin as described in Section 1.2.2. If the pin has a tight seat, heat the piston in hot water (to 60° C/140° F). **Do not use a blow lamp.**
- Using a pair of piston ring pliers, as shown in Fig. 1.14, remove the piston rings carefully from the pistons (over the crown) and keep them matched if they are to be re-used. If no piston ring pliers are available, insert some metal strips under the piston ring to be removed, on opposite sides of the piston and lift the ring this way over the piston crown. Clean all parts thoroughly, avoiding abrasive or sharp tools that might scratch the pistons.
- Piston ring grooves can be cleaned with a broken-off piston ring, which should be ground or filed flat at the broken end. Go around the circumference of the groove, being careful not to lift off any metal.

Carry out the inspections given below, all data being given in Section 1.4.1.0.

1.4.1.2. Measuring the Cylinder Bores

Measurement of the cylinder bores should be made in conjunction with the data given in Section 1.4.1.0. Bores should be measured in both transverse and longitudinal planes and

33

at the three positions down the bore, as shown in Fig. 1.41. With other words, six measurements must be carried out and each value written down. The worst measurement must be taken into consideration when deciding on the size for re-machining. All bores must be re-machined, even if only one of the cylinders is outside the limits.

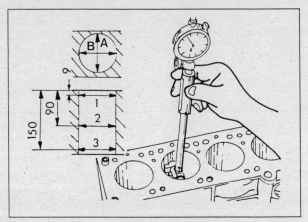

Fig. 1.41. — Measuring a cylinder bore.

The final dimension of a cylinder bore is determined by measuring the outside diameter of the piston and adding the piston running clearance to this dimension.

The running clearance is 0.01 - 0.03 mm (0.0004 - 0.0012 in in.). A dimension of 0.02 mm (0.0001 in.) must be added to the final value to allow for the honing of the cylinders. Cylinders must not be out-of-round or tapered by more than 0.02 mm (0.0001 in.)

1.4.1.3. Checking Pistons and Connecting Rods

- Check the clearance of the piston rings in their grooves as shown in Fig. 1.42. The grooves must be thoroughly cleaned before this check is carried out. If the values are not within the dimensions given, replace the piston ring in question or in severe cases replace the piston. Oversize piston rings are available in the same sizes as pistons.
- Check the ring gap by inserting the ring into the cylinder bore as shown in Fig. 1.42, on the R.H. side. Make sure that the ring is inserted squarely — use the crown of a piston to press the ring down. Note that the gap is measured at the bottom end of the cylinder bore. Compare with the values given in Section 1.4.1.0.
- Check the piston pins and the bores of the connecting rods for wear. The piston fit must be so that the well oiled piston pin can be pushed with thumb pressure through the piston pin bore at room temperature. The pin has a press-fit in the connecting rod small end.
- The piston crown is marked with an arrow which points to the front of the engine. This installation direction is of importance as the piston pin is offset to one side. Oversize pistons have their size marked in the piston crown (for example "25", "50", etc.). Letters and numbers in the piston crown refer to the engine type.
- Check the connecting rods for damage. Never repair a damaged connecting rod but always replace. Re-useable connecting rods should be checked in an alignment fixture to make sure it is not bent by more than 0.05 mm (0.002 in.) or twisted by more than 0.10 mm (0.004 in.). Twisted or bent connecting rods should not be straightened and we recommend that a complete new set is fitted, if the values are exceeded.

34

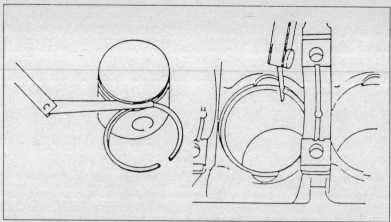

Fig. 1.42. — Checking the side clearance of the piston rings by means of a feeler gauge on the left. The R.H. view shows the checking the piston ring gap with a feeler gauge. The ring is inserted into the bottom of the cylinder bore.

1.4.1.4. Checking the Big End Bearing Running Clearance

Before bearing shells for the connecting rod bearings are ordered, it must be established to which size the crankpins have to be re-ground. Clean the crankshaft thoroughly and inspect the journals for signs of wear or damage. Measure the journals at two positions around the circumference and along its length. Out of round and taper of more than 0.03 mm (0.0012 in.) will mean that the crankshaft will have to be re-ground. All dimensions are given in the "Technical Data", Section 1.4.2.0. Several undersize bearing shells are available.

The running clearance of the big end bearings must be between 0.02 - 0.05 mm (0.0008 - 0.0020 in.), with a wear limit of 0.10 mm (0.004 in.). The clearance can be checked with "Plastigage" plastic filament as follows:

- Rotate the crankshaft until two of the crankpins are at bottom dead centre if the shaft is still fitted to the engine.
- Remove all dirt and grease from the journals and the shells.

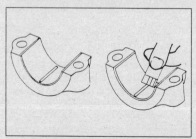

Fig. 1.43. — Checking the big end bearing running clearance. In the left-hand view the "Plastigage" wire is inserted into the bearing shell. In the right-hand view the flattened "Plastigage" wire is measured with the scale provided in the "Plastigage" kit.

- Place a length of "Plastigage" wire along the complete length of the journal and fit the shell and bearing cap.
- Tighten the nuts to a tightening torque of 3.2 - 3.5 kgm (24 - 25 ft.lb.). Do not move the connecting rod after tightening the nuts. The pressure of the bearing shell will compress the "Plastigage" and flatten it.
- Now remove the bearing cap in question and take off the bearing shell. Compare the width of the compressed "Plastigage" wire with the scale provided, as shown in Fig. 1.43. The smallest width of the "Plastigage" indicates the largest running clearance.

35

● If the clearance is excessive, the crankshaft bearing journals must be re-ground and undersize bearing shells fitted. Your dealer will advise you about availability.

1.4.1.5. Assemling Piston and Connecting Rods

The special tool shown in Fig. 1.15 must be used to assemble the pistons to the connecting rods. The piston pin must be pressed in with a pressure of 500 -1500 kg (1100 - 3300 lb.) and

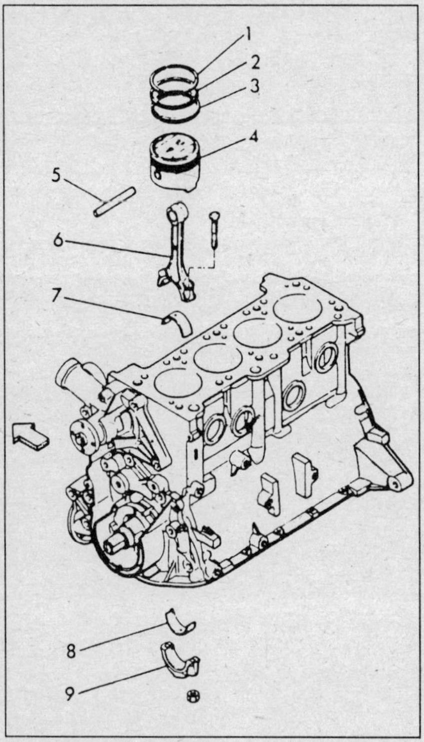

Fig. 1.44. — Exploded view of cylinder block, piston and connecting rod.

1 Top compression ring	6 Connecting rod
2 2nd compression ring	7 Bearing shell
3 Oil control ring	8 Bearing shell
4 Piston	9 Big end bearing cap
5 Piston pin	

it may be better if the parts are assembled in a workshop with the proper tools.

● Lubricate the outside of the piston pin and the inside of the connecting rod small end with engine oil.

● Align the connecting rod and the piston so that the "Front" mark of both components are facing towards the top. The piston has an arrow in the crown and the connecting rod is marked with a number in the shank.

● Press the piston pin in position with the special fixture. Connecting rod and/or piston pin must be replaced, if the pin slides into the connecting rod before the pressure given above is reached.

● After the piston pin has been pressed in position, check that the connecting rod can be moved to and fro without binding.

1.4.1.6. Fitting Pistons and Connecting Rods

Refer to Fig. 1.44 for the following operations. If parts are re-used, make sure to fit them into their original position. If cylinder bores have been re-bored, fit the new piston into the relevant cylinder bore.

● Arrange the connecting rods with the number in the shank facing towards the front of the engine.

● Fit the three-part oil control ring. Install the spacer expander with a pair of piston ring pliers. Fit the upper and lower side rails, but do not use the piston ring pliers as the rings may be broken if such a method is employed. To install the side rails, first insert one end of the side rail between the piston ring groove and the spacer expander, hold it down firmly and then press down the portion which is to be inserted into the groove with a finger as shown in Fig. 1.45. In this manner the side rail can be easily fitted. The upper side rail is fitted first. After installation, check that both side rails can be turned smoothly. The size mark and the maker's mark in the side rails must be facing towards the piston crown after installation. Arrange the gaps so that the expander

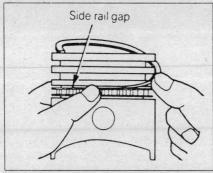

Side rail gap

Fig. 1.45.—Fitting the two side rails of the three-part oil control ring. Fit the upper side rail first as shown.

spacer gap is arranged 45° away from the two side rail gaps.

● Fit the centre piston ring (compression ring) and the upper compression ring with a pair of piston ring pliers, with the size mark and the maker's mark facing towards the piston crown. Note that the two compression rings are not identical, although of the same size. The chrome-plated piston ring is fitted to the upper groove. Fig. 1.46 shows a sectional view through piston and piston rings for reference.

● Arrange the piston ring gaps in accordance with Fig. 1.46 on the circumference of the piston skirt. Make sure the "Front" mark points to the front of the engine.

● A piston ring compressor is required to fit the pistons to the cylinder bores. Place the compressor around the piston rings (without disturbing their position) and push the piston rings into their grooves. A compressor can be hired out from most tool hire companies. Never try to fit pistons without compressing the piston rings.

● Insert the corrrect connecting rod into the cylinder bore, check that the arrow in the piston faces towards the front and guide the connecting rod, with the bearing shell inserted, into the cylinder bore. The lug in the bearing shell must be engaged into the cut-out of the connecting rod. The connecting rod bolts must be fitted. Small pieces of rubber or plastic sleeve can be fitted over the two bolts to prevent scratching of the cylinder bore.

● Insert the piston into the bore up to the piston ring area and carefully guide in the piston rings, at the same time pushing off the compressor and guiding the big end bearing over the crankpin. The cylinder block should be on its side to facilitate the installation.

● Insert the big end bearing shell into the cap, with the lug on the rear face into the cut-out of the cap and generously lubricate the bearing shell face with engine oil. Do not use a brush to oil the shells, as bristles could enter the bearing.

● Make sure that the connecting rod is in position on the crankpin and fit the bearing cap with the shell over the crankpin and against the connecting rod. Check that the two cut-outs in connecting rod and cap are on the same side. Tap the cap in position with a rubber or plastic mallet.

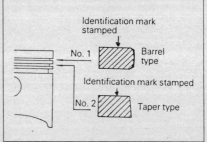

Identification mark stamped

No. 1   Barrel type

Identification mark stamped

No. 2   Taper type

Fig. 1.46.—The correct arrangement of the piston ring gaps.

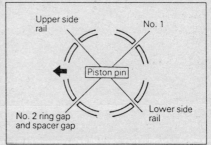

Upper side rail

No. 1

Piston pin

No. 2 ring gap and spacer gap

Lower side rail

Fig. 1.47.—The correct arrangement of the piston ring gaps.

- Fit the bearing cap nuts and alternatively tighten them to 3.2-3.5 kgm (24-25 ft.lb.).
- After fitting the connecting rod, measure the end float of the big end bearing on the crankpin by inserting a feeler gauge between the big end bearing and the thrust face of the crankpin as shown in Fig. 1.48. The nominal value is 0.10- 0.25 mm (0.004-0.010 in.).
- Fit the remaining connecting rod and piston to the crankpin at bottom dead centre position in the manner described above.

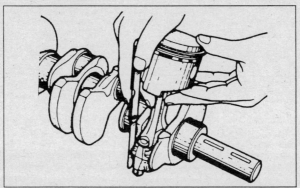

Fig. 1.48.—Measuring the end float of a connecting r end float of a connecting rod on the assembled big end bearing. Push the rod to one side and measure on the other side.

- Rotate the crankshaft by one turn and fit the two remaining assemblies in the manner described above.
- Rotate the crankshaft a few times and check for hard spots. To rotate the engine, fit two bolts to the crankshaft end flange and turn the crankshaft with a strong screwdriver.

1.4.2.   CRANKSHAFT AND BEARINGS

1.4.2.0.   Technical Data

Number of bearings: 5
Main journal diameter: . . . . .57.00 mm (2.2441 in.)
Crankpin journal diameter: . . . . .45.00 mm (1.7717 in.)
Max. permissible out-of-round: . . . . .0.01 mm (0.0004 in.)
Crankshaft end float:
   Nominal: . . . . 0.05 - 0.18 mm (0.002 - 0.0071 in.)
   Wear limit: . . . . 0.25 mm (0.0098 in.)
Crankshaft thrust taken at: . . . . Centre main bearing
Main bearing running clearance: . . . . .0.02 - 0.05 mm (0.0008 - 0.0002 in.)
   Wear limit: . . . . .0.10 mm (0.004 in.)
Big end bearing running clearance: . . . . .0.02 - 0.05 mm (0.0008 - 0.0020 in.)
   Wear limit: . . . . .0.15 mm (0.006 in.)

1.4.2.1.   Inspection of the Crankshaft

The crankshaft is forged of steel and runs in five bearings. An oil seal is fitted to the flywheel end. The oil seal on the opposite end is inserted into the front housing into the front cover. Removable bearing caps secure the crankshaft to the cylinder block and contain the two bearing shells for each bearing.

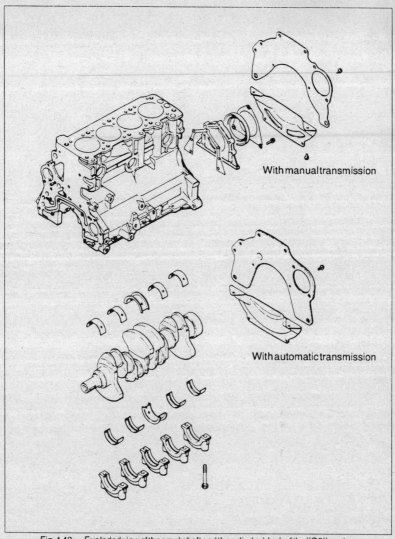

With manual transmission

With automatic transmission

Fig. 1.49. —Exploded view of the crankshaft and the cylinder block of the "G3" engine.

The end float of the crankshaft is controlled by the flanged bearing shells of the centre bearing.

Fig. 1.49 shows an exploded view of the crankshaft and the cylinder block for a "G3" engine. Thoroughly clean the crankshaft in paraffin or petrol and check that all oil drillings are free of obstructions. Clamp the crankshaft between the centres of a lathe or place the two end journals in "V" blocks and with a dial gauge, measure the run-out at the centre journal as shown in Fig. 1.50. The max. permissible indication is 0.05 mm (0.0002 in.). Note that the shaft should be

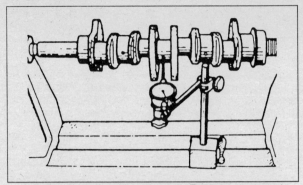

Fig. 1.50. — Checking a crankshaft for run-out. The shaft can be clamped between the centres of a lathe or the end journals are placed in "V" blocks.

rotated by two complete turns. Half of the indicator valve is the actual run-out.

Check the crankshaft main bearing journals and crankpin journals for grooves or other damage (seized bearings). If no obvious damage is seen, measure the diameters of all journals with a micrometer. Take care not to place the jaws of the micrometer against any of the oil drillings.

From the result decide if the crankshaft can be re-ground. Various undersize bearing shells are available and can be used as required.

1.4.2.2.   Crankpins

Apart from the nominal size big end bearing shells there are a number of undersize shells available. The selection of the correct undersize shells depends on the condition of the individual crankpins as it is sometimes possible that the first undersize shell is not enough. Therefore, measure the crankpin diameters, compare with the nominal values and from the

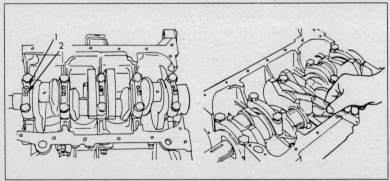

Fig. 1.51. — The L.H. view shows the fitted crankshaft. Arrow No. 1 points to the arrow cast into the main bearing cap. Arrow No. 2 shows the bearing cap numbering. The R.H. shows the measuring of the crankshaft end float at the centre main bearing. A feeler gauge is inserted between the flanged bearing shell and the crankshaft thrust face.

result decide to which undersize the journals must be ground. This also applies to the main bearings below.

40

1.4.2.3.   Main Bearing Journals

Apart from the nominal size main bearing shells there are a number of undersize bearing shells available.

1.4.2.4.   Main Bearing Running Clearance

The main bearing running clearance is between 0.02 - 0.05 mm (0.0001 - 0.0020 in.), with a wear limit of 0.10 mm (0.004 in.). All bearings have the same running clearance (also known as radial clearance) and can be measured as described in Section 1.4.1.4. for the big end bearings.

All bearings can be checked at the same time. The main bearing bolts must be tightened to 5.0 - 5.5 kgm (36 - 39 ft.lb.). Do not rotate the crankshaft after the bearing caps have been tightened with the "Plastigage" under the bearing shells.

1.4.2.5.   Installation of Crankshaft

Fig. 1.51 shows how the main bearing caps are numbered, with No. 1 bearing at the crankshaft pulley end and No. 5 at the flywheel end. All bearing caps are also marked with an arrow which must be facing towards the front of the engine. The following points should be noted during installation:

- All arrows must be facing towards the front of the engine. This is important to note, as the caps can be fitted in position the wrong way round.
- Bearing shells of No. 3 bearing have a flange to control the crankshaft end float. The crankshaft end float must be measured after installation as shown in Fig. 1.51. To do this, push the crankshaft to one side, using a strong screwdriver and measure on the other side between bearing shell flange and crankshaft thrust face with a feeler gauge. The end float should be between 0.05 and 0.18 mm (0.002 and 0.007 in.), but a wear limit of 0.25 mm (0.010 in.) is acceptable.
- If the same bearing shells are re-used, make sure they are inserted into their original bearing bores. The bearing shells and the main bearing journals have formed a wear pattern which should not be disturbed.

The installation of the crankshaft is carried out as follows:

- Generously lubricate the bearing shell surfaces with engine oil.
- Insert the lugs at the back faces of each bearing shell into the cut-out of the locating bores of the crankcase. Make absolute sure that each bore receives the correct bearing shell and remember that No. 1 bearing is at the crankshaft pulley end..
- Carefully lift the crankshaft into the bearing shells and rotate it a few times to settle the bearings.
- Fit the lower bearing shells in the same manner into the main bearing caps and place the bearing caps with the shells in position over the crankshaft journals and the crankcase. Fit the cap screws and tighten them finger-tight.
- Commencing at the centre bearing cap and working towards the outside, tighten the bolts to a torque reading of 5.0 - 5.5 kgm (37 - 39 ft.lb.). The correct order of tightening is: Centre bearing, bearing No. 2, bearing No. 4, front bearing and rear bearing.
- After all bearings caps have been tightened as described, rotate the crankshaft a few times to check for binding.
- Lubricate the sealing lip of a new rear oil seal with grease and drive the seal into the rear oil seal flange. The oil seal is driven in from the outside and then secured with the retainer, as shown in Fig. 1.52.

- Fit the oil seal flange with a new gasket and attach the rear engine plate.
- Clean the crankshaft flange with a clean rag and fit the flywheel. Tighten the flywheel bolts to 13.0 - 14.0 kgm (94 - 101 ft.lb.). On models with automatic transmission, fit the drive plate (Fig. 1.52).

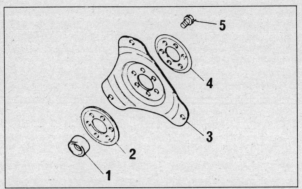

Fig. 1.52. — The component parts of the driven plate for an automatic transmission model.

1 Crankshaft pilot bush	4 Adaptor plate
2 Adaptor plate	5 Driven plate bolt
3 Driven plate	

1.4.2.6. Checking the Cylinder Block

Thoroughly clean the top of the cylinder block and check the surface for distortion. Place a steel ruler on the top face of the block in the directions shown in Fig. 1.32, similar as for the cylinder head. Using a feeler gauge measure the gap between the ruler and the block. The cylinder block should be re-ground or, in severe cases, replaced, if the gap is more than 0.10 mm (0.004 in.).

Note: The maximum combined amount that can be removed from the block and cylinder head is 0.2 mm (0.008 in.).

1.4.2.7. Checking the Flywheel

The flywheel is designed for the particular engine. The flywheel bolts are also of different length. The bolts are marked with "50" in their heads.

Check the face of the flywheel for ridges and check that the flywheel run-out is within 0.13 mm (0.005 in.).

Check the teeth on the flywheel ring gear for wear and damage. If it is in poor condition, also check the starter motor pinion. An excessively worn or damaged ring gear should be renewed.

To remove, drill a hole between two of the teeth and then split the ring, using a chisel. Protect your eyes during this operation.

Heat the new ring gear to 260 - 280° C (500 to 536° F) and shrink-fit to the flywheel.

The pilot bearing in the end of the crankshaft can be replaced. Remove the old bearing with a suitable puller and drive the new bearing into the crankshaft. Grease the bearing before installation.

Flywheel bolts are tightened to 13-14 kgm (94-101 ft.lb.). Counterhold the flywheel during the tightening operation. If the oil sump is removed, insert a block of wood between one of the crankshaft throws and the wall of the cylinder block.

1.4.2.8. Drive Plate (Automatic)

Fig. 1.52 shows the component parts of the drive plate. No pilot bearing is fitted into the end of the crankshaft, if an automatic transmission is used with the engine, but a bush is fitted which can be removed with a threaded tab. Cut a thread of suitable size into the bush, screw in a bolt and withdraw the bush with a pair of pliers or similar.

When fitting the drive plate note the position of the two washers (4). Only use genuine Mitsubishi bolts. Tighten the bolts to the same torque as given for the flywheel above.

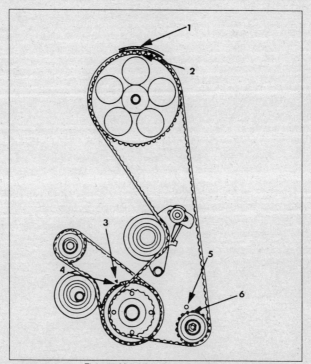

Fig. 1.53. View of the fitted timing belt .

1. Timing mark in rear cover	4. Timing mark in timing gear
2. Timing mark in timing gear	5. Timing mark in oil pump cover
3. Timing mark	6. Timing mark in pump drive gear

1.4.3. CAMSHAFT AND TIMING DRIVE

1.4.3.0. Technical Data

Drive: . . . . Toothed belt
End float of camshaft: . . . . 0.05 - 0.20 mm (0.002 - 0.008 in.)

Cam Heights: . . . . See Section 1.4.0.0.
Diameter of fuel pump eccentric: . . . . 40.0 mm (1.57 in.)
  Min. diameter: . . . . 39.5 mm (1.555 in.)
Bearing journal diameter: . . . . See Section 1.4.0.0.
Bearing running clearance: . . . . 0.05 - 0.09 mm (0.002 - 0.0035 in.)
Camshaft identification number: . . . . See Section 1.4.0.0.
Max. run-out of shaft: . . . . 0.10 mm (0.004 in.)

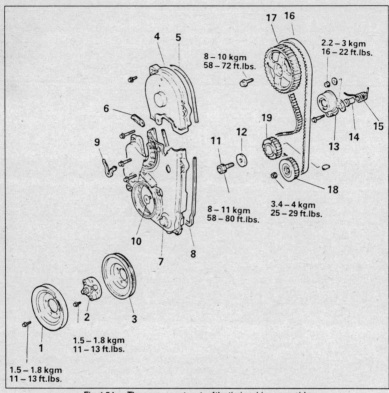

Fig. 1.54. — The component parts of the timing drive assembly.

1 Damper pulley	8 Gasket	15 Tensioner spring
2 Adaptor	9 Gasket	16 Timing belt
3 Crankshaft pulley	10 Access cover	17 Camshaft sprocket
4 Upper belt cover	11 Sprocket bolt	18 Oil pump sprocket
5 Gasket	12 Special washer	19 Crankshaft sprocket
6 Gasket	13 Belt tensioner	
7 Lower belt cover	14 Tensioner spacer	

1.4.3.1. Short Description

The camshaft is mounted in five bearings and driven by a toothed belt, as shown in Figs. 1.53.
The belt also drives one of the balance shafts and is kept under tension by a belt tensioner,
fitted to the centre of its run. A second belt, having its own belt tensioner, drives the second
balance shaft.

44

The drive gear for the distributor is fitted to the front of the camshaft. The gear is secured to the camshaft. 1.54 shows the individual parts of the timing gear assembly with the location of parts. A number identification in the rear face of the shaft indicates for which engine the shaft is suitable. Shafts for this engine are marked with "6" (U.K. models) or "1".

1.4.3.2.   Removal of the Camshaft

- Withdraw the breather hoses.
- Remove the air cleaner.
- Carry out all operations described in Section 1.2.1 until the camshaft can be lifted out of the cylinder head. There is no need to dismantle the rocker shaft assembly, unless work is to be carried out on the rocker shaft or levers at the same time. Take care not to drop the half-moon shaped sealing rubber in the cylinder head. The camshaft oil seal must be replaced.

1.4.3.3.   Inspection of Parts

Clamp the camshaft between the centres of a lathe or place the end journals into "V" blocks (in a similar manner as shown in Fig. 1.50 for the crankshaft) and apply a dial gauge to the centre bearing journal. Rotate the camshaft by two revolutions and read off the indication. One half of the value is the run-out of the camshaft which should not exceed 0.05 mm (0.002 in.). Replace the shaft if the reading is outside the given value.

Check the cam surfaces on each side, top and bottom and if in good condition, measure the height of each cam with a micrometer as shown in Fig. 1.55 and compare the results with the values given in Section 1.4.0.0.

Measure the camshaft end float as follows:

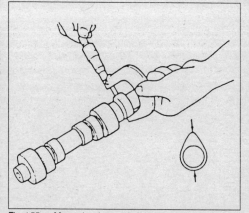

- Fit the camshaft to the engine and attach a dial gauge so that the end of the stylus rests against the end of the camshaft face. Move the camshaft into one direction, set the dial gauge to zero and push the camshaft into the other direction. The reading is the end float and should be between 0.05 - 0.15 mm (0.002 - 0.006 in.), with a limit of 0.3 mm (0.012 in.).
- If no dial gauge is available, use a feeler gauge between the flange of the No. 1 journal and the No. 1 bearing on the cylinder head side, as shown in Fig. 1.56. The gap must be the same as given above.

Fig. 1.55. — Measuring the cam height with a micrometer. Apply the micrometer jaws at the points shown by the arrows in the inset.

Check the camshaft journals for wear. If the journals are worn, replace the camshaft without any further checks. In this case, also check the bearing bores in the cylinder head as these may also be damaged. Replace the cylinder head if necessary.

Check the teeth of the distributor drive gear for wear. The distributor drive gear of a engine can be replaced separately. The eccentric drive for the fuel pump should also be checked for wear.

45

1.4.3.4. Fitting the Camshaft

- Coat the camshaft bearing journals and the cams with engine oil and also the bearing faces in cylinder head and bearing caps.
- Place the camshaft into the cylinder head and rotate a few times to settle the shaft into the bearings.
- Fit the rocker shaft assembly as described in Section 1.4.0.5.
- Fit the timing belt and adjust the timing as described in the following section.

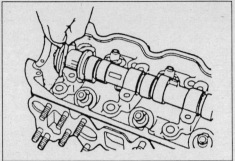

Fig. 1.56. — Measuring the camshaft end float by means of a feeler gauge.

1.4.4. ADJUSTING THE VALVE TIMING

The component parts of the timing mechanism can be replaced when the engine is in the vehicle, as described during the dismantling of the engine. Also refer to the illustrations in this section for particulars.

The component parts of the timing mechanism are shown in Figs. 1.54 and all number references refer to this illustration, unless otherwise mentioned.

The following description assumes that the components of the timing mechanism are completely removed, as this is the case during an engine overhaul or during replacement of parts.

- Fit the balance shaft timing gear and provisionally fit the bolt.
- Place the crankshaft timing wheel over the end of the crankshaft. Align the timing marks of all timing wheels as shown in Fig. 1.57.

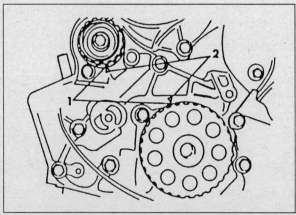

Fig. 1.57. — Details of fitting the timing wheels.
1. Timing marks in timing gears   2. Timing marks in housing

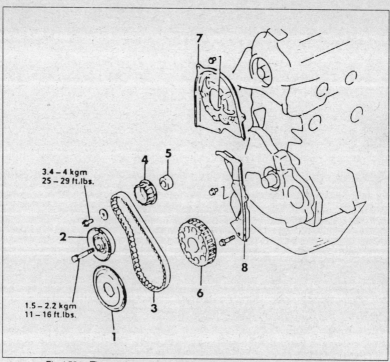

Fig. 1.58. — The component parts of the timing mechanism for the balance shafts.

1 Guide flange	4 Balance shaft sprocket	7 Rear belt cover
2 Belt tensioner	5 Spacer bush	8 Rear belt cover
3 Small toothed belt	6 Crankshaft sprocket	

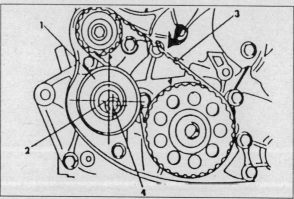

Fig. 1.59. — Fitting the tensioner pulley for the small timing belt.

1. Tensioner roller	3. Timing belt
2. Centre of tensioner roller	4. Centre of bolt

47

- Place the timing belt over the two drive wheel so that the tensioner side is tight.
- Fit the belt tensioner. The centre point of the tensioner pulley must be located at the left-hand side of the mounting bolt. The pulley flange must be directed towards the front of the engine. Fig. 1.59 shows the tensioner pulley in fitted position.
- Fit the oil pump drive wheel and tighten the nut to 3.4-4.0 kgm (24.5-29 ft.lb.). Now rotate the shaft until the two timing marks, i.e. the one in the oil pump wheel and the other one in the timing housing, are opposite each other, as shown in Fig. 1.60.

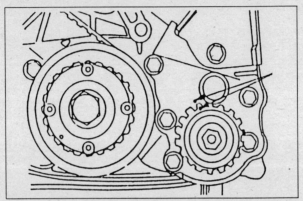

Fig. 1.60. — After fitting the oil pump drive wheel, turn the shaft until the two timing marks (arrows) are opposite each other.

- After aligning the timing marks, insert a screwdriver into the opening on the left-hand side of the cylinder block as shown in Fig. 1.61. If the screwdriver blade (approx. 8 mm/0.3 in. in diameter) can be inserted by approx. 60 mm (2.4 in.), the alignment is correct. If it can be inserted only by 25 mm (1 in.), rotate the oil pump drive wheel by one revolution and again

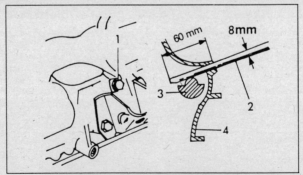

Fig 1.61. — Details for the removal and installation of the L.H. balance (silent) shaft.

1 Plug	3 Balance shaft
2 Screwdriver	4 Cylinder block

align the timing marks. Keep the screwdriver in position until the timing belt has been fitted.
- Fit the tensioner pulley with spacer sleeve and spring. Temporarily tighten the tensioner pulley nut.

- Push the flange located underneath the tensioner in the direction of the arrow in Fig. 1.62 until the two bolts "A" and "B" can be screwed in position. Each end of the tensioner spring should be engaged in the correct position. Engage the front end end of the spring (bent at right angle) on the projection of the tensioner and the other end (straight) on the water pump body, as shown by the arrow in Fig. 1.62.

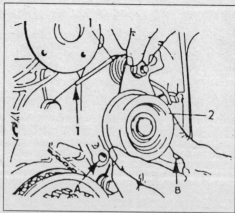

- Grip the tensioner pulley with one hand and pull it into the direction of the arrow in Fig. 1.12 until it is near the water pump and temporarily tighten the pulley nut in this position.

- Place the timing belt in position. The belt should be installed first over the crankshaft timing wheel, then over the oil pump drive wheel and finally over the camshaft timing wheel. Before fitting the belt, check once more that all timing marks are still in line. Take care that the belt is not slackened during installation.

- Remove the screwdriver inserted into the cylinder block and temporarily fit the crankshaft pulley to prevent misalignment when the crankshaft is turned.

Fig. 1.62. — Fitting the tensioner pulley (2) for the long timing belt. The straight end (arrow) of the spring (1) is hooked into the water pump housing.

- Slacken the tensioner mounting bolt and nut. While doing so, the tensioner will normally be pushed by the spring and will apply tension to the belt. Push the tensioner up by hand against the mounting nut to make sure that the belt comes into complete mesh with the tim-

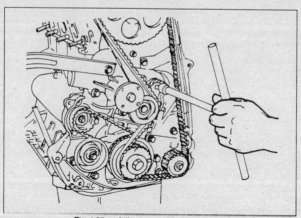

Fig. 1.63. — Adjustment of the timing belt.

ing wheel. Tighten the tensioner mounting nut and then the bolt (Fig. 1.12). This order of tightening is important.

- Re-check that all timing marks are in line, rotate the crankshaft by one revolution in normal direction of rotation and check the timing marks once more. Never turn the crankshaft against the normal direction of rotation.
- To check the belt tension, grip the belt as shown in Fig. 1.64 between thumb and forefinger. Move the belt as shown. Re-adjust the tension as described above if the movement is less than 12 mm (0.47 in.).

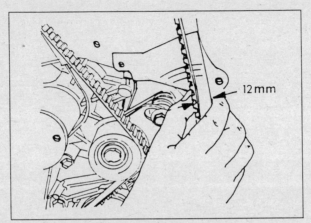

12 mm

Fig. 1.64. — Checking the timing belt tension.

- Carry out all other operations in reverse order to the removal procedures.

1.4.5. BALANCE SHAFTS

Two balance shafts are fitted to this engine, one at the top of the R.H. side of the cylinder block and the other one at the bottom L.H. side of the block. The shafts are driven by means of two belt wheels, one by the large toothed belt and the other one by a smaller toothed belt. Fig. 1.65 shows the layout of the balance shafts.

The front housing, which must be removed to take out the shafts, contains the oil pump and the oil relief valve. An oil suction strainer is fitted to the bottom of the housing. The oil pump cover is fitted in front of the front housing.

The R.H. shaft rotates in the same direction as the crankshaft; the L.H. shaft rotates in opposite direction. Both shafts are rotating with twice the speed of the crankshaft.

The shafts are running in bearings at the front end rear. The front end of the L.H. shaft is located in the front housing. The R.H. shaft is located at front and rear in a bearing bush, fitted to the cylinder block. The rear end of the L.H. shaft has a similar location. The removal of the shafts has already been described during the dismantling of the engine.

Before fitting the shafts check the front housing for cracks or other damage. Check the bearing bore for the L.H. shaft in the housing. If worn, replace the front housing.

If the engine has been overhauled, replace the oil seals for crankshaft, R.H. balance shaft and oil pump. Otherwise replace the oil seals if the sealing lips are no longer in good condition.

Measure the outside diameter of the bearing journals and the inside diameter of the bearing bores in the cylinder block. If the difference between the two dimensions is excessive the bushes in the block must be replaced. This is a job for a specialist shop.

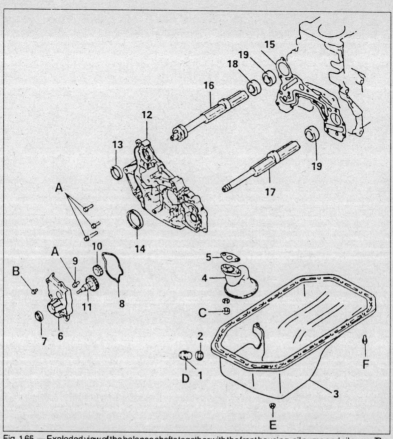

Fig. 1.65. — Exploded view of the balance shafts together with the front housing, oil pump and oil sump. The letters refer to the tightening torques.

1 Oil drain plug	8 Gasket	15 Front case gasket
2 Drain plug gasket	9 Flange bolt	16 Balance shaft, right
3 Oil sump	10 Oil pump driven gear	17 Balance shaft, left
4 Oil suction screen	11 Oil pump drive gear	18 Balance shaft bearing
5 Oil screen gasket	12 Front case	19 Rear bearing
6 Oil pump cover	13 Shaft oil seal	
7 Oil pump oil seal	14 Cranshaft front seal	

A = 1.5 - 1.8 kgm (11 - 13 ft. lb.)   D = 3.5 - 4.5 kgm (25 - 33 ft. lb.)
B = 1.5 - 1.8 kgm (11 - 13 ft. lb.)   E = 0.5 - 0.7 kgm (3.6 - 5.1 ft. lb.)
C = 1.8 - 2.5 kgm (13 - 18 ft. lb.)   F = 0.6 - 0.8 kgm (4.3 - 5.8 ft. lb.)

Fit the balance shafts as follows:

- Insert the two oil pump gears from the front into the front housing, aligning the marks as shown in Fig. 1.66. The two alignment marks must be opposite each other.
- Lubricate the pump gears with engine oil and insert the L.H. balance shaft into the driven

51

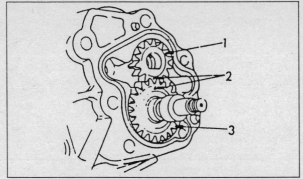

Fig. 1.66.—Aligning the timing marks when fitting the oil pump gears.
1. Driven gear   2. Timing mark   3. Drive gear

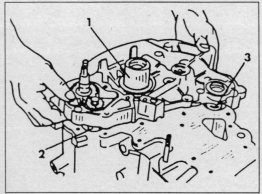

Fig. 1.67.—Fitting the front housing.
1. Guide for oil seal   L.H. balance shaft   3. R.H. balance shaft

pump gear. Provisionally fit and tighten the screw.

● Lubricate the bearing journals of the R.H. shaft with engine oil and insert into the cylinder block. Wrap masking tape around the end of the crankshaft and place the front housing gasket in position.

● Insert the L.H. shaft into the cylinder block at the same time place the housing over the cylinder block, as shown in Fig. 1.67.

● Insert a screwdriver into the block, as shown in Fig. 1.68) to lock the shaft in position and tighten the shaft bolt.

● Fit a new "O" seal ring into the groove of the oil pump cover and fit the cover. Tighten the cover bolts to 1.5 - 1.8 kgm (11 - 13 ft. lb.). These are the bolts (5) in Fig. 1.69, which have a length of 40 mm. The bolt heads are marked with the number "4". Fit the front housing bolts, again noting their different length, given in Fig. 1.69 (same torque).

● Fit the oil suction pipe with a new gasket and tighten

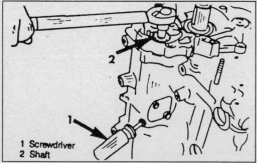

1 Screwdriver
2 Shaft

Fig. 1.68.—Tightening the balance shaft nut. A screwdriver must be inserted into the side of the block to prevent the shaft from rotating.

52

the nuts to 1.8-2.5 kgm (13-18 ft. lb.).

- Coat the oil sump with sealing compound at the points shown in Fig. 1.70 and fit a new gasket. Tighten the 20 bolts to 0.6-0.8 kgm (4.5-5.5 ft. lb.). Do not over-tighten these bolts.

- Fit the rear timing belt guard and the lower guard panel. Tighten the lower screw to 1.5-1.8 kgm (11-13 ft. lb.). This screw also secures the oil pump. The torque of the other screws is less.

- Place the spacer over the front end of the R.H. balance shaft. The chamfer must be towards the inside. Refer to Fig. 1.71 on the next page to check the direction of installation. Coat the outside of the spacer with engine oil. Take care not to damage the oil seal lip.

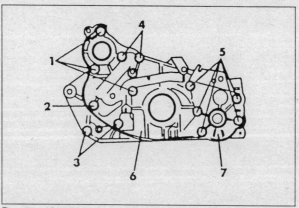

Fig. 1.69. — View of the front housing to show the length of the various securing bolts).

1 = 20mm	5 = 40mm
2 = 25mm	6 = Front housing
3 = 40mm	7 = Oil pump cover
4 = 25mm	

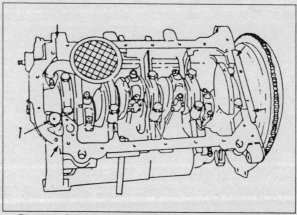

Fig. 1.70. — Coat the points indicated by the arrows with sealing compound. The oil relief valve (1) must be inserted before the oil sump is fitted to the cylinder block.

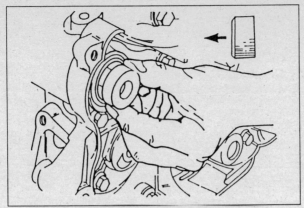

Fig. 1.71. — Fitting the spacer to the front end of the balance shaft.

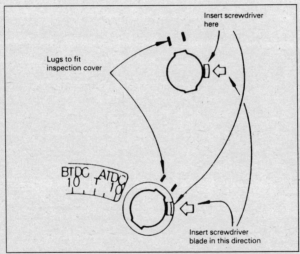

Fig. 1.72. — Position of the two inspection holes to adjust the timing belt tension.

1.4.6. ADJUSTING THE TIMING BELT TENSION — ENGINE FITTED

The lower timing belt cover has two openings which enable the adjustment of the timing belt tension without removal of the timing cover. Fig. 1.72 shows details where the closing covers for these openings are located. The belt tension does not require adjustment under normal circumstances. The tension of the drive belt for the R.H. balance shaft cannot be adjusted. Adjust the timing belt tension as follows:

● Remove the upper timing belt guard.
● Turn the crankshaft in the normal direction of rotation until the mark "A" in the camshaft

54

timing gear is in line with the timing mark in the rear cover of the cylinder head. If mark "A" is not visible, align the second tooth before the camshaft timing gear mark with the timing mark in the rear cover. Fig. 1.73 shows the two possibilities.

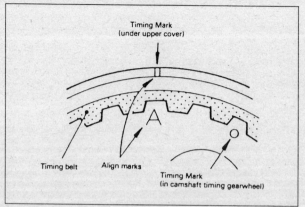

Fig. 1.73.—Aligning the timing marks.

NOTE: When the camshaft timing gear is aligned in the position described, the crankshaft will be in a position which brings the No. 1 piston slightly below the top dead centre and the slack side of the timing belt is on the side of the timing belt tensioner. If the mark "A" is used, do not attempt to rotate the crankshaft to the left, as this would tension the timing belt and prevent correct adjustment of the tension.

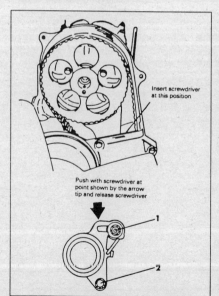

Fig. 1.74.—Adjusting the timing belt tension.

- Remove the two closing covers for the inspection holes by applying a screwdriver at the positions shown in Fig. 1.72.
- Insert a suitable socket with an extension through the opening, and slacken the nut and bolt securing the belt tensioner by no more than ½ of a turn. Use a piece of sticky tape to attach the socket to the extension to prevent it from slipping off.
- Insert a screwdriver against the belt tensioner as shown in Fig. 1.74, push the tensioner into the direction shown by the arrow and then release. The belt tension will be automatically adjusted by the action of the tensioner return spring. The "help" with the screwdriver is necessary in case that the tensioner is sticking to the cylinder block.
- Tighten the upper nut (1) in Fig. 1.74 and then the bolt (2). The order of tightening is important, as the tension can change if the bolt is tightened first.
- Fit the two closing covers. To do this, insert the covers from above between the

two guides until the locking tabs engage.

1.5.   EXHAUST SYSTEM

1.5.0.   Removal

The exhaust system should only be removed completely if parts of it must be replaced. The system consists of two sections, i.e. the front section with the front exhaust pipe and the front silencer and the rear section with the rear silencer and the end pipe. Different exhaust systems are fitted for petrol and diesel models.

Replace the parts of the system as described below. The car should be jacked up and supported at a suitable heigth to gain access to the connections and mountings from underneath the vehicle.

● **Rear Silencer and Pipe:**   Support the end of the exhaust pipe from underneath with suitable wooden planks or blocks or by other means and unscrew the bolts connecting the rear pipe to the rear end of the front silencer. Two bolts are used. Unhook the suspension rubbers, remove the suspension brackets and withdraw the end silencer together with the end pipe. A tight connection can be sprayed with rust-dissolving fluid. Wait a few minutes to allow the fluid to act.

● **Front Pipe and Silencer:**   Remove the rear exhaust pipe with the silencer as described above. Unscrew the front pipe from the exhaust manifold connection. Spray the manifold bolts with rust-dissolving fluid if necessary. Unscrew the front exhaust pipe-to-transmission bracket and take out the assembly.

1.6.1   Installation

Loosely attach all sections of the exhaust system to their mountings. Fit the front pipe to the exhaust manifold, the clamp at the clutch housing and the silencer clamp connection and finally fit the rear pipe with the silencer. Seal the joining faces of all pipes with heat-resistant sealing compound.

Check the correct layout of all pipes, to ensure that there is a gap of at least 20 - 30 mm (0.8 - 1.2 in.) between all pipes and other chassis or body parts. The rubber suspension rings must not be under tension.

1.6.   Engine — Tightening Torque Values

Cylinder head bolts:
Engine cold: . . . . .7.0 - 7.5 kgm (51 - 54 ft.lb.)
Engine warm: . . . . .8.0 - 8.5 kgm (58 - 61 ft.lb.)
Camshaft bearing caps: . . . . .1.9 - 2.1 kgm (14 - 15 ft.lb.)
Camshaft timing gear bolt: . . . . .8 - 10 kgm (58 - 72 ft.lb.)
Inlet and exhaust manifold: . . . . .1.5 - 1.9 kgm (11 - 14 ft.lb.)
Locknut for valve adjusting screws: . . . . .1.2 - 1.7 kgm (8.5 - 12 ft.lb.)
Main bearing cap bolts: . . . . .5.0 - 5.5 kgm (36 - 40 ft.lb.)
Big end bearing cap nuts: . . . . .3.2 - 3.4 kgm (23 - 24.5 ft.lb.)
Crankshaft pulley bolts: . . . . .1.5 - 1.8 kgm (11 - 13 ft.lb.)
Crankshaft timing gear bolt: . . . . .8 - 10 kgm (58 - 72 ft.lb.)
Oil pump drive gear nut: . . . . .3.4 - 3.9 kgm (25 - 29 ft.lb.)
Belt tensioner nut: . . . . .2.2 - 3 kgm (16 - 22 ft.lb.)

Balance shaft timing gear bolt: . . . . 3.5-4.0 kgm (25-30 ft.lb.)
Front housing bolts: . . . . 1.5-1.7 kgm (11-12 ft.lb.)
Flywheel bolts: . . . . 13-14 kgm (94-101 ft.lb.)
Drive plate bolts (automatic): . . . . 13-14 kgm (94-101 ft.lb.)
Oil pump cover: . . . . 1.5-1.7 kgm (11-12 ft.lb.)
Oil pressure switch: . . . . 1.5-2.1 kgm (11-14 ft.lb.)
Oil sump bolts: . . . . 0.6-0.7 kgm (4.5-5 ft.lb.)
Sump oil drain plug: . . . . 3.5-4.5 kgm (25-33 ft.lb.)
Oil filter . . . . 1.1-1.2 kgm (8-8.5 ft.lb.)
Oil pressure relief valve: . . . . 4-5 kgm (30-36 ft.lb.)
Water temperature sender unit: . . . . 3-4 kgm (21-30 ft.lb.)
Starter motor bolts: . . . . 2.2-3.1 kgm (14.5-30 ft.lb.)
Alternator mounting: . . . . 2.0-2.4 kgm (14.5-15 ft.lb.)
Alternator belt adjusting link: . . . . 2-3 kgm (14-21 ft.lb.)
Spark plugs: . . . . 2-3 kgm (14-30 ft.lb.)
Exhaust tube to manifold: . . . . 2.0-3.0 kgm (15-21 ft.lb.)
Exhaust tube to silencer: . . . . 2.0-3.0 kgm (15-21 ft.lb.)
Other exhaust attachments: . . . . 1.0-1.5 kgm (7.2-11 ft.lb.)
Engine and transmission mountings:
    L.H. mounting bracket to engine: . . . . 5-6.5 kgm (36-47 ft.lb.)
    L.H. mounting bracket to body: . . . . 6-8 kgm (43-58 ft.lb.)
    Front roll stopper bracket to engine: . . . . 5-6.5 kgm (36-47 ft.lb.)
    Front roll stopper bracket to crossmember: . . . . 4-5 kgm (29-36 ft.lb.)
    Rear roll stopper bracket to crossmember: . . . . 6-8 kgm (43-58 ft.lb.)
    Rear roll stopper stay to bracket: . . . . 3-4 kgm (22-29 ft.lb.)
    L.H. mounting to body: . . . . 3-4 kgm (22-29 ft.lb.)
    Rear mounting bracket to engine: . . . . 3-4 kgm (22-29 ft.lb.)
    Transmission mounting bracket to body: . . . . 4-5 kgm (29-36 ft.lb.)
    Transmission mounting to transmission: . . . . 6-8 kgm (43-58 ft.lb.)
Engine damper (diesel) to engine: . . . . 3-4 kgm (21-29 ft.lb.)
Engine damper (diesel) to crossmember: . . . . 5-6.5 kgm (36-47 ft.lb.)
Clutch bolts: . . . . 1.5-2.2 kgm (11-18 ft.lb.)
Transmission case to engine: . . . . 4.3-5 kgm (31-36 ft.lb.)

2.   THE LUBRICATION SYSTEM

2.0.   Technical Data

Oil Pump:
    Type: . . . .   Gear-type oil pump, fitted to front housing, driven through toothed belt. L.H. balance shaft driven from pump gearwheel

Oil Pump Clearances:
    Clearance between gearwheel and pump body bore:
        Driven gearwheel: . . . . 0.10-0.70 mm (0.004-0.027 in.)
        Drive gearwheel: . . . . 0.20-0.70 mm (0.008-0.027 in.)
    Side clearance: . . . . 0.06-0.12 mm (0.0024-0.0047 in.)
    Clearance between shaft and cover: . . . . 0.02-0.05 mm (0.0008-0.002 in.)

Relief Valve Spring:
    Free length: . . . . 47.0 mm (1.8504 in.)
    Fitted load: . . . . 4.3 kgm (9.46 lbs.)

2.1.   The Oil Pump

A gear-type oil pump is used inside the engine. The oil pump is located in the front cover and

57

consists of a drive gear and a driven gear. The pump is driven by a toothed belt from the crankshaft. One of the balance shafts is fitted to the driven pump gear and rotates against the normal direction of crankshaft rotation.

2.1.0.   REMOVAL AND INSTALLATION

The removal of the oil pump is carried out together with the balance shafts and these operations have already been described in Section 1.4.5.

2.1.1.   OIL PUMP OVERHAUL

- Remove the two screws and take off the oil pump cover. Take out the gearwheels.
- Unscrew the oil pressure relief valve plug and take out the spring and the plunger.

Thoroughly clean all parts and check for wear. Pay attention to grooves inside the pump housing and on the contact areas of the pump gearwheels. Check all openings and bores in the pump body for obstruction and clear, if necessary with compressed air. If the pump cover shows signs of wear replace it.

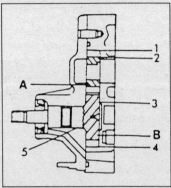

Check the clearances of the oil pump in accordance with Fig. 2.1. The specific values are given in the "Technical Data" section (2.0).

Insert the relief valve plunger into the bore and check for freedom of movement. Check the spring for distortion or fatigue.

The assembly of the oil pump is a reversal of the removal procedure. Lubricate the gearwheels and pump body with oil before assembly. When fitting the oil pump gearwheels, align the two mating marks as shown in Fig. 1.66. The final installation is carried out together with the front housing.

Rotate the gearwheels a few times after installation. 10 c.c. of engine oil can be filled into the pump to prime it for its first minutes of operation.

Fig. 2.1. — Sectional view of the oil pump with the checking positions for the gear clearances.
1 Clearance between teeth tips
2 Radial clearance
3 Radial clearance
4 Clearance between teeth tips
A = Driven gearwheel
B = Drive gearwheel

2.2.   Oil Filter

The oil filter is fitted to the cylinder block. The oil filter is removed with a special filter wrench, similar as the one shown in Fig. 2.2 or a universal filter wrench is used, which can be purchased at most accessory shops. If no special appliance is available, drive the blade of a strong screwdriver through the side of the oil filter and use the handle as a lever to unscrew the filter.

After removal thoroughly clean the filter seat on the front housing. Coat the gasket of the new oil filter with engine oil and screw the filter in position until the rubber seal touches the filter seat. From this position tighten the filter by a further 2/3 of a turn, using the hands only. No filter wrench should be used for this operation.

Check the engine oil level in the sump and start the engine. After the engine has been running for a while, check the filter connection for oil leaks.

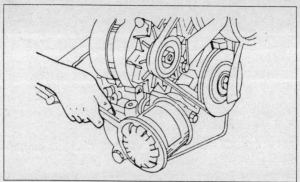

Fig. 2.2. — Removal of the oil filter. Shown is the special tool which engages into the ribs of the filter cartridge.

2.3.   Checking the Oil Level

The oil level can only be checked properly if the vehicle is parked on a level ground. If the engine has been running, wait a few minutes. This gives the oil time to flow back into the oil sump.

Withdraw the oil level dipstick and wipe off with a clean cloth or tissue paper. Re-insert the dipstick and withdraw once more. The oil level mark will now appear on the dipstick.

If necessary, top-up with the recommended engine oil. Check the oil level once more. The oil should be up to the "H" mark on the dipstick. Never run the engine when the oil level is below the "L" mark. Overfilling of the oil sump will serve no useful purpose as the additional oil will be burnt very quickly.

2.4.   Oil Pressure Switch

The oil pressure switch is connected by means of a lead with the oil pressure warning light in the dashboard. If a new switch is fitted, coat the threads with sealing compound. Tighten the switch to 1.5 - 2.2 kgm (11 - 15 ft.lb.).

To check the operation of the oil pressure switch, connect a 12 volt test lamp between the switch terminal and a good earthing point. Start the engine and check if the warning light comes on. If this is not the case, replace the switch.

3.	COOLING SYSTEM

A thermo-syphon cooling system is used for the engine, consisting of a tube and fin radiator, an expansion tank, a centrifugal water pump and a wax thermostat. An oil cooler for the engine lubrication system is fitted to diesel-powered models; an oil cooler for the transmission is fitted to models with automatic transmission. Both coolers are cooled through the engine cooling system. Fig. 3.1 shows the layout of the cooling system for the petrol model. The layout for the diesel model is similar, but the expansion tank is located on the other side of the radiator.

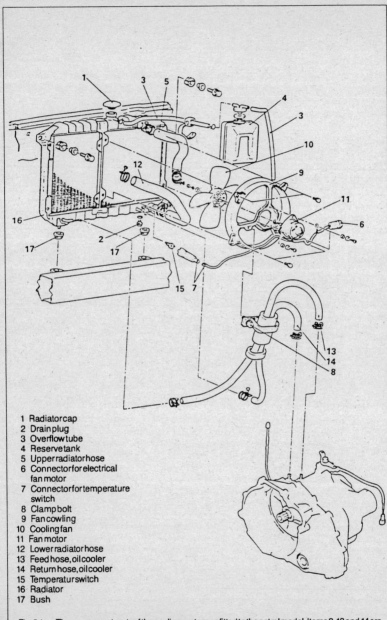

1 Radiator cap
2 Drain plug
3 Overflow tube
4 Reserve tank
5 Upper radiator hose
6 Connector for electrical
   fan motor
7 Connector for temperature
   switch
8 Clamp bolt
9 Fan cowling
10 Cooling fan
11 Fan motor
12 Lower radiator hose
13 Feed hose, oil cooler
14 Return hose, oil cooler
15 Temperature switch
16 Radiator
17 Bush

Fig. 3.1. — The component parts of the cooling system as fitted to the petrol model. Items 8, 13 and 14 are only fitted to models with automatic transmission.

The radiator functions together with an electrically operated cooling fan. The water pump is driven via a drive belt from the crankshaft.

The thermostat is located in the water outlet elbow. The thermostat is closed when the coolant has a low temperature. This enables the coolant to by-pass the radiator, thereby ensuring a quick warming up of the engine.

3.0.   Technical Data

Type: ....   Thermo-syphon system with centrifugal water pump, thermostat, electro-magnetic cooling fan, controlled through switch in side of radiator

Radiator
Type: ....   Fin and tube, oil cooler fitted to bottom in case of automatic transmission. Separate oil cooler for engine in case of diesel model.

Cooling system capacity: ....See Section 0.3

Opening pressure of filler cap: ....0.75 - 1.05 kg/sq. cm. (10.7 - 15 psi.)

Thermostat
Opening temperature:
  Marked "82" (diesel): ....80.5 - 83.5° C
  Marked "88" (petrol): ....86.5 - 89.5° C
Fully open at:
  Marked "82": ....95° C
  Marked "88": ....100° C

Water pump belt tension: ....See Section 3.3.2

3.1.   Draining and Filling the Cooling System

● Remove the filler caps from radiator and expansion chamber. The engine must be cold. On a hot engine, turn the radiator filler cap to the first detent and allow the vapour to blow off. Use a thick rag to protect the hands.

● The anti-freeze in the cooling system can be collected in a clean container if still in good condition. There is no need to drain the cooling system for certain operations. It is for example sufficient to drain the system to the level of the upper water hose or the thermostat if only these parts are to be replaced.

● Set the heater control lever in the dashboard to the "Warm" position and unscrew the drain plug at the bottom of the radiator (2, Fig. 3.1) and, if fitted on the side of the cylinder block.

● After the cooling system has been completely drained, close the drain tap.

If the cooling system has not been drained for a long time it should be flushed through with clean water. To do this, open the drain tap and insert a water mains connected hose into the radiator filler neck. Turn on the water and let it run until the water flowing from the drain tap opening is clean and free from contamination. Start the engine to assist the circulation.

To refill the system:

● Refit the drain plug. Check the sealing washer and replace if necessary.

● Prepare the anti-freeze solution in accordance with cold weather to be expected. A mixture of 50% anti-freeze and 50% water will cover normal temperatures below zero.

● Fill the radiator through the filler neck to the bottom of the neck and also fill the expansion chamber. Fit the two filler caps.

61

- Start the engine and let it run until the temperature gauge shows that the operating temperature of the engine has been obtained.
- Wait for the engine to cool down and re-check the coolant level in the radiator. If necessary fill in additional anti-freeze.
- Fill the expansion chamber to the "'Full'' mark (Fig. 3.2). When the engine is cold, the coolant level on the expansion tank must be between the "Full" and the "Low" mark.

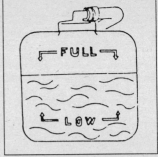

3.2. The Radiator

3.2.1. REMOVAL AND INSTALLATION

Fig. 3.2. — View of the cooling system expansion chamber. The coolant must be within the two marks when the engine is cold. Note the different type in Fig. 3.1.

Carry out the following operations by referring to Fig. 3.1:

- Drain the cooling system as described in Section 3.1.
- Slacken the hose clips and remove the upper and lower radiator hoses from the radiator and also from the engine connections.
- Disconnect the battery.
- Disconnect the overflow hose from the expansion chamber.
- If an automatic transmission is fitted, disconnect the oil cooler hoses. Place a container underneath the connections to collect any transmission fluid running out. Fig. 3.1 shows where the pipes are connected.
- Disconnect the fan motor connector, free the clip from the cable harness and disconnect the wiring from the temperature switch for the fan operation.
- Remove the radiator securing screws on each side of the radiator and lift out the radiator. Take care not to damage the radiator core on any of the surrounding parts. The fan motor remains on the radiator during removal. If necessary unscrew the motor together with the fan cowling from the radiator.

Check the radiator hoses for cracks, porosity or other damage. Replace a doubtful hose as it may split whilst on the road with the consequent inconvenience. Check the radiator for rusty areas, indicating in most cases a leak. Leaking radiators can be repaired in a specialist shop.

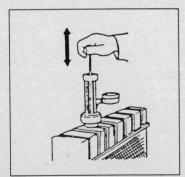

Fig. 3.3 — Checking the cooling system for leaks (loss of pressure) with the radiator test pump.

If a radiator pressure testing pump is available, check the radiator cap. Attach the pump to the radiator cap and build-up pressure until the valve inside the cap opens. This should take place at a pressure of 0.8 - 1.0 kg/sq.cm. (11 - 14 psi.).

The same pump can also be used to test the fitted radiator and the connecting hoses for leaks. In this case, attach the pump to the radiator filler neck (Fig. 3.3) and operate the pump to build-up a pressure of 1.6 kg/sq.cm. (23 psi.). Observe the dial on the pump. There should be no visible drop-off of pressure for a considerable time. If a loss of pressure can be detected, drive the vehicle over a dry area to facilitate the tracing of the leak.

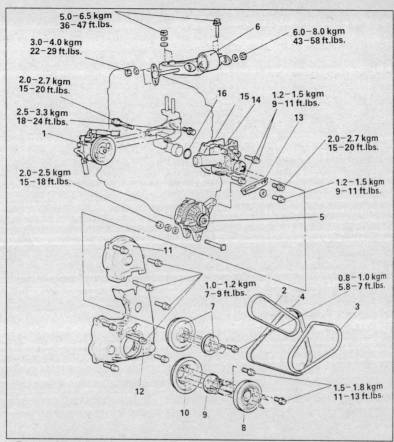

Fig. 3.4. — Details for the removal and installation of the water pump. Observe the tightening torques.

1 Steering pump	7 Water pump pulleys	13 Alternator link
2 Steering pump V-belt	8 Crankshaft pulley	14 Water pump
3 Compressor V-belt	9 Adaptor plate	15 Gasket
4 Water pump V-belt	10 Crankshaft pulley	16 "O" sealing ring
5 Alternator	11 Upper belt guard	
6 L.H. mounting bracket	12 Lower belt cover	

3.2.2.   Installation

The installation of the radiator is a reversal of the removal procedure. Guide the pins at the bottom of the radiator into the rubber mounting bushes. When fitting the radiator hoses push them over their respective connections, ensuring that enough length of the hose is pushed over the radiator and engine elbows. The same applies to the small overflow hose. Tighten the hose clips without overtightening them. An overtightened hose clip will cut into the hose and may create water leaks.

Fill the cooling system as described in Section 3.1, start the engine and check all connections for leaks after the engine has reached its operating temperature.

3.3.   Water Pump

There is no provision to overhaul the water pump. A new unit must be fitted if the original pump is damaged in any way. The only check on the water pump is for excessive clearance of the shaft bearing. If excessive side play can be noticed, the pump must be replaced.

3.3.1.   REMOVAL AND INSTALLATION OF THE PUMP

Fig. 3.4 shows the parts to be removed to unscrew the water pump from the engine, in the case of the petrol engine. The removal and installation of the pump is carried out in a similar manner for the petrol and diesel engine. In the case of the diesel engine lower the engine and transmission as far as necessary before removal of the pump. Refer to the instructions for the removal of the engine in Section 16.1 for details of removal.

- Remove the steering pump (1) and take off the pump drive belt (2). If an air conditioner is fitted, remove the drive belt (3) for the compressor.
- Remove the drive belt (4) for the alternator and water pump and remove the alternator (5) from the mounting bracket.
- Remove the L.H. mounting bracket (6).
- Unscrew the water pump pulleys (7). If an air conditioning system is fitted, remove the crankshaft pulley (8) and the adaptor (9). In the case of all models, remove the crankshaft pulley (10).
- Remove the timing belt upper guard (11), followed by the lower guard (12) and take off the alternator adjusting link (13).
- Remove bolts securing the water pump. Note that not all bolts are of the same length and they should be marked in accordance with their position. Remove the pump from the engine and take off the gasket (15) and the "O" sealing ring (16). Immediately clean the gasket face on pump and cylinder block.

Always use a new gasket and a new "O" sealing ring when refitting the pump. The installation of the pump is a reversal of the removal procedure. Observe all tightening torques shown in Fig. 3.4. Adjust the fan belt tension as described in Section 3.3.2. Finally refill the cooling system (Section 3.1) and check the cooling system for leaks.

3.3.2.   DRIVE BELT TENSION (See also Section 3.6)

Always tension the drive belt whenever the alternator or water pump or the drive belt have been removed or slackened for any reason. The drive belt is properly tensioned when the deflection shown between the arrows is 6.5 - 8.0 mm (0.26 - 0.31 in.) when a belt has been fitted or between 8.0 - 11.0 mm (0.31 - 0.43 in.) when the belt tension is just being checked. A used belt should be tensioned to a deflection of approx. 10 mm (0.4 in.). Move the belt to and fro, gripped between forefinger and thumb. A pressure

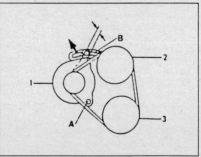

Fig. 3.5. — Details of the drive belt tension. The belt must have the deflection given between the two arrows. Move the alternator in the direction of the large arrow to tension the belt (see also Section 3.6).

of 10 kg (22 lb.) should be applied to the belt when this check is carried out. To check the tension professionally it is therefore possible to hook a spring scale to the belt and pull on the scale with the value given. Check that the belt deflects as above.

When a new belt has been fitted, it is as well to re-check the tension after a few hundred miles have been covered.

Signs of a slipping drive belt are a squealing noise from the engine compartment when the engine is accelerated suddenly. The belt will slip in the pulleys, thereby producing a noise.

To adjust the fan belt tension on an arrangement as shown in Fig. 3.5, slacken the alternator securing bolts and the bolt and nut securing the drive belt tensioning link (points "A" and "B" in Fig. 3.5) and move the alternator towards the outside by inserting a strong screwdriver or a tyre lever at the drive end of the unit. Never apply the leverage at any other point of the alternator. Re-tighten the securing bolts and the adjusting link and re-check the tension. Finally tighten the bolt and nut on the link to 1.2-1.5 kgm (9-10 ft.lb.) and the lower alternator bolts and nuts to 2.0 -2.5 kgm (15- 18 ft.lb.). Refer to Section 3.6 for latest models.

3.4. Thermostat

The thermostat is located behind the water outlet elbow, at the end of the upper water hose. To remove the thermostat, partially drain the cooling system, remove the two elbow securing screws and take off the upper radiator hose. Lift out the thermostat.

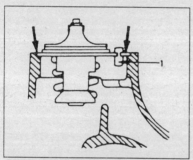

Fig. 3.6. — Correct installation of the thermostat.

The average opening temperature is stamped into the thermostat. "82" signifies an opening temperature of 82° C and this thermostat is used for diesel engines. Petrol engines have a thermostat with a higher opening temperature, marked "88".

A thermostat can be tested by immersing it into a container of cool water and gradually raising the temperature to check that it opens properly.

Suspend the thermostat on a piece of wire so that it does not touch the sides or the bottom of the container. A thermometer must also be suspended in the same manner. Observe the thermometer and check that the thermostat opens at around 82° C (180° F) and is fully open at 95° C (203° F) or 88° C, depending on the engine. A thermostat failing this test must be replaced. It is possible to drive without thermostat for a short while if one is not handy for immediate installation. When fitting the thermostat coat both sides of the gasket with sealing compound. Make sure that the "jiggle pin" (1) is in the position shown in Fig. 3.6. Finally fill the cooling system.

3.5. Engine Oil Cooler — Diesel Models

To remove the oil cooler for the engine oil, fitted to the above models, proceed as follows, referring to Figs. 3.7 for details:

- Remove the union nuts (1) connecting the oil cooler feed tube (6) and the return tube (7) to hoses.
- Remove the banjo bolts (2), remove the sealing washers (3) and disconnect the two oil cooler tubes from the oil cooler. The welded-in connections must be held with an open-ended spanner when the banjo bolts are slackened.
- Remove the oil cooler mounting bolts and remove the oil cooler (5). Be careful not to spill

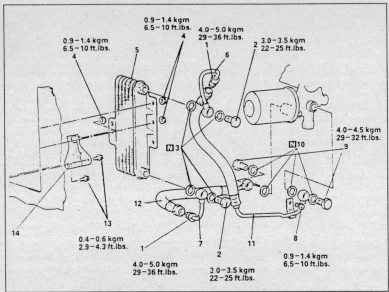

Fig. 3.7. — The component parts of the engine oil cooler, fitted to diesel models.

1	Union nuts	8	Clamp securing bolt
2	Banjo bolts	9	Banjo bolts
3	Sealing washers	10	Sealing washers
4	Securing nuts	11	Oil cooler feed hose
5	Engine oil cooler	12	Oil cooler return hose
6	Oil cooler return tube	13	Bracket securing bolts
7	Oil cooler feed tube	14	Oil cooler bracket

any of the oil inside.

● Remove other parts of the oil cooler assembly by referring to the illustration.

If the same oil cooler is refitted, check it for leaks, blockages or damage. Replace the sealing washers for the banjo bolts, if not in good condition.

The installation of the oil cooler is a reversal of the removal procedure. Refer to the tightening torques in Figs. 3.7 when tightening the banjo bolts and other attachmemts of the oil cooler. After installation, start the engine to bleed the air out of the oil cooler system.

Check the oil level in the engine and replenish with fresh engine oil if necessary. Check all pipe and hose connections for leaks. Change the sealing washers if oil leaks can be noticed. Do not tighten above the specified torque in order to cure an oil leak.

3.6.   Water Pump Drive Belt — With Belt Adjuster

Latest models are fitted with an adjuster for the alternator and water pump drive belt. Further-more, a ripped belt is used on some models. When fitting this type of belt, make sure that the belt is centred in the centre of the pulley groove during installation.

To adjust the belt tension, if an adjuster is fitted, refer to Fig. 3.8. First slacken the alternator moun-ting bolt at the bottom to enable the alternator to swivel towards the inside or outside.

Slacken the lock bolt for the adjuster by a few turns. If the belt has been replaced, check for pro-per engagement in the grooves of the pulleys.

66

Use the adjuster bolt in Fig. 3.8 to adjust the belt tension. Turn the bolt clockwise to increase the belt tension or anti-clockwise to decrease the belt tension. The tension of a used belt must be between 8 and 11 mm (0.31 and 0.43 in.). Diesel models can also be fitted with the adjuster, but have a V-belt. The deflection of the belt should be 10 - 13 mm (0.4 - 0.5 in.).

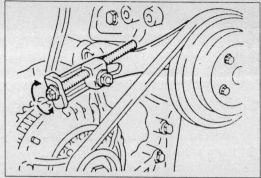

Fig. 3.8. — Adjusting the water pump and alternator drive belt tension on an engine with adjuster. Turn the adjuster bolt in the direction of the arrow (see text).

4.   THE CARBURETTOR FUEL SYSTEM

The fuel system consists of a mechanically operated diaphragm fuel pump, the carburettor (either manufactured by Aisan or Mikuni), the air cleaner, the fuel tank and hoses and pipes to connect the various components. The fuel pump is operated via an eccentric on the camshaft which acts directly onto the operating lever of the pump.

The fuel is drawn from the tank through a replaceable filter. A float, fitted to the tank, operates the fuel gauge in the dashboard.

A two-barrel downdraught carburettor is fitted. A fuel return line between the carburettor and the tank has been added. The fuel return line runs parallel to the fuel feed line and care should be taken not to interchange the two pipe connections on the tank if these have been separated for any reason.

4.0.   Technical Data

Fuel Pump:
Type: . . . . Mechanical diaphragm pump
Delivery pressure: . . . . 0.26 - 0.36 kg/sq.cm. (3.7 - 5.1 psi.)
Delivery amount: . . . . 1.3 litres (2.3 Imp. pts.)/min. at engine speed of 5000 rpm

Carburettor
Manufacturer: . . . . Aisan or Mikuni
Starting device: . . . . Automatic

4.1.   The Fuel Pump

4.1.1.   REMOVAL AND INSTALLATION

Refer to Fig. 4.1:

- Remove the air cleaner (Section 4.4).
- Disconnect the two hoses from the fuel pump connectors.

- Remove the two pump securing screws and take off the pump together with the two gaskets and the intermediate flange.

The installation of the fuel pump is a reversal of the removal procedure. Observe the following points:

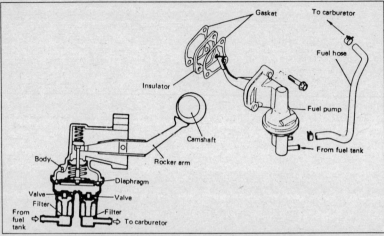

Fig. 4.1. — Sectional view of the fuel pump and details of the mounting.

- Rotate the engine until the piston of No. 2 cylinder is at T.D.C. position in the firing stroke. Fit the pump together with the gaskets and the intermediate flange. Start the engine and check all fuel line connections for leaks.
- Carry out all other operations in reverse order to the removal procedure.
- Start the engine and check all fuel hose connections for leaks. Allow the engine to idle and accelerate to check for proper fuel supply.

4.1.2.   FUEL PUMP TEST

A low delivery pressure or delivery amount or failure to supply fuel to the carburettor could be traced to the fuel pump. Before the pump is removed for inspection, carry out the following tests:

Check all fuel lines for obstructions and check the fuel filter for blockage. The fuel pump must be tested with the engine at operating temperature and running at idle speed. Proceed as follows:

- Insert a "T"-piece into the fuel line at the carburettors, as shown in Fig. 4.2 and

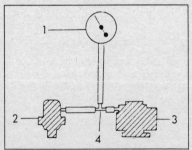

Fig. 4.2. — Checking the fuel pump delivery pressure.
1. Pressure gauge   3. Carburettor
2. Fuel pump   4. "T"-piece

connect a piece of hose of not more than 150 mm (6 in.) between the "T"-piece and a pressure gauge. A longer hose may collect fuel and additional weight of fuel would be added to the pressure of the pump, resulting in inaccurate reading.

68

- Connect a revolution counter (tachometer) and start the engine. Run the engine at idle speed and check that a reading of 0.26 - 0.36 kg/sq.cm. (3.7 - 5.1 psi.) is obtained on the pressure gauge.
- The pressure should remain constant or return to zero slowly when the engine is switched off. An immediate return to zero indicates a leaky delivery valve.
- If the pressure is below the min. value given above, check the diaphragm spring for weakness.

4.2.   Fuel Filter

The fuel filter is clipped in position as shown in Fig. 4.3. The filter should be replaced when the fuel tank is nearly empty to prevent loss of fuel.

To remove the filter, disconnect the two hoses and remove the filter. Remove the fuel filter from the filter clamp. Push the fuel hoses 25 - 30 mm (1 - 1.12 in.) over the connector and tighten the hose clamps. Start the engine and check the connections for fuel leaks.

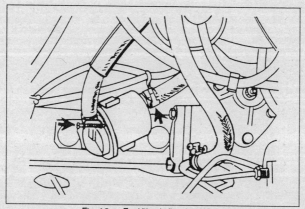

Fig. 4.3. — Fuel filter in fitted position.

4.3.   The Carburettor

All Mitsubishi engines are fitted with a two-barrel downdraught carburettor with manual or automatic choke, accelerator pump and enrichment system. The carburettor has been modified at various stages between the introduction of the the petrol model and now. Fig. 4.4 shows a view of the carburettor fitted before 1988. Figs. 4.5 and 4.6 show views of the carburettor as fitted at present (as of model year 1988).

The carburettor operates with the first stage during normal conditions and with the second stage when the engine is under full load. All jets and drillings are determined during the production of the engine to achieve the best power under all operating conditions. The carburettor jet settings should therefore not be altered for normal use. A larger number on a jet denotes a large jet size. Main and idle fuel jets with larger numbers, therefore, produce a richer fuel/air mixture, whereas air jets with larger numbers produce a weaker mixture.

4.3.1.   Carburettor — Removal and Installation

- Remove the air cleaner (Section 4.4.).

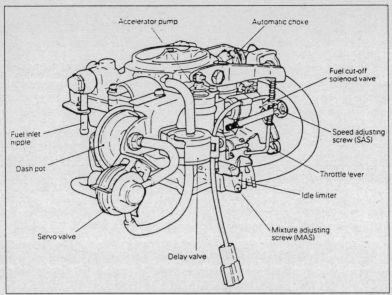

Fig. 4.4. — View of the carburettor fitted before 1988.

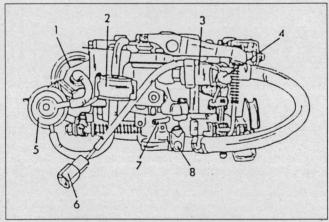

Fig. 4.5. — View of the carburettor (1988 on) from one side.

1. Throttle damper
2. Delay valve
3. Idle cut-off valve
4. Idle speed adjusting screw
5. Servo valve
6. Fuel cut-out solenoid plug
7. Vacuum connection, distributor
8. Mixture adjusting screw

● Disconnect the throttle cable. To do this, slacken the two adjusting nuts at the bracket, release the cable end and unhook the cable end from the throttle operating lever.

● Disconnect the vacuum pipe for the ignition distributor from the carburettor connection.

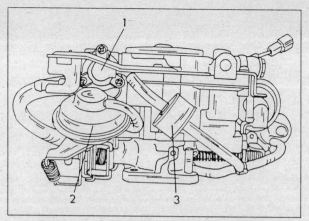

Fig. 4.6. — View of the carburettor (1988 on) from the other side.

1. Choke breaker
2. Depression (vacuum) chamber
3. Choke breaker delay valve

- Disconnect the fuel feed pipe and the return pipe. Do not interchange the connections. Disconnect the choke cable (if fitted).
- Disconnect the electrical connector from the idle fuel cut-off valve.
- Partially drain the cooling system or pinch the hoses on the carburettor with a suitable clamp and disconnect the hoses from the carburettor.
- Remove the carburettor securing nuts at the base of the carburettor, take off the washers

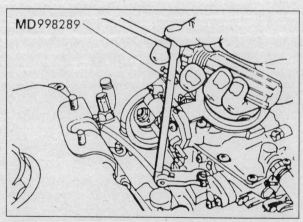

Fig. 4.7. — Removal of the carburettor securing nuts with the special wrench.

and lift the carburettor off the manifold. Remove the gasket between carburettor and manifold and immediately cover the manifold opening with a clean cloth to prevent entry of foreign matter. A special wrench is used to reach the carburettor nuts (Fig. 4.7.). If this tool is not available, suitably bend an open ended spanner in the manner shown to reach the nuts.

The installation of the carburettor is a reversal of the removal procedure. Use a new carburettor gasket. Check both mounting faces for signs of dirt or foreign matter. Do not use sealing compound. Make sure that the fuel return pipe is connected to the correct nipple. After installation of the carburettor, carry out the adjustments described in Section 4.3.3.

4.3.2. CARBURETTOR — DISMANLLING AND ASSEMBLING

It is not intended to describe the dismantling and assembling of the carburettor. Once the carburettor is removed it will be evident how to remove the carburettor cover to reach the jets located underneath the cover. The illustrations of the carburettors show where the individual parts are located and removal and installation of these parts is quite straight forward. Once a jet is removed, make sure to refit it to its original bore. Take great care not to interchange jets between the first and second carburettor stage. New gaskets must be used if the old gaskets show any signs of deterioration or other damage.

4.3.3. CARBURETTOR ADJUSTMENTS

Idle Speed: The position of the two screws used for the slow-running or idle adjustment are shown in Fig. 4.8. The mixture adjusting screw must never be screwed-in too hard, as this would damage the tip of the screw. After the carburettor has been refitted, always adjust the idle speed. The adjustment is also necessary if the engine stalls continuously when the throttle pedal is released or if the engine idles too quickly.

A special tool may be required to adjust the mixture adjusting screw (different for earlier and later models). A limiter cap is placed over the screw and the tool is used to rotate the cap.

The ignition timing point, valve clearances and spark plug gaps must be in order before the idle speed can be adjusted.

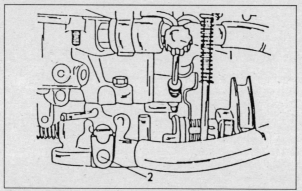

Fig. 4.8. — The location of the idle adjusting screw (1) and the mixture adjusting screw (2). The screw (1) is adjusted with a screwdriver in the case of models after 1988.

Adjust the idle speed as follows:

- Set the gearchange lever into neutral (manual) or into position "N" (automatic).
- Switch off the headlamps and all other electrical consumers.
- Connect a CO meter and a revolution counter in accordance with the instructions of the manufacturer.
- Start the engine and run until the operating temperature is reached. Check the tem-

perature gauge in the dashboard which should show "Normal". If a power-assisted steering is fitted, set the front wheels into the straight-ahead position.

- Adjust the ignition timing to the value given on the sticker in the engine compartment.
- Rev the engine two or three times to 2000-3000 rpm and allow it to return to the idle speed. This will stabilise the idling.
- Check the reading on the revolution counter. The idle speed must be adjusted if outside 800 ± 50 rpm. in the case of a vehicle with manual transmission or automatic transmission before model year 1988. From 1988 the idle speed is set to 750 ± 50 rpm. in the case of models with manual transmission or 800 ± in the case of models with automatic transmission.
- Using the special tool, shown in Fig. 4.9 (shown on the latest carburettor), turn the mixture adjusting screw until the CO content is within 1.5 ± 0.5%.

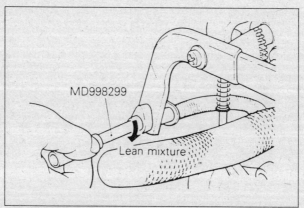

Fig. 4.9. — Adjusting the limiter cap for the mixture adjusting screw on models from 1988, using the special tool.

- Turn the throttle stop screw (1) in Fig. 4.8 (either the knurled screw or with a screwdriver on models from model year 1988) until the correct idle speed has been obtained.

Throttle Damper Adjustment If the engine fails to return to the idle condition after having been accelerated, there is a possibility that the throttle damper must be adjusted. Ignition timing point and idle speed must be correctly adjusted before the setting is checked. A stopwatch is required for the check.

- Run the engine until operating temperature is reached. The headlamps and all other current consumers must be switched off. The cooling fan must not operate. Engage "N" or "P" on an automatic transmission.
- Connect a revolution counter in accordance with the instructions of the manufacturer and start the engine. Allow the engine to idle.
- Move the throttle lever until the lever (1) in Fig. 4.10 is completely free of the throttle damper push rod (2).
- Slowly release the throttle lever until the damper lever just contacts the throttle damper push rod and read off the engine speed. This is referred to as the contact speed.
- Prepare the stop watch and release the throttle lever, at the same time starting the stop watch. Note the elapsed time for the engine to return to the engine speed given below and compare the result.

73

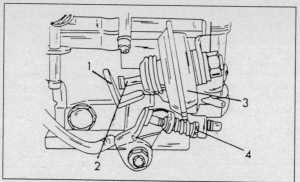

Fig. 4.10. — Details for the adjustment of the throttle damper.

1. Damper lever   3. Throttle valve damper
2. Push rod   4. Adjusting screw

Engine	Contact Speed	Standard Speed	Elapsed Time
Manual transmission	1600-2000 rpm	900 rpm	2.5-5.5 sec.
Automatic transmission	1300-1700 rpm	900 rpm	1.5-4.5 sec.
Manual transmission, from 1988	1600-2000 rpm	900 rom	3.6-6.5 sec.

● If the standard speed is outside the value given, turn the adjusting screw (4) of the throttle damper; if the elapsed time is outside the limits, adjust the contact speed within the adjustment range.

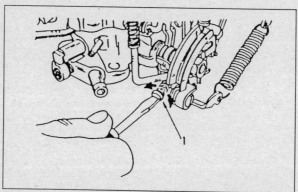

Fig. 4.11. — Turn the adjusting screw (1) for the fast idle speed as shown.

Fast Idle Speed: The engine must be cold before this adjustment is checked:

● Start the engine and check that the fast idle speed is slowly increasing, as the engine warms up. The idle speed must, of course, be correctly adjusted.

● If the fast idle is excessive, turn the screw shown in Fig. 4.11 towards the left, if the speed is too low, turn it towards the right.

Float Level Adjustment: The following instructions are only valid for the Aisan carburettor. The float adjustment must be checked in in raised position and in the lowered position. A drill

74

bit shank can be used for the first check, a feeler gauge of 0.8 - 1.0 mm thickness for the second check. Proceed as follows:

- Invert the carburettor cover to allow the float to lie flat and insert a drill bit shank of 8 mm diameter between the lower edge of the float and the carburettor cover face, as shown in Fig. 4.12 in the L.H. view. If necessary bend the float tongue (1) to adjust the float level. The shank of the drill bit should just slide in, without lifting the float off the cover face.
- For the second check hold the carburettor in the position shown in Fig. 4.12 on the R.H. side and insert a feeler gauge between the float needle valve pin (3) and the float lip. If necessary, bend the float tongue (2), until the gap if between 0.8 - 1.0 mm (0.03 -0.04 in.).

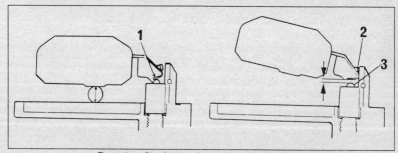

Fig. 4.12. — Checking the float level (see Section 4.3.4).
1. Float tongue   2. Float tongue   3. Float needle valve tip

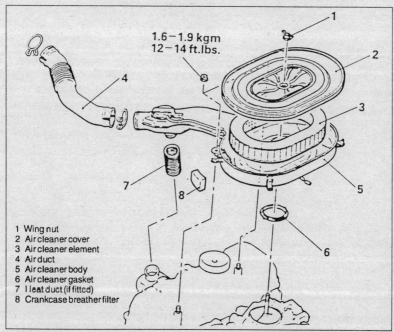

1.6 − 1.9 kgm
12 − 14 ft.lbs.

1 Wing nut
2 Air cleaner cover
3 Air cleaner element
4 Air duct
5 Air cleaner body
6 Air cleaner gasket
7 I leat duct (if fitted)
8 Crankcase breather filter

Fig. 4.13. — Exploded view of the air cleaner.

4.4. Air Cleaner

Fig. 4.13 shows details of the air cleaner. The air cleaner contains a paper filter element. The element cannot be cleaned in liquid. Slightly soiled elements can be blown out with an air line from the inside towards the outside.

To remove the air cleaner element, unscrew the lid and take out the element. Immediately cover the opening of the carburettor bore with a clean rag as long as the filter is removed.

Carefully remove all dust particles from the inside of the air cleaner casing. Check that the two rubber sealing rings are in good condition. If the element appears to be in fairly good condition, tap it onto a wooden surface to remove collected dust from the inside.

Fit the air cleaner element in dry condition and refit the lid.

5. THE IGNITION SYSTEM

The ignition system of the petrol engine covered in this manual is of the so-called CEI type (constant energy ignition system). The ignition distributor contains a centrifugal and a vacuum ignition advance mechanism. The centrifugal advance responds to the speed of the engine; the vacuum advance to the load of the engine. When the engine speed is increased, the flyweights of the centrifugal mechanism are thrown towards the outside, against the force of small return springs and rotate the distributor cam in relation to the distributor shaft, thereby progressively advancing the ignition timing point.

The vacuum unit is connected by a small hose to the carburettor. The ignition timing point is advanced when there is a high vacuum in the inlet manifold and is retarded when the engine is under high load.

The igniter is part of the ignition distributor.

5.0. Technical Data

Fitted Distributor MD079462

Ignition Timing Points (at idle speed): . . . . 13° before tod dead centre

Distributor Data
Direction of rotation: . . . . Clockwise
Firing order: . . . . 1—3—4—2

5.1. The Ignition Distributor

5.1.0. MAINTENANCE

Clean the outside and the inside of the distributor cap at regular intervals to remove carbon deposits, dust and moisture. Also clean the distributor rotor. Use a petrol-moistened cloth to clean the components. After cleaning check the cap and rotor for cracks or so-called "tracking". These a very thin black lines between the various metal segments inside the cap which lead to voltage jumping across, thereby shortening out some of the current.

Replace the distributor rotor if the contacts are badly corroded. Under no circumstances redress the brass contacts.

With the distributor cap and rotor removed, lubricate the inside of the distributor shaft with

2 or 3 drops of oil to lubricate the distributor bearings.

Keep the outside of all H.T. cables free of moisture to ensure proper electrical conduct through the ignition system. Withdraw all H.T. leads from time to time out of their connections and check and clean the connection ends. H.T. leads must not be shortened to rectify bad ends. Always replace the leads.

5.1.1.   DISTRIBUTOR — REMOVAL AND INSTALLATION

The distributor is driven by the camshaft by means of a skew gear. The distributor is fitted into the cylinder head.

To remove the distributor, proceed as follows:

- Disconnect the battery.
- Withdraw the spark plug cables from the distributor or remove the complete distributor cap after springing back the two clips. Place the cap to one side.
- Take off the L.T. wire and then pull off the tube at the vacuum unit.
- Rotate the engine until the piston of the No. 1 cylinder is at top dead centre in the compression stroke (check on the timing marks at the crankshaft pulley) and suitably mark the outside edge of the distributor housing opposite the tip of the distributor rotor with a scriber or screwdriver blade.
- Unscrew the distributor clamp nut and pull the distributor upwards until it is free to be removed.

If the engine has not been rotated and no overhaul of the distributor has been carried out, fit the distributor in its original position, observing the marks made during removal. If the distributor is refitted after overhaul work, proceed as follows:

- Set the engine at T.D.C. position. To do this, turn the crankshaft by applying a socket to the crankshaft pulley bolt, until the notch in the crankshaft pulley is opposite the "T" mark on the timing scale. To make sure that the correct position has been obtained, remove the rocker cover and check that both valves of No. 1 cylinder have some clearance.
- Turn the distributor drive shaft until the two marks in distributor shaft and distributor housing are opposite each other, as shown in Fig. 5.1.

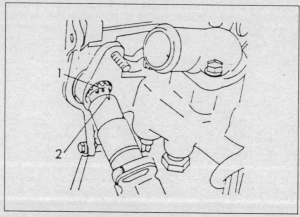

Fig. 5.1. — When fitting the distributor, align the mark (1) on the shaft with the mark (2) on the distributor housing.

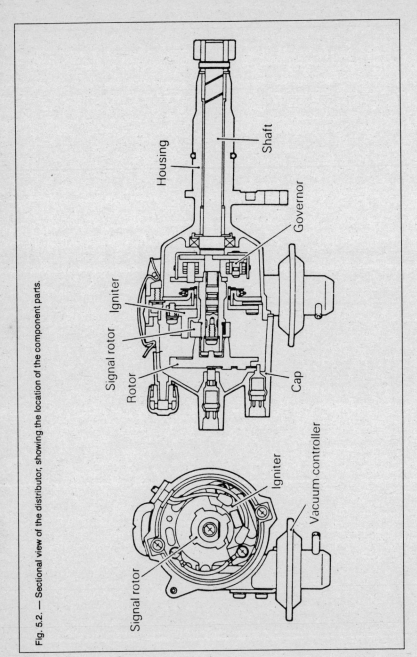

Fig. 5.2. — Sectional view of the distributor, showing the location of the component parts.

Housing

Shaft

Governor

Igniter

Signal rotor

Rotor

Cap

Igniter

Vacuum controller

Signal rotor

- Insert the distributor in this position and check that the mark made in the housing edge is opposite the signal rotor tip. The distributor drive gear will turn slightly due to the effect of the skew gear and the shaft should be turned back by approx. 60° to offset this effect. After installation, check that the the mark on the rotor finger is once more in line with the mark in the rim of the distributor housing.

5.1.2.   DISTRIBUTOR—TESTING

To test the vacuum advance mechanism, disconnect and re-connect the vacuum tube while the stroboscopic timing light is aimed at the notch in the crankshaft pulley and check if the notch "moves" when the tube is connected and disconnected. A failure of the timing to alter, is a sign that the unit is not functioning.

We suggest that your dealer should be asked to overhaul the distributor, as he has test instruments to check the centrifugal and vacuum advanced curves to ensure the correct operation of the distributor and the ignition system.

5.1.3.   Distributor — Overhaul

Refer to Fig. 5.3 for the following operations:

- Remove the distributor cap after springing back the clips, if not already carried out. Take off the seal (3).
- Remove the rotor (5). Unscrew the vacuum unit (6) and disconnect the linkage at the inside. Unscrew the earth cable (7) and the supply cable (8).
- Unscrew the igniter (9).
- Remove the screw inside the distributor shaft and remove the rotor shaft (10) from the upper end of the distributor. Withdraw the signal rotor (11) from the end of the shaft. Unscrew the breaker plate from the distributor housing. The flywheel mechanism can be removed after carefully disengaging the flyweight springs.
- From the other side of the distributor drive the retaining pin (16) out of the drive pinion (17). To do this, place the pinion over the partly opened jaws of a vice and drive the pin with a cylindrical mandrel through the pinion and the distributor shaft. Any burrs at the end of the shaft must be removed before the pinion is withdrawn.
- Remove the distributor shaft from the inside. If necessary remove the oil seal and the washer.

CAUTION!   Do not use any solvent on the vacuum unit or the electrical component parts.

Distributor Cap: Inspect the cap for cracks, tracking or other damage. Faulty caps must always be replaced. Clean corroded high tension terminals.

Distributor Rotor: Inspect the rotor for cracks or excessive burning at the end of the metal strip. Faulty rotors must always be replaced.

Flyweight Mechanism: Check the flyweight mechanism for freedom of movement. Make sure that the maximum clearance of 0.2 mm (0.008 in.) exists between the flyweight and the pin.

Distributor Shaft: Check the shaft for wear and proper fit in the distributor housing. The run out of the shaft should not exceed 0.05 mm (0.002 in.). Assemble the distributor shaft, washers and drive gear with the retaining pin to the distributor body and check the end float of the distributor shaft, using a dial gauge or feeler gauge. The clearance should be between 0.15 and 0.50 mm. If the clearance exceeds the upper limit, correct by inserting new adjusting washers.

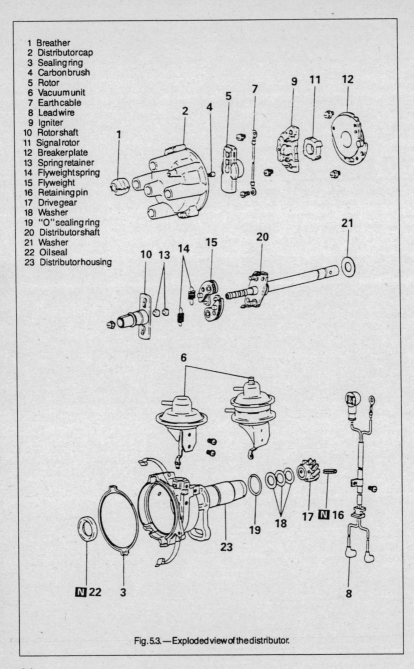

1 Breather
2 Distributor cap
3 Sealing ring
4 Carbon brush
5 Rotor
6 Vacuum unit
7 Earth cable
8 Lead wire
9 Igniter
10 Rotor shaft
11 Signal rotor
12 Breaker plate
13 Spring retainer
14 Flyweight spring
15 Flyweight
16 Retaining pin
17 Drive gear
18 Washer
19 "O" sealing ring
20 Distributor shaft
21 Washer
22 Oil seal
23 Distributor housing

Fig. 5.3. — Exploded view of the distributor.

Lubricate the shaft with oil and insert it into the distributor housing. Fit the washers onto the end of the shaft and attach the drive gear and the retaining pin to the bottom shaft end and rivet the pin ends to the gear collar.

Assemble the flyweight mechanism to the plate, making sure that the flyweight springs are properly located. Refit the lock clips. Lubricate all moving parts with engine oil and check for freedom of movement.

The signal rotor is pressed over the end of the distributor shaft. A dowel pin in the rotor and a groove in the distributor shaft must be aligned. Fit the igniter to the distributor and turn the signal rotor until one of the lobes is in the position shown in Fig. 5.4. Use a feeler gauge and adjust the gap between the lobe and and igniter is 0.8 mm (0.031 in.). Move the igniter accordingly and tighten the screws.

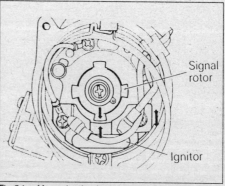

Signal rotor

Ignitor

Fig. 5.4. — Measuring the air gap between the signal rotor and the ignitor.

5.2.   Adjusting the Ignition Timing

It is essential that the ignition timing is finally adjusted with a stroboscopic timing light with the engine running at idle speed. Do not attempt this procedure unless a tachometer (revolution counter) is available.

The engine must be at normal operating temperature before the ignition timing can be adjusted. Check the idling speed and adjust if necessary.

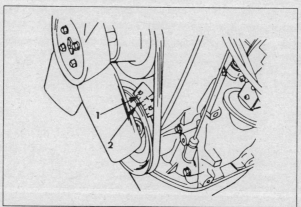

Fig. 5.5. — The notch in the crankshaft pulley (2) must be in line with the correct mark on the ignition timing scale (1), when the timing point is checked with a strobe light.

● Check at the crankshaft pulley that the notch in the outside edge of the pulley is visible. If necessary use chalk or a spot of white paint to highlight the notch.

- Connect a stroboscopic timing light in accordance with the instructions of the manufacturer and start the engine.
- Run the engine at idle speed. Aim the flash of the timing light at the front of the crankshaft pulley and check that the timing mark (see Section 5.0) is in line with the notch in the pulley (Fig. 5.5).
- If necessary, slacken the distributor securing nut and turn the distributor until the two timing marks are in line. To do this, grip the distributor as shown in Fig. 5.6 and turn it clockwise to retard the ignition or anti-clockwise to advance the ignition point. Re-check the timing, re-connect the vacuum hose and finally disconnect the stroboscopic timing light.

Fig. 5.6. — Rotating the distributor to adjust the ignition timing (see text)

5.3.   Spark Plugs

The following spark plugs are used in the engine covered in this manual:

NGK: BPR6ES
Nippon-Denso: W20EPR
Champion: RN-9Y

If spark plugs are removed, make sure that the surrounding area is clean to prevent foreign matter from falling into the plug holes as soon as the plugs are unscrewed. Clean the plug face with a wire brush and check the electrodes for wear or burns.

Use a feeler gauge to check the electrode gap (Fig. 5.7) and close the gap if necessary, by tapping the outside electrode with the handle of a screwdriver. To open up a plug gap, insert the blade of a small screwdriver and bend up the side electrode. Never bend the centre electrode in order to correct plug gaps as this will damage the insulator. The gap should be set to 0.7 - 0.8 mm (0.028 - 0.031 in.).

Inspect the condition of the insulator tip and the electrodes. Following there are a few examples to interpret the condition of plugs removed from the engine.

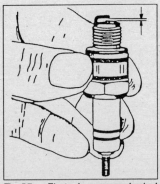

Fig. 5.7. — Electrode gaps are checked between the arrows.

82

Normal Plug Face: The colour of the of the insulator should appear greyish-brown or tan-coloured. The electrodes should be black or sooted. These are signs of a plug which has been used under normal conditions with alternative short and long driving periods. White or yellow deposits mean that the car has been used for long periods at high speeds and can be ignored.

Worn Plug Appearance: Insulator tip and electrodes are burnt off. All plugs which show this condition must be replaced. Always replace the whole set and make sure to fit the correct plug.

Oiled-up Appearance: Normally this condition is recognised by wet oil deposits which have been left by excessive ingress of oil into the combustion chamber (worn piston rings or pistons, inlet valves or valve guides, worn bearings, etc.). Hotter plugs are normally able to overcome the fault, but in serious cases an overhaul of the engine is necessary.

Burnt or Overheated Appearance: Burnt or overheated plugs can normally be recognised by their electrodes being coloured white or being burnt, or by the presence of blisters on the insulator or the electrodes. Electrodes may also be burnt off. Faults can be traced to the cooling system or improper ignition timing.

---

6. CLUTCH

6.0. Technical Data

Type: . . . . Single disc with diaphragm spring
Operation:
   Petrol engine: . . . . By clutch cable
   Diesel engine: . . . . Hydraulic system

Free play at clutch pedal:
   Mechanical operation: . . . . 15 - 20 mm (0.8 - 0.8 in.)
   Hydraulic operation: . . . . 6 - 13 mm (0.25 - 0.5 in.)

Clutch pedal height, all models: . . . . 176.0 - 181.0 mm (6.9 - 7.1 in.)

Clutch Lining Dimensions:
   Outer diameter: . . . . 200 mm (7.8 in.)
   Inner diameter: . . . . 130 mm (5.12 in.)

The dry single plate clutch is of the diaphragm spring type for all engines covered in this Workshop Manual. The operation of the clutch is by a mechanical clutch cable on models with petrol engine or by hydraulic system with master and slave cylinder on models with diesel engine.

The clutch is balanced as an assembly during manufacture and it is essential that all parts are refitted in their original positions to retain the balance.

6.1. Clutch — Removal

Refer to the section on the transmission and follow those instructions to remove the unit. If the engine or transmission is removed for any other reason, always unscrew the clutch to check it over. Remove the clutch as follows:

● Mark the clutch cover and the flywheel face to ensure correct re-assembly. This is carried out with a centre punch. Mark two punch dots at opposite points in flywheel and clutch cover.

- Remove the bolts carefully, a little at a time until the spring pressure is released and take off the clutch cover and the driven plate. Do not allow grease or oil to get on the lining faces or other parts. If necessary, the flywheel can also be removed from the engine.

- Immediately clean the inside face of the flywheel with a clean cloth and check the flywheel friction face. If the clutch linings are worn down to the rivet heads, there is the danger that the rivets have left grooves in the friction face.

6.2.   Inspection of Parts

The parts must not be washed in solvent. Dirt should be removed with a stiff brush and an air line. Oily and greasy surfaces, except the friction surfaces, may be wiped down with a cloth moistened with fuel or suitable solvent.

The driven plate must be renewed if it is mechanically damaged, the linings excessively worn or if the linings are contaminated with oil or grease. Check that the damper springs are secure and that the splines on the hub are not worn so that they allow side clearance.

The driven plate should be mounted on a mandrel between a lathe and the run-out checked by applying a dial gauge at the outer edge as shown in Fig. 6.1. Rotate the disc slowly and read off the deflection of the dial gauge. The run-out should not exceed 0.5 mm (0.02 in.).

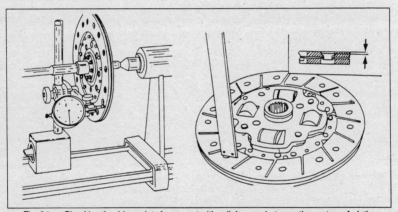

Fig. 6.1. — Checking the driven plate for run-out with a dial gauge between the centres of a lathe on the left. The R.H. view shows the measurement of the clutch lining thickness.

Replace if any of the faults are found. Check the fit of the splines to the gearbox input shaft. At the outer edge of the disc the backlash on the splines must not exceed 0.4 mm (0.016 in.).

Using a depth gauge, measure the distance from the clutch lining surface to the rivet heads on both sides of the driven plate. If this dimension is less than 0.3 mm (0.012 in.), replace the disc. The disc should also be replaced if this min. dimension is nearly reached.

Inspect the ends of the diaphragm spring for wear. If excessive, the complete cover assembly will have to be replaced. The height of the ends of the diaphragm spring must all be at the same level. If necessary, the ends can be bent (carefully) by using a strip of steel with a slit in the end to take the spring thickness.

6.3.   Clutch — Installation

To install the clutch, the use of an alignment mandrel or a spare main driveshaft is necessary.

Clutch alignment mandrel sets can be hired from tool hire companies and one of the mandrels will fit your clutch. Note that the long end of the clutch disc hub must face towards the rear, away from the flywheel.

If the flywheel has been removed, refit it to the crankshaft flange. Counterhold the flywheel by inserting a screwdriver into the teeth of the starter motor ring gear and evenly tighten the flywheel bolts to the torque setting given in Section 1.5. Before inserting the driven plate, have a last look to make sure that no foreign matter remains in the flywheel.

When refitting the original clutch align the punch mark in the flywheel and the clutch cover and install the six bolts. Tighten the clutch securing bolts in a diagonal pattern to a torque reading of 1.5 - 2.2 kgm (11 - 15 ft.lb.).

6.4. Clutch Adjustments

Two checks must be carried out on models with clutch cable, i.e. the pedal height and the adjustment of the clutch pedal free play.

6.4.0. ADJUSTING THE CLUTCH PEDAL HEIGHT

The pedal height "a" in Fig. 6.2 is given in Section 6.0. The adjustment of the clutch pedal height is the same for all models. The pedal height is only adjustable on L.H. drive models.

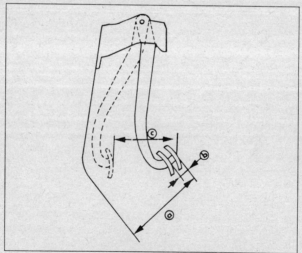

Fig. 6.2. — Details for the clutch pedal height adjustment (a).
a. Pedal height
b. Pedal free play
c. Pedal travel

There is no provision to adjust the pedal on R.H. models. To adjust the pedal height on L.H. drive models, slacken the locknut of the pedal stop bolt (1) and adjust the stop bolt until the correct dimension is obtained. The height can be measured as the stop bolt is adjusted, as shown in Fig. 6.3.

6.4.1. ADJUSTING THE CLUTCH PEDAL CLEARANCE

The free play of the clutch pedal must be adjusted if the clutch does not disengage properly or if parts of the clutch mechanism have been replaced. Proceed as follows for the two types of clutch release:

Cable Operation: From the inside of the engine compartment pull the clutch cable outer sleeve towards the outside and check if there is a free play of 0-1 mm (0-0.04 in.) as shown in Fig. 6.4.

If this is not the case, turn the adjuster wheel shown in Fig. 6.4 until the given free play of 15-20 mm (0.6-0.8 in.) is obtained.

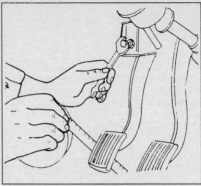

Fig. 6.3. — Measuring the clutch pedal height. Adjust the pedal stop bolt (L.H. drive only) at the same time.

Depress the clutch pedal a few times and check that the clutch pedal free play is still as specified.

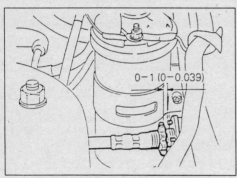

$0-1 (0-0.039)$

Fig. 6.4. — Adjusting the clutch pedal free play.

Hydraulic Operation: Grip the clutch pedal pad between forefinger and thumb and move the pedal to and fro. The play thus indicated is the play at the clutch pedal clevis pin which should be between 1 to 3 mm (0.04 to 0.12 in.). If this play cannot be felt, proceed as follows:

Slacken the locknut of the clutch pedal stop bolt and unscrew the bolt until it is no longer in contact with the clutch pedal lever.

Adjust the clutch pedal height to the value given in Section 6.0 by turning the clutch cylinder push rod, using a pair of pliers. The locknut must be slackened and re-tightened after adjustment.

Now go back to the push rod and screw the push rod in or out until the slight play at the clutch pedal tip, is between 1 to 3 mm (0.04-0.12 in.) when measured between forefinger and thumb. Take care not to push the push rod into the master cylinder when carrying out the clearance check, as this will give a wrong indication.

Operate the clutch pedal a few times and re-check the clutch pedal free play as described above. If the clearance at the push rod and at the clutch pedal cannot be obtained, bleed the clutch system or check the clutch master and/or slave cylinders.

6.5. Replacing the Clutch Cable

- In the inside of the engine compartment unscrew the adjuster wheel from the end of the cable outer sleeve (Fig. 6.4).
- In the inside of the passenger compartment slacken the locknut for the clutch pedal stop bolt (Fig. 6.3) and unscrew the bolt as far as possible.
- Disconnect the clutch operating cable from the clutch release lever on the transmission, as shown in Fig. 6.5 and then unhook it from the top of the clutch pedal. The instrument

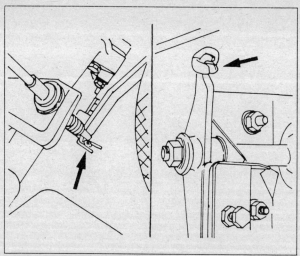

Fig. 6.5. — The attachment of the clutch operating cable. On the L.H. side on the clutch release lever and on the R.H. side on the clutch pedal.

panel undercover and the lap heater duct must be removed to gain access to the clutch cable connection. Withdraw the cable towards the engine compartment.

Check the clutch cable for rough movement, if it is to be refitted. The rubber boot must be in good condition. Wear on the clutch cable eyelet can also take place. Lubricate the new cable with engine oil. The cable should also be lubricated every 12,000 miles. Refit the clutch cable in reverse order to the removal procedure. Adjust the clutch pedal height and the clutch pedal clearance as described in Section 6.4, noting the differences between models with and without cruise control system.

6.6.　　　Hydraulic Clutch Control

6.6.0.　　CLUTCH MASTER CYLINDER

Fig. 6.6 shows the arrangement of the clutch master cylinder together with the hydraulic pipe and hose. The following operations are carried out by referring to the illustration.

Removal and Installation:

- Jack up the front end of the vehicle and push a bleeder hose over the bleeder screw of the clutch slave cylinder. Insert the other end of the hose into a jar. Open the bleeder screw and ask a helper to operate the clutch pedal until the clutch system is drained of fluid.

- Remove the splint pin (1) from the master cylinder push rod clevis pin (3), remove the washer (2) and withdraw the clevis pin.

- Disconnect the fluid line from the master cylinder by unscrewing the banjo bolt (4) and remove the two sealing washers (5). If necessary unscrew the union nut connecting the clutch hose (10) to the clutch hydraulic pipe (6). Remove the spring plate (8) securing the clutch hose to the bracket and remove the hose after opening the hose clamp (9). Unscrew the cylinder from its mounting. Remove the cylinder, taking care that no brake fluid is allow to drip onto painted areas of the vehicle.

The installation is a reversal of the removal procedure. Lubricate the clutch pedal clevis pin

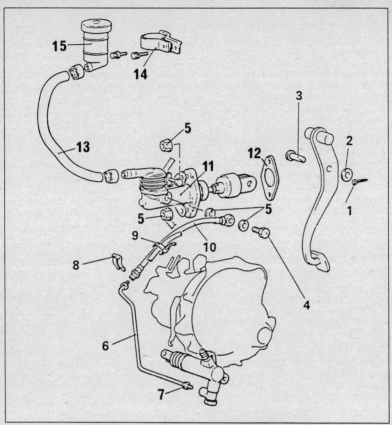

Fig. 6.6. —View of the component parts for the hydraulic clutch control.

1	Split pin	9	Hose clamp
2	Washer	10	Clutch hydraulic hose
3	Clevis pin	11	Clutch master cylinder
4	Banjo bolt	12	Gasket
5	Securing nut	13	Connecting hose
6	Clutch hydraulic pipe	14	Reservoir bracket
7	Union nut	15	Fluid reservoir
8	Spring plate		

with chassis grease. Tighten the master cylinder securing nuts to 1.0 - 1.5 kgm (7 - 11 ft.lb.). The two union nuts are tightened to 1.3 - 1.7 kgm (9 - 12 ft.lb.); the banjo bolt to 2.0 - 2.5 kgm (14.5 - 25 ft.lb.). Finally fill the system with fresh brake fluid and bleed the system as described in Section 6.6.2.

Cylinder Overhaul: Clamp the cylinder into a vice, with the opening towards the top, and push the push rod towards the inside until the snap ring (1) in Fig. 6.7 can be removed from the cylinder bore. Remove the push rod and extract the piston out of the cylinder bore.
Using the fingers only, remove the piston cup from the piston. Mark the hose connector for

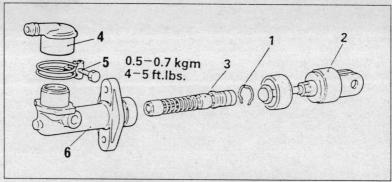

Fig. 6.7. — Exploded view of the clutch master cylinder.

1	Snap ring	4	Fluid hose connector
2	Damper and push rod	5	Connector clamp
3	Piston assembly	6	Master cylinder

the fluid reservoir in suitable manner in relation to the cylinder body, slacken the clamp and withdraw the connector. If the reservoir is to be replaced, disconnect the hose.

Thoroughly clean all parts in brake fluid or white spirits and check for wear. If piston or cylinder bore show signs of seizure or other damage, fit a new cylinder.

Coat a new piston cup with brake fluid and, using the fingers only, fit the cup to the piston. The sealing lip must be facing towards the inside.

Push the piston carefully into the piston bore without damaging the edge of the sealing lip. Use the push rod to push the piston fully in and secure the piston with the retaining snap ring. Make sure the ring enters the groove fully.

Fit the rubber boot to the cylinder end. Fit the connector for the reservoir, align the marks made before removal and tighten the clamp.

6.6.1.   CLUTCH SLAVE CYLINDER

Removal and Installation: Jack up the front end of the vehicle and place chassis stands in position. Push a bleeder hose over the slave cylinder bleeder screw and insert the other end of the hose into a jar.

Open the bleeder screw and ask a helper to operate the clutch pedal until all fluid contained in the system has been ejected.

Disconnect the fluid pipe from the slave cylinder, unscrew the two securing bolts and take the cylinder away from the transmission.

The installation of the cylinder is a reversal of the removal procedure. Fill the system with fresh brake fluid and bleed of air as described in the next section.

After the completed installation check the operation of the clutch with the engine running. Grating noises indicate a malfunction of the clutch assembly.

Cylinder Overhaul: No problems should be encountered to overhaul the slave cylinder. Shake out the piston after removal of the dust cap. Clean and check all parts as described for the master cylinder. Either replace the cylinder or assemble with new parts.

6.6.2.   BLEEDING THE CLUTCH SYSTEM

The system must be bled of air if fluid lines have been disconnected or parts of the system have been removed. Proceed as follows:

- Fill the fluid reservoir to the correct level and jack up the front end of the vehicle (vehicle on chassis stands).
- Remove the dust cap from the slave cylinder bleed screw, push a bleeder hose over the screw and insert the other end of the hose into a glass jar, filled partially with brake fluid.
- Ask a helper to operate the clutch pedal with slow and even strokes and open the bleeder screw a little, when the pedal is being held on the floor. Close the bleeder screw.
- Repeat this pumping operation, until the fluid flowing into the glass jar is free of air bubbles.
- During the bleeding operation keep the fluid level in the reservoir to its max. mark by continuously adding fresh brake fluid. A reservoir allowed to run empty will require a re-start with the bleeding process.
- Finally top-up the reservoir once more and remove the bleeding hose. Fit the dust cap.

7. MANUAL TRANSMISSIONS

7.0. Technical Data

Type: — To end of Model Year 1987: .... 5-speed transmission KM-162 (petrol) with linkage gearchange mechanism or KM-163 (diesel) with cable gearchange mechanism.

Type — From Model Year 1988: .... 5-speed transmission KM-201 (petrol) with cable gearchange mechanism, KM-206 (diesel) with new gearchange cable layout.

Gear Ratios:

	KM-162/KM-163	KM-201/KM-206
1st speed	4.226 : 1	3.454 : 1
2nd speed	2.365 : 1	1.946 : 1
3rd speed	1.285 : 1	1.285 : 1
4th speed	1.105 : 1	0.939 : 1
5th speed	0.855 : 1	0.756 : 1
Reverse:	4.109 : 1	3.083 : 1

Lubrication Oil:
Filling capacity:
KM-162 transmission: .... 2.1 litres 3.75 Imp. pts.)
KM-163 transmission: .... 2.3 litres (4.0 Imp. pts.)
KM-201 and KM-206 transmissions: .... 2.5 litres (4.5 Imp. pts.)

Final Drive Ratios:
To 1987, petrol model: .... 3.470 : 1
To 1987, diesel model: .... 3.466 : 1
From 1988, petrol model: .... 4.018 : 1
From 1988, diesel model: .... 4.018 : 1

A five-speed transmission of the type given above is fitted, with linkage-type gearchange mechanism to the end of model year 1987 when a petrol engine is fitted. A new transmission of type KM-200 is fitted with the introduction of the 1988 model year. The gearchange mechanism is cable-operated on all models, but the transmission fitted to diesel models has a new cable system for the gearchange.

90

7.1. Transmission — Removal

The transmission is removed without the engine. The vehicle must be suitable jacked up and support to carry out the necessary operations from underneath the vehicle.

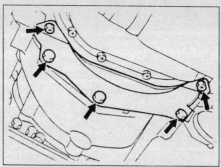

- Disconnect the battery, remove the battery and remove the battery carrier.

- In the case of the diesel model, push a bleeder hose over the bleeder screw of the clutch slave cylinder, place the other end of the hose into a suitable container and open the bleeder screw. Ask a second person to operate the clutch pedal until all clutch fluid has been discharged.

Fig. 7.1. — The arrows show the securing bolts for the clutch slave cylinder and the connector for the selector switch harness.

- Remove the cooling system expansion tank and the windscreen washer reservoir.
- If a diesel engine is fitted, disconnect the clutch pipe from the clutch slave cylinder. If a petrol engine is fitted, disconnect the clutch operating cable from the clutch release lever on the transmission and disconnect the speedometer cable (unscrew the knurled nut and withdraw the cable).
- Disconnect the selector switch harness and remove the selector control valve with the vacuum tank.
- Disconnect the electrical lead from the reversing light switch and from the selector switch at the top of the transmission case.
- Disconnect the electrical cables from the starter motor. Push the cables to one side. Then remove the starter motor.
- Remove the upper bolts securing the engine to the transmission. The location of the bolts is shown in Fig. 7.2.

Fig. 7.2. — The engine to transmission mounting bolts. Note the hidden bolt on the L.H side.

- Remove the actuator for the selector switch assembly.
- Remove the complete air cleaner assembly if a diesel engine is fitted.
- Jack up the front of the vehicle, place chassis stands under the sides of the body and remove both front wheels.
- Remove the undercover from the front of the vehicle and unscrew the drain plug from the side of the transmission (see Fig. 7.3). Place a suitable container underneath the transmission to collect the oil. Refit the plug after the oil has drained out.

- Disconnect the L.H. and R.H. drive shafts. To do this, disconnect the steering knuckle from the lower suspension ball joint and disconnect the steering track rod from the lever on the steering knuckle. Refer to Section 10 (Front Suspension) for the necessary instructions. Remove the drive shafts as described in Section 9.1.

- On models with linkage gearchange disconnect the gearchange linkage in accordance with the instructions in Section 7.3.0 and push the linkage and the and the extension strut away from the vehicle. If a cable system for the gearcnage is fitted, refer to Section 7.31 and disconnect the two gearchange control cables.
- From underneath the vehicle remove the clutch bell housing cover (see Fig. 7.4) and

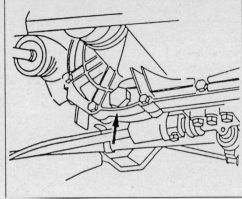

Fig. 7.3. — The oil drain plug in the side of the transmission.

remove the bolts securing the transmission to the engine at the bottom.

- Place a mobile jack underneath the transmission and lift the box slightly until the load is removed from the transmission mountings. Insert a piece of hardwood between the jack head and the transmission to prevent damage.
- Remove the bolt and nut securing the transmission to the transmission mounting bracket and then unscrew the mounting bracket from its attachment. Lift out the bracket. Fig. 1.6 shows with (1) and (2) where the mounting bracket is secured. The bolts are accessible from the R.H. front wheel arch after the covering panel has been removed.

Fig. 7.4. — The arrows point to the engine to clutch cover securing screws.

- Withdraw the transmission from the engine towards the right and lower the unit to the ground. The engine should be suspended on a rope to retain it in its approximate fitted position. Take care not to rest the weight of the transmission on the clutch shaft, as this might damage the driven plate or bend the clutch shaft.

The installation is a reversal of the removal procedure. Refer to Fig. 7.5 for the important tightening torques, to be observed during the installation. Tighten the gearchange extension to the transmission to 6.0 - 7.0 kgm (43 - 51 ft. lb.) and the bolt for the gearchange linkage coupling to 3.3 kgm (24 ft. lb.). Use locking wire to secure the bolt in position. If the transmission is fitted to a model with diesel engine and turbocharger, fill the transmission with the correct amount of transmission oil and fill the clutch system with hydraulic fluid. Bleed the clutch system as described in Section 6.6.2.

On models with clutch operating cable adjust the clutch pedal free play as described in Section 6.4.

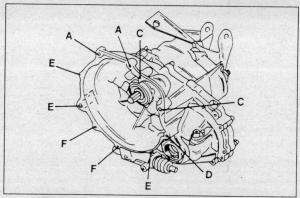

Fig. 7.5.—The letters indicate the tightening torque values.

A = 5.0 kgm (36 ft. lb.)
B = 5.0 kgm (36 ft. lb.)
C = 2.7 kgm (19.5 ft. lb.)

D = 3.2 kgm (23 ft. lb.)
E = 1.1 kgm (8 ft. lb.)
F = 1.9 kgm (14 ft. lb.)

7.2. Transmission Overhaul

As special tools are necessary to overhaul the transmission and, also the differential, we do not intent to describe the dismantling and assembling of the unit. If faults are experienced with the transmission of the final drive, we recommend to fit an exchange unit or have the original assembly overhauled at your dealer who has the necessary special tools to assemble and adjust the transmission.

7.3. Gearchange Control

A gearchange cable system is fitted to models with diesel engine and to the petrol model from model year 1988. With the fitting of the new transmission type from model year 1988 the transmission lever, the gearchange cable and the gear selector cable have been changed on diesel models, compared to the earlier version.

Models with petrol engines are fitted with a linkage gearchange system. A gearchange linkage and an extension rod are fitted between the gearchange lever and the transmission. The console must be removed in order to remove the gearchange linkage or the selector cables.

7.3.0. Removal and Installation — Rod Linkage

Fig. 7.6 shows the component parts of the linkage gearchange system. Proceed as follows to remove parts of the gearchange system:

- Unscrew the gearchange lever knob and remove the floor console.
- Remove the nuts (4) securing the gearshift rod mounting bracket to the floor panel and remove the bracket (5).
- Refer to Fig. 7.7 and remove the extension rod (18) to the side of the transmission. After removing the lock wire, remove the screw securing the gearchange rod to the transmission (Fig. 7.8) and disengage the gearchange rod and the extension as one assembly from the transmission.

If further dismantling of the gearchange is required, refer to the illustration.

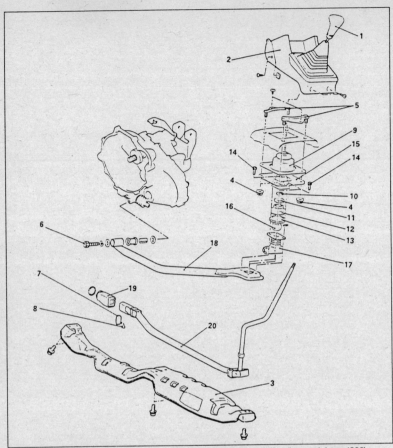

Fig. 7.6. — Layout of the gearchange linkage system (petrol models before model year 1988).

1 Gearchange lever knob	8 Lock screw	15 Insulator
2 Floor console	9 Gearchange lever cover	16 Fulcrum ball
3 Heat shield (not U.K.)	10 Snap ring	17 Cover
4 Change rod securing nuts	11 Washer	18 Extension rod
5 Bracket	12 Rubber insulator	19 Dust cover
6 Extension rod bolt	13 Spring seat	
7 Lock wire	14 Bolts	

Check the gearchange rod joint for wear, and sticking or rough movement, all rubber parts for wear or deterioration and the fulcrum ball and cap for damage. Fully dismantle the mechanism if necessary, to replace the parts in question.

The installation of the gearchange mechanism is a reversal of the removal procedure. Grease the inside of the dust cover, the gearchange lever and the contacting surface and the gearchange lever sliding portion with M.P. grease. When inserting the lock screw for the gearchange rod connection make sure that the tip of the screw engages with the indentation of the rod. Secure the screw with lock wire.

94

Fig. 7.7. — Removal of the gearchange linkage extension from the side of the transmission.

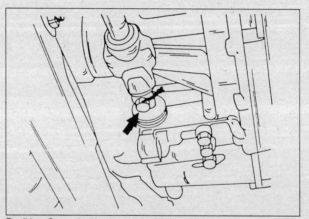

Fig. 7.8. — Separating the gearchange rod from the shaft in the transmission. Secure the bolt with lock wire after installation.

7.3.1.   Cable Mechanism — Removal and Installation

Fig. 7.9 shows the component parts of the gearchange mechanism, as fitted to diesel models before model year 1988. The layout of the gearchange control cables is similar on later models, but some parts have been modified.

- Remove the gearchange lever knob and the floor console box. If electrically heated seats are fitted, disconnect the cables from the switch and remove the switch.
- Refer to Fig. 7.10 and disconnect the gear selector cable and the gearchange cable from their levers, remove the bolts securing the shift lever and remove the complete assembly. The connection points for the cables and the securing bolts are shown by the arrows in the illustration.
- Refer to Fig. 7.11 and remove the two retainers (3) and (18) in Fig. 7.9. Two screws (16) hold the retainer (7). Remove the retainer clips from the gearchange cables, using a screwdriver. The

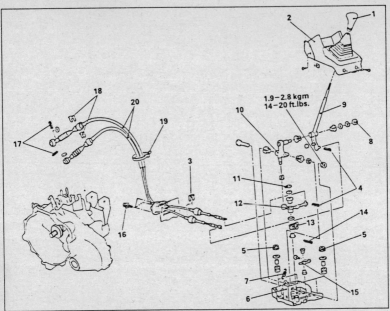

Fig. 7.9. — Layout of the gearchange cable system on the diesel model before model year 1988.

1 Gearchange lever knob
2 Floor console
3 Clips (gearchange lever side)
4 Control cable securing clips (gearchange lever side)
5 Securing nuts
6 Bracket assembly
7 Spring
8 Nut, 2.5 kgm (18 ft.lb.)
9 Gearchange lever
10 Gearchange lever
11 Snap ring
12 Gearchange lever
13 Spring
14 Split pin
15 Gearchange lever
16 Securing screws
17 Control cable mounting clips (transmission side)
18 Clips (transmission side)
19 Cable band
20 Gearchange control cables

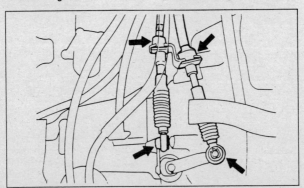

Fig. 7.10. — The arrows show where the gearchange cables are attached at the transmission side.

96

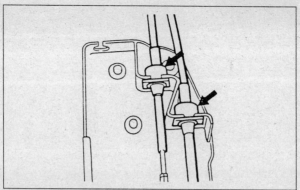

Fig. 7.11. — The arrows show where the two gearchange control cables are secured to the gearchange lever bracket.

cables are connected to the levers on the transmission by means of split pins and washers. Remove these parts and disconnect the cables.

- Withdraw the gearchange cables towards the inside of the vehicle. If necessary, dismantle the gearchange lever assembly into the component parts shown in Fig. 7.9. Immediately check all parts for re-use. The rubber parts must show no signs of wear or deterioration. Levers (10) and (12) in Fig. 7.9 must not be distorted. There must be no kinks in the two cables.

During installation grease all sliding parts of the gearchange lever assembly with M.P. grease. Refit the two cables ends to their transmission levers as shown in Fig. 7.10, but note the order of installation of the cables, with the transmission gearchange lever in the "Neutral" position:

- Connect the two cables to the gearchange levers on the lever bracket, fit the cables outer sleeves and secure with the two spring plates.

- Fit the retaining clamp with the rubber insulator and tighten the screws.

- Connect the two cables to the transmission bracket and fit the two spring plates. Make sure that the cables are not twisted. An adjusting turnbuckle on each cable enables the ends to be aligned without stress.

- Connect the cable ends to the transmission levers as shown in Fig. 7.12. An "O" ring is fitted over each transmission lever pin before the cable end is pushed over the pin.

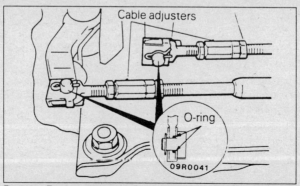

Fig. 7.12. — The arrows show where the two cables can be adjusted. The two "O" rings are shown in the position shown.

Before fitting the remaining parts check the operation of all gears. The gearchange lever must operate smoothly. If one of the cables needs adjustment, adjust the cable length by using the turnbuckle adjuster in Fig. 7.12 after slackening the locknuts. There is no need to disconnect the cable end from the transmission lever. Tighten both locknuts after adjustment. The remaining installation is a reversal of the removal procedure.

8.   AUTOMATIC TRANSMISSION

8.0.   Technical Data

Type: . . . . KM 170
Gear Ratios:
   1st speed: . . . . 2.846 : 1
   2nd speed: . . . . 1.581 : 1
   3rd speed: . . . . 1.00 : 1
   Reverse speed: . . . . 2.176 : 1
Axle Ratio: . . . . 3.597 : 1
Oil capacity: . . . . 5.6 litres (10.4 Imp. pts.)
Recommended fluid: . . . . Dexron II or Dexron

The automatic transmission is a complicated piece of equipment. Any dismantling or repairs should be entrusted to a dealer who has the necessary knowledge and special tools required to overhaul the transmission. Only the operations described on the following pages should be carried out.

8.1.   Gearchange Control — Removal and Installation

Fig. 8.2 shows the component parts of the gearchange control. The following operations are carried out with reference to this illustration.

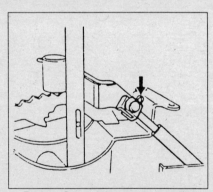

Fig. 8.1. — Removal of the gearchange cable.

- Remove the floor console. Screws are fitted to the rear end and to the sides of the console.
- Remove the gear selector handle from the end of the selector lever. A grub screw is inserted into the side of the handle which must be removed with an Allen key or a cross-headed screwdriver.
- Remove the two screws at the front and rear of the gear position indicator cover and take off the cover. Disconnect the connector for the position indicator lamp.
- Disconnect the gearchange cable from the lever after removal of the split pin and the clevis pin.
- Unscrew the bolts securing the bracket to the floor panel.
- Jack up the front end of the vehicle and from underneath remove the nut and bolt securing the selector cable to the floor panel and pull the control cable towards the lower part of the chassis. Remove the control cable securing bolt and clip from the floor panel.

98

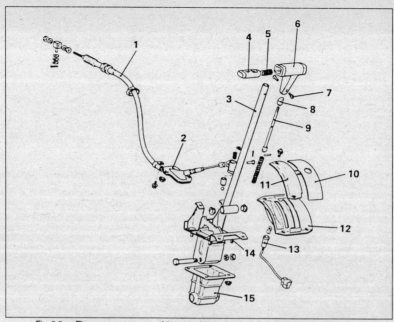

Fig. 8.2. — The component parts of the gearchange control of an automatic transmission.

1 Gearchangecable	6 Pushbutton	11 Positionindicator
2 Cableend	7 Grubscrew	12 Indicatorpanel
3 Selectorlever	8 Sleeve	13 Positionindicatorlamp
4 Selectorleverhandle	9 Connectingrod	14 Plateassembly
5 Spring	10 Slider	15 Dustcover

● The control cable is now attached to the transmission bracket and the transmission lever. Remove a nut and a washer, take off the square block and

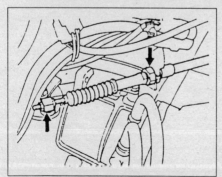

Fig. 8.4. — The arrows show the attachment of the gearchange cable. Tighten the nut shown by the L.H. arrow to take any slack out of the gearchange cable.

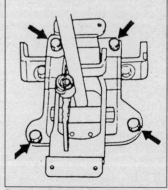

Fig. 8.3. — The arrows show the securing bolts for the selector lever bracket.

further in on the cable slacken the nut securing the cable to the bracket. Fig. 8.4 shows where the cable is attached.

Check the detent plate and the pin at the end of the selector lever for wear. Check also the contact surfaces of the push button and sleeve and the condition of the control cable.

The installation is a reversal of the removal procedure. All sliding parts must be coated with grease. Adjust the gearchange as follows:

- Fit the selector lever handle so that the push button is on the driver's side.
- Place the selector lever to the "N" position.
- Move the selector lever and the inhibitor switch to the "N" position and fit the gearchange cable. Fig. 8.5 shows how the lever and switch must be aligned. Turn the adjusting nut at the cable end to remove slack from the cable.
- A toothed washer is used for the gearchange cable connection at the transmission mounting bracket. The teeth of this washer must face towards the bracket. Tighten the nut shown by the R.H. arrow in Fig. 8.4 to attach the cable.
- Check that the gearchange lever operation is smooth, that the correct gear is selected at each position of the lever and that the correct position mark is indicated in each position. To check the correct engagement, move the gear selector lever through the gears and each time check that the corresponding position mark is indicated at each position.

8.2.   Automatic Transmission — Removal — Installation

- Disconnect the battery cable, remove the battery and unscrew the battery carrier.
- Remove the expansion tank for the cooling system and also the windscreen washer reservoir.
- Referring to Fig. 8.4, disconnect the control cable from the side of the transmission and push it to one side.
- Disconnect the speedometer cable and the inhibitor switch cable from the transmission.
- Disconnect the oil cooler hoses from the transmission. **Plug the hoses and the transmission to prevent dirt, etc. from entering**.
- Disconnect the starter motor wiring and remove the bolts securing the upper portion of the transmission to the engine. One of the bolts secures a pipe. Remember which one it is. The starter motor can also be removed.

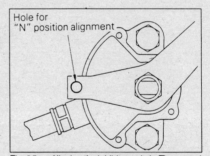

Fig. 8.5. — Aligning the inhibitor switch. The neutral position alignment hole (1) must be as shown.

- Raise the front end of the vehicle and support securely. Remove the undercover and then drain the transmission fluid.
- Disconnect the steering knuckle from the lower suspension ball joint and disconnect the reaction strut and the stabiliser bar from the steering knuckle lever. Remove the two drive shafts as described in Section 9.1.
- Remove the bell housing cover. This will expose the torque converter and the drive plate. Remove the three bolts securing the converter to the drive plate. Turn the crankshaft at the crankshaft pulley bolt with a socket until each bolt appears in the opening, as shown in Fig. 8.6 and remove the bolt. Push the torque converter away from the engine to prevent it from sticking to the engine.
- Support the lower part of the transmission and remove the remaining bolts securing the transmission to the engine. Use a piece of hardwood between jack head and transmission to prevent damage to the transmission oil sump.

- Remove the transmission mounting bracket and the transmission mount. Fig. 8.7 shows the points of attachment. To gain access to the transmission mounting and the mounting bracket, remove the cover from the inside of the R.H. wheel arch. First remove the nut and bolt securing the transmission mounting to the bracket and then unscrew the bracket.
- Slide the transmission assembly to the right and then lower it to remove from the vehicle. A second person should be available to lift the transmission to the ground.

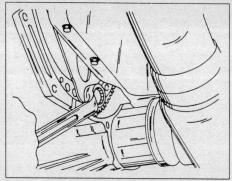

Fig. 8.6. — Removal of the torque converter from the drive plate.

The installation is the transmission is a reversal of the removal procedure. To prevent damaging the transmission oil seals, the torque converter must be connected to the transmission first and then to the engine.

Refill the transmission with the correct fluid as described below, noting that about 3 litres (5.2 pts.) will have remained in the transmission.

Adjust the control cable to take up any free play. Ensure that the inhibitor switch wiring is not in contact with the transmission mounting bracket.

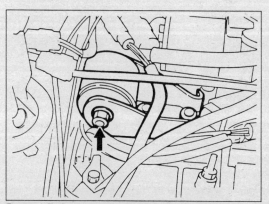

Fig. 8.7. — The arrow shows the long bolt securing the transmission mounting to the mounting bracket. A nut is fitted to the bolt.

Check that the engine will not start with the selector lever in any position other than "N" or "P".

8.3.   Fluid Change

The fluid should be hot before it is drained from the automatic transmission. If the transmission is cold, give the vehicle a short run to warm it up. Proceed as follows:

- Jack up the front end of the vehicle and place a suitable container underneath the transmission.
- Remove the two drain plugs from the automatic transmission and drain the fluid into the container. Immediately clean the plugs and screw back in position. Note that the tightening torque of the upper of the two plugs is 3.0 - 3.4 kgm (22 - 25 ft.lb.). The torque for the bottom plug on the other hand is only 2.6 - 2.9 kgm (19 - 21 ft.lb.). Do not make mistakes.
- Fill the transmission with Dexron II automatic transmission fluid. The total capacity is 5.7 litres (12 Imp. pints), but it should be noted that some of the fluid remains inside the

101

transmission and that a lot less may be needed.

● With the vehicle on a flat level surface, start the engine and allow to idle. Move the selector lever from "P" to "L" and then to "N" and stop the engine. Re-check the oil level.

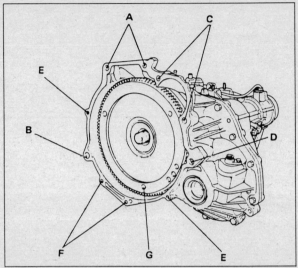

Fig. 8.8. — The tightening torques to be observed during the installation of the automatic transmission.

A = 4.3-5.5 kgm (31-40 ft.lb.)   E = 1.0-1.2 kgm (7-9 ft.lb.)
B = 4.3-5.5 kgm (31-40 ft.lb.)   F = 1.5-2.2 kgm (11-16 ft.lb.)
C = 2.2-3.2 kgm (16-23 ft.lb.)   G = 3.5-4.2 kgm (25-30 ft.lb.)
D = 3.0-3.5 kgm (22-25 ft.lb.)   H = 0.2 kgm (1.4 ft.lb.)

8.4.   Automatic Transmission — Tightening Torques

Transmission to engine bolts: .... See Fig. 9.7
Transmission Mounting Bolts: .... 4.3-5.5 kgm (31-40 ft.lb.)
Starter motor bolts: .... 2.2-3.2 kgm (16-23 ft.lb.)
Bell housing cover to transmission:
    20 mm bolts: .... 1.5-2.2 kgm (11-16 ft.lb.)
    14 mm bolts: .... 1.0-1.2 kgm (77-9 ft.lb.)
Torque converter to drive plate: .... 3.5-4.2 kgm (25-30 ft.lb.)

9.   DRIVESHAFTS

9.0.   Technical Data

Type   — Outer C.V. Joint:
   Petrol model .... Birfield joint
   Diesel model: .... Birfield joint or Rzeppa joint, L.H. shaft, with diesel engine)
Type — Inner C.V. Joint:
   Petrol models: .... Ball-type joint
   Diesel models: .... Ball-type joint or tripod joint, L.H. shaft with diesel engine

Drive Shaft Length (joint to joint):
Petrol Model to 1987:
    R.H. shaft: .... 365.0mm (14.37 in.)
    L.H. shaft: .... 690.0mm (27.17 in.)
Petrol Model from 1988:
    R.H. shaft: .... 367.5mm (14.47 in.)
    L.H. shaft: .... 686.0mm (27.00 in.)
Diesel Model to 1987
    R.H. shaft: .... 351.0mm (13.82 in.)
    L.H. shaft: .... 685.0mm (26.97 in.)
Diesel Model — From 1988:
    R.H. shaft: .... 352.0mm (13.86 in.)
    L.H. shaft: .... 685.0mm (26.97 in.)

Grease Quantity in Joints:
    Birfield joint — petrol engine: .... 90-120 grams (3.2-4.2 oz.)
    Birfield joint, diesel engine: .... 80-100 gr (2.8-3.5 oz.) from 1988
    Ball joint: .... 70-100g (2.5-3.5 oz.) — 90-100g (3.2-2.53 oz.) from 1987
    Tripod joint, case outer diameter 78mm: .... 150-170g (5.3-6.0 oz.)
    Tripod joint, case outer diameter 85.5mm: .... 180-200mm (6.3-7.1 oz.)

Drive Shaft Boot Refit Length:
    Ball-type joint — L.H. side: .... 83 ± 3mm (3.19 ± 0.12 in.)
    Ball-type joint — R.H. side: .... 88 ± 3mm (3.46 ± 0.12 in.)
    Ball-type joint (diesel model) — R.H. Side: .... 88 ± 3mm (3.46 ± 0.12 in.)
    Tripod joint (diesel model) — L.H. side: .... 84 ± 3mm (3.31 ± 0.12 in.)
    New Shafts — From 1988 (petrol model):
        L.H. shaft: .... 85 ± 3mm (3.35 ± 0.12 in.)
        R.H. shaft: .... 90 ± 3mm (3.54 ± 0.12 in.)
    New Shafts — From 1988 (diesel model):
        L.H. shaft: .... 84 ± 3mm (3.31 ± 0.12 in.)
        R.H. shaft: .... 90 ± 3mm (3.54 ± 0.12 in.)

Wheel Bearings:
    Type: .... Taper roller bearings
    Dimensions (O.D. x I.D.): .... 65 x 38mm (2.56-1.50 in.)
    Hub axial play: .... 0.2mm (0.008 in.)
    Hub starting torque: .... 13 kgcm (11 in. lbs.)

9.1. Drive Shafts — Removal and Installation

Note that different drive shafts are used in models covered in this publication. Always ensure to fit the correct shaft, if replacements are necessary.

- Remove the centre cap from the wheel hub, remove the shaft nut split pin and slacken the shaft nut by a few turns before the vehicle is jacked up.
- Jack up the front end of the vehicle, remove the wheels and support the vehicle on stands. Remove the undercover, if fitted.
- Withdraw the split pin from the track rod ball joint nut, remove the nut and, using a suitable ball joint extractor, separate the track rod from the steering knuckle lever.
- Remove the nut securing the suspension arm ball joint from the steering knuckle and disconnect the stabiliser bar from the lower suspension arm. Separate the ball joint from the steering knuckle, as described in Section "Front Suspension". Remove the nuts and bolts securing the reaction strut to the front suspension arm.
- Drain the transmission oil.
- Attach the puller shown in Fig. 9.1 to two studs of the wheel hub and withdraw the wheel hub by tightening the centre spindle. The hub must be held against rotation during the removal operation. Keep the spacer.
- When pulling out the R.H. drive shaft from the transmission, use two screwdrivers, as shown

103

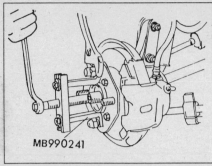

Fig. 9.1. — Removal of a wheel hub with the special puller.

(tripod-type) joint drive shaft. Reckless bending of the joint will damage it.

● Withdraw the shaft towards the inside from the swivel joint and remove from the suspension.

NOTE: Do not remove the drive shaft with a hammer or a drift.

Check the drive shaft boots for damage or deterioration. Check the ball joint for excessive play and the splines for wear or damage.

in Fig. 9.2 and push the shaft out of engagement.

● When pulling out the L.H. drive shaft, insert the wheel nut wrench supplied with the vehicle or a similar lever between the transmission and the case of the inner C.V. joint as shown in Fig. 9.3 (not more than 7 mm/0.28 in.) and with a short push against the lever, towards the transmission, disengage the drive shaft. Do not pull the hub assembly outwards to prevent possible deformation of the circlip in the joint. Take extra care when removing a T.J.

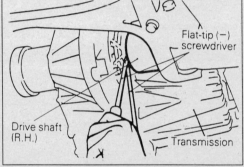

Fig. 9.2. — Removal of the R.H. drive shaft with two screwdrivers. Push the drive shaft towards the outside.

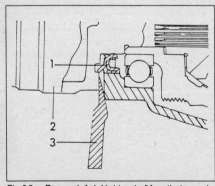

Fig. 9.3. — Removal of a L.H. drive shaft from the transmission. Take care not to damage the oil seal (1) by inserting the lever too far into the gap.

1. Oil seal   2. CV joint   3. Lever

The rubber boots can be replaced, if necessary (Section 9.2). If the boot of the inner joint has been replaced, set the length of the boot as specified in Section 9.0, measured between the centres of the grooves.

The installation of the drive shaft is a reversal of the removal procedure. Tighten the parts on the lower suspension arm, stabiliser, track rod ball joint, reaction struts, etc. to the correct torque settings.

Tighten the drive shaft nut provisionally and finally tighten to 20-26 kgm (145 -188 ft.lb.) when the wheels are back on the ground. Use a new split pin to secure the nut. As the torque of 26 kgm (188 ft.lb.) must not be exceeded, tighten the nut to the lower value and try to insert the split pin. If the holes are not in line, tighten to the next slot and insert the pin. If a T.J./R.J.type drive shaft is fitted, make sure that the joint operates properly.

9.2. Drive Shaft Rubber Boot and C.V. Joint Replacement

Different repair kits are available to repair drive shafts. Your dealer will be able to advise you regards availability and suitability for your particular model. As already mentioned, different shaft joints are fitted over the years, but note that Birfield joints and Rzeppa joints must not be dismantled.

9.2.1. Double Offset and Birfield Joint

Remove the drive shaft from the vehicle as described in Section 9.1 and clamp the shaft into a vice. Using a screwdriver, as shown in Fig. 9.4, remove the retaining clamp for the inner joint rubber boot and withdraw the rubber boot from the joint.

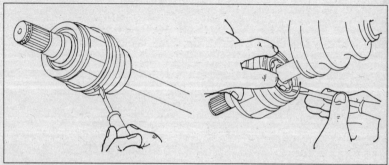

Fig. 9.4. — Removal of the retaining clamp for the rubber boot (left) and removal of the snap ring securing the ball cage to the joint housing (right).

Clean the inside of the C.V. joint and with a small screwdriver, as shown in Fig. 9.4 on the right, remove the retaining ring from the joint housing. Thoroughly clean the end of the shaft.

With a pair of circlip pliers, as shown in Fig. 9.5 remove the circlip from the end of the shaft and withdraw the inner cage together with the balls from the shaft. Mark the parts for re-assembly. Immediately check the balls and inner cage for damage and replace if they are defective.

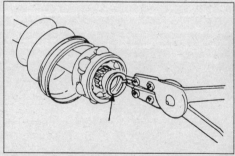

Fig. 9.5. — Removal of the circlip from the end of the shaft.

If the outer joint rubber boot is to be replaced, remove the two retaining clamps and take the boot off the shaft. Note that rubber boots are not the same for all models.

Depending on the extent of the repair necessary, obtain the correct repair kit and assemble the shaft as described below:

● Remove all grease from the splined portion of the shaft and wrap vinyl tape around the splined portion to prevent the boot from damage. The rubber boot with the two bellows is used for the inner joint (the outer one has three)

● Assemble the inner race, the outer cage and the joint balls in accordance with the marks

105

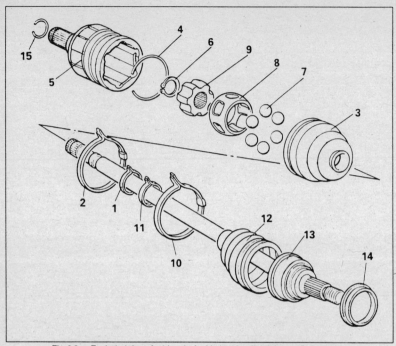

Fig. 9.6. — Exploded view of a drive shaft with double-offset joint and Birfield joint.

1	Small rubber boot band	9	Ball joint inner race
2	Large rubber boot band	10	Large rubber boot band
3	Rubber boot	11	Small rubber boot band
4	Circlip	12	Rubber boot, Birfield joint
5	Outer race, ball-joint	13	Birfield joint assembly
6	Circlip	14	Dust cover
7	Steel balls	15	Circlip
8	Cage, double-offset joint		

made during dismantling and slide the inner race over the shaft. Fit the circlip as shown in Fig. 9.5, making sure it enters its groove properly.

- Apply approx. half of the grease (provided in the repair kit) to the outer housing and insert the drive shaft. Check that the balls, cage and inner race have been fitted fully in the outer housing.

- Apply the other half of the remaining grease into the outer housing and fit the retaining ring into the groove of the outer housing. The grease must be spread inside the joint as shown in Fig. 9.7. Only use the grease supplied in the repair kit.

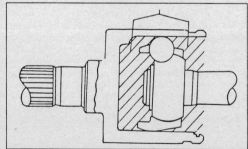

Fig. 9.7. — Fill the shaded area with grease during assembly of the drive shaft joint (double-offset type).

- Place the rubber boot over the joint and stretch the joint until the dimension specified in Section 9.0 for the L.H. and R.H. drive shaft is obtained. Measure between the centre of the securing clamps, as shown in Fig. 9.8. This will provide the necessary movement for the boot during operation of the shaft. Fit the retaining clamps and tighten.
- Fit the rubber boot to the outer joint if it has been removed.

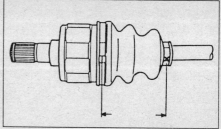

Fig. 9.8. — The length of the rubber boots is measured between the two clamp bands, as shown by the arrows.

10.2.2.   Drive Shafts with Rzeppa and Tripod Joints

The shaft shown in Fig. 9.10 is fitted to the diesel model on the L.H. side. The Rzeppa joint cannot be dismantled.

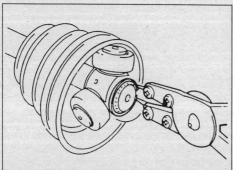

Fig. 9.9. — Removal of the circlip from the end of the spider journal.

Remove the retaining band for the rubber boot, using a screwdriver and remove the boot from the joint housing.

Clean the grease from the joint, remove the circlip from the end of the shaft and remove the spider assembly. Fig. 10.9 shows where the circlip is located. Remove the retaining clamp securing the dynamic damper and the outer rubber boot.

To assemble the shaft, wrap tape around the spline part of the drive shaft and install the inner and outer boots over the shaft. The boots and boot bands are different for Rzeppa and tripod joints. Take care not to interchange them.

Fill the inside of the Rzeppa joint and the rubber boot with 130 - 140 g (4.6 - 4.9 oz.) of the grease contained in the repair kit. Do not use any other grease. Place the rubber boot over the Rzeppa joint and then secure the boot with the small and the large band.

Assemble the dynamic damper to the drive shaft. Slide the damper along the shaft until a dimension of 430 - 436 mm (16.9 - 17.2 in.) is obtained between the front face of the joint face to the other face of the damper. Secure the damper with the retaining clamp in this position. Coat the spider assembly of the tripod joint and fit the spider over the end of the shaft. Fit a new circlip, making sure it enters the groove.

Fill the case of the tripod joint case with the grease supplied in the repair kit. 200 - 210 g (7.1 - 7.4 oz.) are required. Fit the rubber boot bands and adjust the length of the rubber boot, measured as shown in Fig. 9.8, to the value given in Section 9.0.

9.3.   Wheel Hub and Steering Knuckle Removal and Installation

- Remove the drive shaft as described in Section 10.1. Remove the spacer ring from the

107

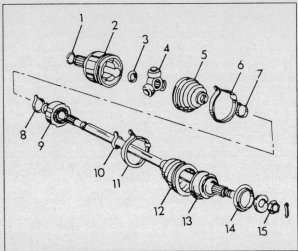

1 Snap ring
2 Inner joint housing
3 Retaining ring
4 Spider assembly
5 Rubber boot
6 Large retaining band
7 Small retaining band
8 Retaining clamp
9 Dynamic damper
10 Small retaining band
11 Large retaining band
12 Rubber boot
13 Outer C.V. joint
14 Dust seal
15 Drive shaft nut

Fig. 9.10. Exploded view of a drive shaft with tripod joint, Rzeppa joint and dynamic damper.

end of the shaft and keep for re-assembly.

● Remove the two brake caliper mounting bolts and suspend the caliper with a piece of wire. Do not allow the caliper to hang on the flexible brake hose.

● Remove the split pin from the castellated nut on the track rod ball joint, unscrew the nut and separate the track rod ball joint with a ball joint extractor.

● Remove the two bolts securing the spring strut to the steering knuckle joint and lift out the hub and steering knuckle as an assembly.

If the bearings are to be replaced, read under the next heading. Replace the oil seal in the rear of the steering knuckle if it shows signs of leakage. The installation of the complete steering knuckle is a reversal of the removal procedure. Refer to the end of Section 10 for the relevant tightening torques.

9.4.   Replacement of Wheel Bearings

Normally a special puller is required to remove the wheel hub from the knuckle and to remove and refit the bearings. The bearings will be damaged if a hammer and drift is used to remove the bearings. Fig. 9.13 shows an exploded view of the bearings for reference. The following text assumed that the special tools shown in Fig. 9.11 are obtainable.

● Remove the brake disc from the wheel hub and clamp the steering knuckle into a vice. Using a plastic mallet drive the wheel hub out of the wheel bearings from the rear of the steering knuckle, but only if the bearings need replacement. Otherwise use the extractor screw as shown in Fig. 9.11. The inner bearing race of the outer bearing will remain on the hub and must be removed with a suitable puller.

● Using a screwdriver, lever the oil seal out of the front of the steering knuckle. Place the wheel hub over the jaws of a partially opened vice and drive the outer bearing races from opposite sides out of the hub. Note that bearings are made by different suppliers and only bearings of the same manufacturer must be fitted.

● Thoroughly clean all parts.

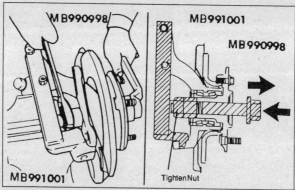

Fig. 9.11. — Use of the special tools to remove and refit the wheel bearings and wheel hub to the steering knuckle.

- Drive the outer races of the new bearings from opposite sides into the steering knuckle. Use a soft-metal drift for this operation.
- Coat the outside of the bearing cages and the inside of the steering knuckle with bearing grease and fit the outer bearing into the knuckle. Drive in the oil seal and wipe off surplus grease.
- Fit the inner bearing cage into the steering knuckle and the wheel hub into the bearings.
- Use the extractor bolt, used for removal into the wheel hub and the bearings and tighten the nut to 20 to 26 kgm (145 - 188 ft.lb.), at the same time counterholding the bolt head (see Fig. 9.11). Rotate the wheel hub a few times during the tightening operation to settle the bearings.

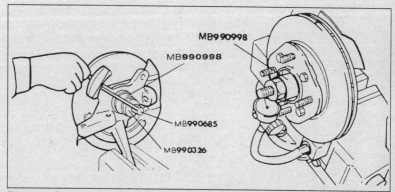

Fig. 9.12. — Checking the starting torque of the wheel hub (left) and the end play of the wheel bearings (right).

- Measure the wheel hub starting torque with a torque wrench as shown in Fig. 9.12 (left) and write down the value. It should be around 11 kg.cm. (10 in.lbs.) or less. Next the end float of the wheel bearings must be measured with a dial gauge, as shown in Fig. 9.12 (right). Move the hub to and fro (the extractor bolt must be still in position) and read off the dial gauge. The play must not exceed 0.2 mm (0.008 in.).

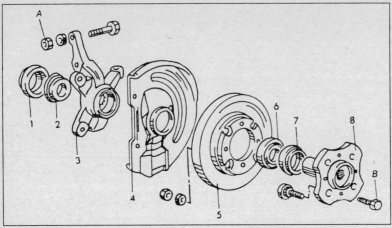

Fig. 9.13. — Exploded view of a front wheel hub together with the steering knuckle. "A" and "B" give the tightening torques.

1	Inner oil seal	6	Outer wheel bearing
2	Inner wheel bearing	7	Outer oil seals
3	Steering knuckle	8	Wheel hub
4	Splash shield	A	77.5 - 9.0 kgm
5	Brake disc	B	5.0 - 8.0 kgm

- If either of these measurements are incorrect, and the nut has been tightened to the correct torque, remove the hub and bearing once more, and start again, as something has not been fitted correctly.

- Remove the special tool, grease the inside of the steering knuckle and the bearing and drive a new oil seal from the drive shaft side into the steering knuckle. Wipe off surplus grease. Make sure to coat the oil seal lip with grease.

- Refit the steering knuckle in reverse order to the removal procedure to the spring strut and the suspension arm and refit the drive shaft.

9.5. Drive Shafts and Hubs — Tightening Torques

Drive shaft nut: . . . . 20 - 26 kgm (145 - 188 ft.lb.)
Hub to brake disc: . . . . 5 - 6 kgm (36 - 43 ft.lb.)))
Support bearing bracket to engine: . . . . 3.5 - 4.5 kgm (25 - 32.5 ft.lb.)
Knuckle to strut assembly: . . . . 8 - 9 kgm (54 - 65 ft.lb.)

10. FRONT SUSPENSION

10.0. Technical Data

Type: . . . . McPherson spring struts with integral shock absorbers, coil springs, reaction struts and front stabiliser bar. Stabiliser bar mounting changed from from 1988 models.

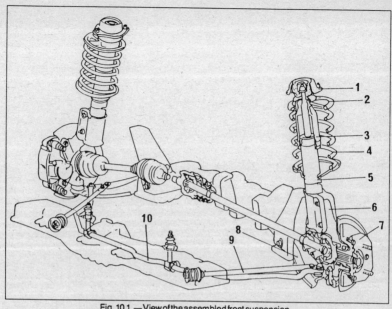

Fig. 10.1. — View of the assembled front suspension.

1 Upper strut bearing	6 Steering knuckle
2 Spring seat	7 Wheel hub
3 Bump rubber	8 Suspension arm
4 Coil spring	9 Reaction strut
5 Spring strut	10 Stabiliser bar

Wheel Alignment

Camber: . . . . 25' ± 30'
Castor: . . . . 48' ± 20'

Toe-in (measured at centre of tyre tread): . . . . 0 ± 3.0 mm (0.12 in.)
Toe-in (measured at rim edge): . . . . 0 ± 1.5 mm (0.06 in.)

Coil Springs

	Petrol Engine (M/T)	Petrol Engine (A/T)
Free Length:	343 mm (13.50 in.)	351 mm (13.81 in.)
Coil Spring Colour Codes:	Sky blue x 1	Sky blue x 2
Wire diameter:	12.3 mm (0.48 in.)	12.5 mm (0.49 in.)
Outer diameter:	152.3 mm (6.0 in.)	152.5 mm (6.0 in.)

Coil Springs — Diesel Engine:

Free Length: . . . . 367 mm (14.45 in.)
Coil Spring Colour Codes: . . . . Violet x 2
Wire diameter: . . . . 12.8 mm (0.50 in.)
Outer diameter: . . . . 152.8 mm (6.02 in.)
M/T = Manual transmission, A/T = Automatic transmission

Shock Absorbers
Type: . . . . Hydraulic, telescopic, double-acting
Max. length: . . . . 492 mm (19.37 in.)
Min. compressed length: . . . . 331 mm (13.03 in.)
Stroke: . . . . 161 mm (6.34 in.)

Diameter: . . . . 22.0 mm (0.87 in.)

Fig. 10.1. shows the assembled front suspension on models before 1988. The illustration shows the simple arrangement of the suspension arms and their attachment to the suspension crossmember. Two spring struts with coil springs, hydraulich telescopic shock absorbers, reaction struts and an anti-roll bar (stabiliser bar) make up the front suspension. The attachment of the stabiliser bar has been changed on all models with the introduction of model year 1988 (connected to the reaction struts, before to suspension arms).

The front hubs are located on taper roller bearings. The two-way acting, hydraulic telescopic shock absorbers cannot be overhauled.

10.1.　　Front Spring Struts
10.1.1.　　Removal

A long socket, which fits the upper nut of the spring strut piston nut, is required to dismantle the spring strut (for example to replace the spring).

- Jack up the front of the vehicle and place support stands under the sides of the body. Remove the wheel on the side in question.
- Disconnect the brake hose from the rigid brake pipe. Plug the open end of the pipe in a suitable manner to prevent entry of dirt. Knock out the retaining plate for the brake hose attachment and withdraw the hose from its bracket on the spring strut. Plug the end of the brake hose to prevent entry of dirt. This can be carried out by wrapping a piece of tape around the hose end.
- From below the vehicle remove the two bolts securing the spring strut to the steering knuckle. Fig. 10.2 shows the attachment of the spring strut.

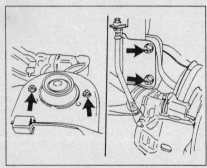

- From the engine compartment remove the two nuts from the upper spring strut mounting (Fig. 10.2) and remove the strut towards the bottom. The strut must be held from below before it is taken out through the wheel arch.

10.1.2.　　Dismantling a Spring Strut

Before a spring strut is dismantled, note the following points before commencement of any work:

- The coil spring of the various models are different. This must be noted when ordering new parts.

Fig. 10.2. — The attachment of the spring strut at the top (left) and at the bottom (right).

- The springs on the R.H. and L.H. sides are not the same and when both springs are removed at once, care should be taken to identify them accordingly.
- Never clamp the spring strut directly into a vice. Make up a plate and attach this to the spring strut. Clamp this plate in the vice.
- The shock absorbers cannot be replaced. A damaged shock absorber means a new spring strut.
- A spring compressor is required to replace parts of the spring strut.
- Referring to Fig. 10.4. compress the spring with the special tool shown or any other

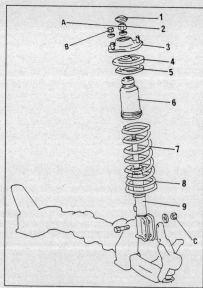

Fig. 10.3. — Exploded view of a spring strut. The letters refer to the tightening torques.

1	Centre cap	7	Coil spring
2	Self-locking nut	8	Lower spring seat
3	Spring strut bearing	9	Spring strut
4	Spring seat	A = 6.0 - 7.0 kgm	
5	Upper spring seat	B = 2.5 - 3.5 kgm	
6	Rebound rubber	C = 7.5 - 9.0 kgm	

spring compressor that can be placed over 3 or 4 coils. Spring compressors can be hired from tool hire companies.

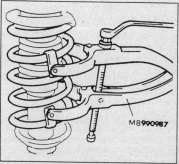

Fig. 10.4. — Compressing a coil spring with the special spring compressor.

● Remove the plastic cap (1) in the centre of the spring strut and remove the nut in the centre of the upper strut bearing. This normally requires the special tools shown in Fig. 10.5. Clamp the spring strut into a vice.

● Remove the parts of the upper bearing (3) and the coil spring (7) from the spring strut. Remove the rebound rubber (6) from the strut.

Thoroughly clean all parts with petrol and dry, if possible, with compressed air. Other lint-free rags to wipe off remaining petrol stains. Make sure that parts are free of dust and dirt. Worn or damaged parts must always be replaced, but ensure that the correct parts are fitted. Your Mitsubishi dealer will have the latest information.

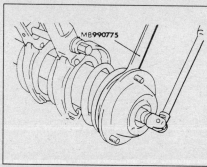

Fig. 10.5. — Removal of the piston rod nut. Use the special tool to counterhold the piston rod against rotation.

10.1.3. Assembling a Spring Strut

Refer to Fig. 10.3. for the following operations, but note the following points:

● Before fitting a spring, check that the same colour mark as seen on the original spring is visible. The mark is approx. in the centre of the coil windings. A further mark, further towards the top, indicates the load rating.

● Fit the rebound rubber in the direction shown in Fig. 10.3.

● Fit the compressed spring over the spring strut, taking care to position it correctly over the spring seat.

113

- Fit the parts over the spring strut in accordance with the exploded view (Fig. 10.3).
- Fit the spring seat (4) and the upper strut bearing (3).
- Fit a self-locking nut to the piston rod and tighten to 6.0-7.0 kgm (43-51 ft.lb.). If possible, use the special tool shown in Fig. 10.5 for this operation.
- Check once more if the top and bottom of the spring is aligned with the respective spring seat grooves and release the spring compressor, ensuring that the spring seats do not become twisted.
- Fit the plastic cap (1) into the centre of the spring strut. The spring strut is now ready for installation.

10.1.4.   Installation of Spring Strut

The installation of the spring strut is a reversal of the removal procedure. After installation turn the steering from one lock into the other to make sure the brake hose caanot touch other parts of the front suspension. Bleed the brake system.

10.2.   Front Wheel Hubs

The front wheel hubs have already been covered in Section 10 together with the drive shafts. Refer to the relevant Section number if the wheel hubs or the wheel bearings are to be removed.

10.3.   Lower Suspension Arm
10.3.1.   Removal

The one-piece rubber bushes of the lower suspension arms should only be removed if replacement is necessary, Fig. 10.6. shows an exploded view of the suspension arm together with its component parts. The suspension arm can easily be removed without dismantling other major parts of the front suspension.

- Support the front end of the vehicle on secure chassis stands. Remove the panel from underneath the front end.
- Remove the mounting bolts for the stabiliser bar and the reaction strut from the suspension arm. On models after model year 1988 remove the clamps securing the stabiliser bar to the reaction strut.

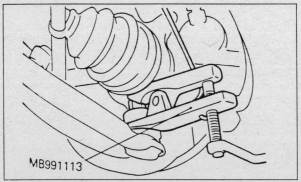

Fig. 10.6. — Separating the suspension ball joint from the steering knuckle with the special extractor. A similar tool can be used.

114

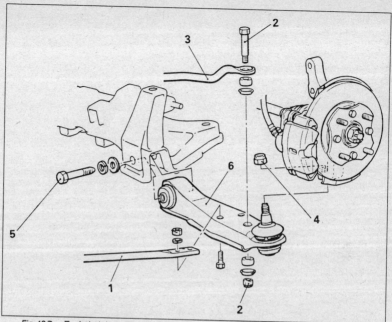

Fig. 10.7. — Exploded view of the suspension arm and the stabiliser bar on models before 1988.

1 Reaction strut bar	4 Ball joint nut, 6.0-7.2 kgm (43-52 ft.lb.)
2 Stabiliser nut and bolt	5 Lower suspension arm shaft
3 Stabiliser bar	6 Lower suspension arm

- Remove the suspension ball joint nut and separate the ball joint connection as shown in Fig. 10.6. Take care not to damage the rubber dust cap of the ball joint. To separate the ball joint, slacken the nut a few turns and then use the extractor as shown. An ordinary ball joint puller can also be used.
- Remove the suspension arm from its inner mounting. Note from which side the fulcrum bolt is fitted before driving out the bolt. Remove the suspension arm from the front suspension.

10.3.2.   Suspension Arm Repairs

The bush in the inner end of the suspension arm can be replaced, if a new bush can be obtained. Remove the old bush under a press with a suitable mandrel. Press in the new bush until centred. Take care not to deform the "U" shape of the suspension arm.

Check the suspension arm for visible damage. If in doubt (for example after an accident), have the arm checked for distortion at your dealer.

Suspension ball joints cannot be dismantled. The end float of the ball joint should not exceed 0.10 mm (0.004 in.). The joint must be replaced, if this is the case. The joint should also be replaced, if the rubber dust cap is torn, as dirt may have entered the joint. Otherwise replace the rubber dust boot. To replace the rubber dust boot, use a screwdriver and pry off the dust cap as shown in Fig. 10.8. Thoroughly clean the inside of the joint. Fill the joint with M.P. grease and fit a new dust cap in position, carefully using a piece of tube of suitable diameter. To replace a ball joint, remove the retaining ring from the upper face of the suspension ball joint and press the joint out of the suspension arm, using a suitable mandrel. Take care not to damage the suspension arm. Press the new ball joint in position and fit the rubber dust cap as described above.

To check the turning torque of a ball joint, a torque wrench with small divisions is required. Fit the nut to the ball joint stud and apply the torque wrench. Rotate the stud with the torque wrench and read off the indication when the ball joint stud starts to rotate. This should be at 120 kgcm (87 in.lb.). When the stud is contiuously turned with a torque wrench, there should be a reading of 30 - 60 kgcm (26 - 52 in.lb.). Remove the ball joint, if it fails the test.

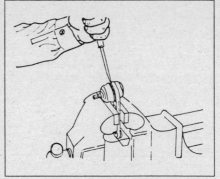

Fig. 10.8. — Removal of the suspension ball joint rubber dust cap.

10.3.3.   Suspension Arm — Installation

Insert the suspension arm into the bracket on the front suspension member, drive in the bolt, with the head in its original position, and tighten the nut finger-tight.

The remaining installation is a reversal of the removal procedure. Use a new nut for the ball joint, if the old one has lost its self-locking feature. Tighten the nut to 6.0 - 7.2 kgm (43.5 - 52 ft.lb.).

Lower the vehicle onto its wheels and tighten the nut of the inner fulcrum bolt to 12 - 15.0 kgm (86 - 108 ft.lb.). This will pre-load the suspension arm bushes to their proper operating position. All other tightening torques are given at the end of this section.

10.4.   Reaction Struts and Stabiliser Bar

10.4.1.   Removal and Installation

It should also be noted that the attachment of the stabiliser bar has been changed on certain models with the introduction of 1988 models. Figs. 10.9 and 10.10 show exploded views of reaction struts and stabiliser bar before and after 1988. To remove the parts, proceed as follows:

- Support the front of the vehicle on secure chassis stands.
- Refer to Fig. 10.9 or 10.10 and remove the nut from the end of the reaction strut bar (9), where it is attached to the body mounting and remove the two bolts and nuts of the bar from the lower suspension arm. Remove the bar towards the front first and take off the mounting parts.
- To remove the stabiliser bar, remove the mounting clamp in the centre and free the rubber mounting from the two suspension arms. Remove the stabiliser bar and take off the rubber parts and metal plate. Note the fitting position of the rubber bushes. If necessary, unscrew the centre bearing from the chassis.

To remove the parts shown in Fig. 10.10 proceed in a similar manner as described above, with the difference that the connecting link between stabiliser bar and reaction strut must be removed. Then remove the centre clamp from the stabiliser bar and take out the bar. If necessary, remove the centre link.

The installation of the stabiliser bar is a reversal of the removal procedure, noting the following points:

116

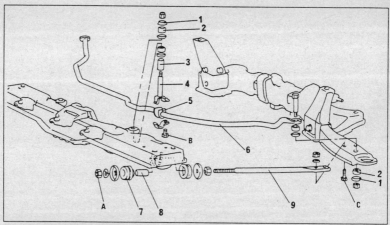

Fig. 10.9. — Exploded view of the reaction strut and stabiliser parts on models before 1988. The letters refer to the tightening torques.

1	Plate washer	4	Connecting bolt	7	Reaction strut bush
2	Rubber bush	5	Rubber bearing	8	Spacer sleeve
3	Spacer sleeve	6	Stabiliser bar	9	Reaction strut

A = 14-16 kgm (101-115 ft.lb.)
B = 1-1.3 kgm (7-9 ft.lb.)
C = 6-7 kgm (43.5-50.5 ft.lb.)

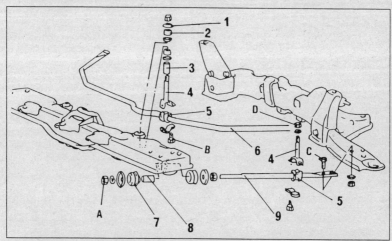

Fig. 10.10. — Exploded view of stabiliser bar and reaction strut on models from model year 1988.

1	Metal plate	4	Connecting link	7	Reaction strut bush
2	Rubber bush	5	Rubber bearing	8	Spacer sleeve
3	Spacer sleeve	6	Stabiliser bar	9	Reaction strut

A = 14-16 kgm (101-115 ft.lb.)
B = 1-1.3 kgm (7-9 ft.lb.)
C = 6-7 kgm (43.5-50.5 ft.lb.)
D = 2-3 kgm (14-21 ft.lb.)

- The reaction strut and the stabiliser bar rubber bushes/bearings can be replaced. Check the bar and the strut for distortion before installation.
- The rubber bushes for the threaded end of the reaction strut bar are symmetrical, but must be fitted as shown in Fig. 10.11.
- Fit the nut to the threaded end of the reaction strut and measure with a depth gauge as shown

117

in Fig. 10.12 a dimension of 78 mm between the end of the strut bar and the front face of the first nut. Turn the nuts accordingly and lock against each other. This adjustment will pre-load the rubber bushes for proper operation.

- Fit the reaction strut to the suspension arm with the projection on the reaction strut facing towards the top.
- In the case of models before 1988, tighten the nut at the bottom of the suspension arm until the bolt thread protrudes by 8 to 10 mm (0.3-0.4 in.).
- If the linkage for the stabiliser moutning (in the centre or at the reaction struts) has been removed, tighten the upper nut as just described.
- Tighten all other connections in accordance with the tightening torques given at the end of this section.

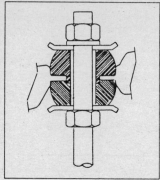

Fig. 10.11. — Correct assembly of the reaction strut bushes. The arrow indicates the front of the vehicle.

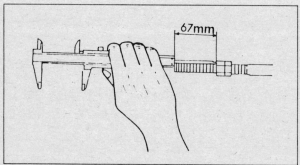

Fig. 10.12. — Measuring the dimension of the strut bar.

10.5. Front Wheel Alignment

The vehicle must be standing on level ground and the tyres must have their correct pressure. Steering, front suspension and wheel bearings must be in proper working order. Excessive play in the wheel bearings or suspension and steering joints will give incorrect readings.

Camber and king-pin inclination cannot be adjusted. If the values obtained are outside the figures given in Section 11.0 it can be assumed that parts of the front suspension are distorted. In this case check the front suspension and replace parts as necessary. The castor setting normally requires no adjustment, but can be adjusted by altering the length of the reaction struts, if necessary.

When checking the camber and castor values have the vehicle at its operating weight, i.e. in the condition it is used on the road. The fuel tank should be full.

10.5.1. Adjusting the Toe-in

The toe-in is adjusted by shortening or lengthening the track rods after slackening the locknuts. The track rod ball joint ends have threads and can rotate on the ball joint on the inside. This will allow the adjustment of the track rods without separating the ball joint connec-

118

tions from the steering levers. Measure the toe-in as follows:

- Place a tracking gauge in height of the front wheel hubs against the centre of the tyres in front of the vehicle. Set the pointers to '"Zero" and mark the tyres with chalk where the pointers are located. The pointers of the tracking gauge can also be placed against the outer edge of the wheel rims, depending what type of tracking gauge is used.

- Remove the tracking gauge and push the vehicle forward by half a turn of the wheels, until the chalk marks are once more at the height of the hubs, but this time at the rear of the tyres.

- Place the tracking gauge in position behind the front wheels and and set the pointers against the centres of the tyres or the wheel rim edges. The difference between the first measurement at the front and the second measurement at the rear should be 0 mm, with a tolerance of plus or minus 3.0 mm (0.12 in.). This value applies when the measurement takes place at the centre of the tyres. If the wheels rims are used, the reading should also be "0", but only a tolerance of 1.5 mm (0.06 in.) is permissible. If the distance at the rear is smaller than at the front, the wheels are adjusted to toe-in; if the distance at the front is greater than at the rear, the wheels have toe-out.

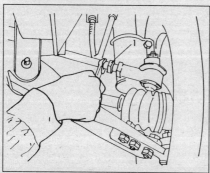

Fig. 10.13. — Adjusting a track rod to correct the toe-in/toe-out of the front wheels.

- To correct the adjustment, slacken the locknut (1) in Fig. 10.13 of both track rods and slacken the outer retaining clamp of both steering gaiters. Turn both track rods with an open-ended spanner. Half a turn of the track rod will alter the setting by approx. 6 mm (¼ in.).

- Re-check the setting as described above and if correct, tighten the locknuts to 5.0-5.5 kgm (36-39 ft.lb.). Also tighten the steering gaiter clamps.

- Check the position of the steering wheel and reset it to the centre position if necessary.

Excessive wear of the tyres on the outside or inside is normally an indication of in incorrect wheel alignment.

10.5.2.   ADJUSTING THE CASTOR

Measure the castor with a conventional castor checking gauge. If the values are outside the figures given in Section 10.0, or the difference between the two wheels is more than 30', adjust the castor as follows:

- Slacken the locknut ot both reaction strut bars (Fig. 10.14) and turn the two nuts either in or out. Re-tighten the locknut and re-check the castor.

- If the castor setting is correct, there is still the possibility that the wheelbase is out of adjustment. To measure the wheelbase, obtain two long nails and a piece of string. Tie one end of the string around one nail. Remove the front hub cap and ask a second person to hold the nail at right angles in the centre of the wheel hub.

- Stretch the string to the rear wheels, remove the hub cap and hold the nail against the centre of the hub. Tension the string and secure it to the nail.

- Hold the two nails against the wheel hubs on the other side of the vehicle. The points of the nails must coincide with the centres of the hubs, but a tolerance of 10 mm (0.4 in.) is per-

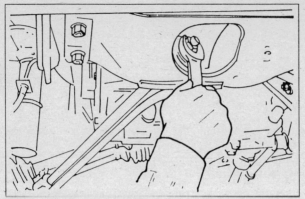

Fig. 10.14.—Slackening or tightening the nut of the reaction strut on the body side.

missible. Measure the length of the stretched string. The dimension must be 2625 mm, but again a tolerance of 10 mm (0.4 in.) is permissible.

10.6.　　Front Suspension — Tightening Torques

Spring strut piston rod nut: .... 6.0 - 7.0 kgm (43 - 51 ft.lb.)
Upper spring strut bearing to body: .... 2.5 - 3.5 kgm (18 - 25 ft.lb.)
Steering knuckle to spring strut: .... 7.5 - 9.0 kgm (54 - 65 ft.lb.)
Reaction strut end nut: .... 13.5 - 16 kgm (98 - 115 ft.lb.)
Stabiliser bar to connecting link: .... 1.0 - 1.3 kgm (7 - 9 ft.lb.)
Reaction strut to suspension arm: .... 6 - 7 kgm (42.5 - 50.5 ft.lb.)
Stabiliser bar linkage to reaction strut: .... 1.0 - 1.3 kgm (7 - 9 ft.lb.)
Suspension arm, inner fulcrum bolt: .... 12 - 15 kgm (86.5 - 108 ft.lb.)
Steering knuckle to ball joint: .... 6 - 7.2 kgm (42.5 - 52 ft.lb.)
Stabiliser to connecting link: .... 2 - 3 kgm (14 - 21 ft.lb.)
Wheel nuts, steel wheels: .... 9 - 11 kgm (65 - 80 ft.lb.)
Wheel nuts, light-alloy wheels: .... 9 - 11 kgm (65 - 80 ft.lb.)
Steering track rod locknut: .... 5 - 5.5 kgm (36 - 39 ft.lb.)

11.　　REAR SUSPENSION

11.0.　　Technical Data

Type: .... Suspension arms with coil springs, hydraulic, telescopic shock absorbers and stabiliser bar

Coil Springs — To End of Model Year 1984:
Wire Diameter (min. x max. diameter): .... 10.2 x 12.0 mm (0.40 x 0.47 in.)
Spring Diameter (min. x max. diameter): .... 117.4 x 121.0 mm (4.6 x 4.8 in.)
Free Length: .... 335.0 mm (13.20 in.)

Coil Springs — From Model Year 1986:
Wire Diameter (min. x max.): .... 10.2 x 12.0 mm (0.40 x 0.47 in.)

Spring Diameter: . . . . 122.0 mm (4.80 in.)
Free Length: . . . . 335.0 mm (13.9 in.)

Shock Absorbers
Max. extended length: . . . . 413.0 mm (16.3 in.)
Min. compressed length: . . . . 282.0 mm (11.1 in.)
Piston stroke: . . . . 131.0 mm (5.16 in.)

Stabiliser bar diameter: . . . . 14.5 mm (0.57 in.)

The rear suspension consists of an axle tube with a suspension arm on either side, coil springs and hydraulic telescopic shock absorbers. A stabiliser bar can be fitted to the rear suspension. Springs have been modified from model year 1986. Remember this, when new parts are required.

Fig. 11.1. shows the assembled rear suspension as fitted to a turbo model, i.e. fitted with stabiliser bar.

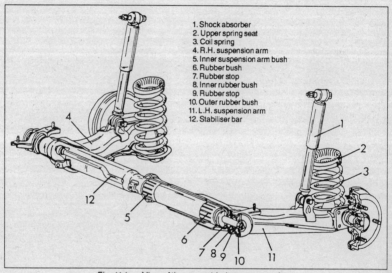

1. Shock absorber
2. Upper spring seat
3. Coil spring
4. R.H. suspension arm
5. Inner suspension arm bush
6. Rubber bush
7. Rubber stop
8. Inner rubber bush
9. Rubber stop
10. Outer rubber bush
11. L.H. suspension arm
12. Stabiliser bar

Fig. 11.1. — View of the assembled rear suspension.

11.1. Rear Suspension

11.1.1. Removal of Rear Coil Springs and Rear Suspension Arms

The left and right rear shock absorbers or the two rear springs should be removed individually if both sides of the rear suspension are to be dismantled as the same time.

- Slacken the wheel nuts and jack up the rear end of the vehicle. Place support stands under the sides of the body.
- Remove the rear brakes as described in Section 13.3.1.
- Place a jack underneath the suspension arm and lift up the arm until the shock absorbers are compressed.
- Remove the lower attachment of the shock absorber (Fig. 11.2.).

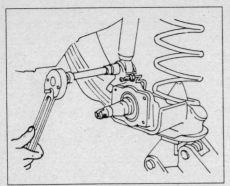

- Slowly lower the jack (ask a second person to do this task), until the rear coil spring can be lifted out (Fig. 11.3). Remove the two spring seats, after marking which one is fitted to the top and which one to the bottom.

- Again raise the jack until the shock absorber can be temporarily refitted to the lower securing point.

- Unscrew the union nut securing the brake pipe to the hose, knock out the retainer plate from the hose and withdraw the hose from the bracket. Plug up the ends of the pipe and the hose (Fig. 11.4)).

Fig. 11.2. — Removal of a shock absorber from the bottom mounting.

- Remove the two bolts in Fig. 11.4 (left arrows). Separate the shock absorber from the lower mounting and withdraw the suspension arm. If the rear suspension is to be removed as one assembly, carry out the same operations on the other side of the vehicle.

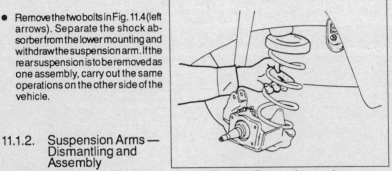

11.1.2. Suspension Arms — Dismantling and Assembly

Fig. 11.3. — Removal of a rear spring.

The suspension arm bushes and the dust cover in the centre of the axle tube can be replaced. The two suspension arms are joined-up in the centre and consist of the component parts shown in Fig. 11.5. The following description assumes that the complete rear suspension must be overhauled.

- Clamp the rear suspension into a vice, using soft-metal jaws and from both sides of the axle remove the nut on the outside of the suspension arm. Discard the nut as it must be replaced on assembly.

- Remove the washer. Note that this washer has a serration which must be facing the suspension arm bush on both sides of the axle.

- Remove the mounting brackets for the suspension arms from the centre shaft. Mark the fitted position of both brackets. This is important for the installation.

- In the centre of the axle tube remove the dust cover clamp. If there is no visible damage of the dust cover, leave it on the right-hand suspension arm.

- Pull the two suspension arm assemblies apart and remove the rubber stopper from the R.H. suspension arm.

- Clamp the left-hand suspension arm into a vice (soft-metal jaws) and using a strong screwdriver, drive out the outer bush as shown in Fig. 11.6.

- Using a drift, drive out the inner bush from the inside of the suspension arm as shown in Fig. 11.7. Both bushes are located in the suspension arm (7) in Fig. 11.5.

122

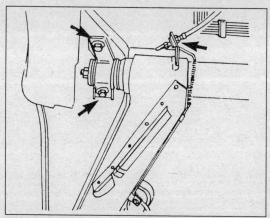

Fig. 11.4. — Removal of a rear suspension arm (left arrows) and the brake pipe to hose connection (right arrow).

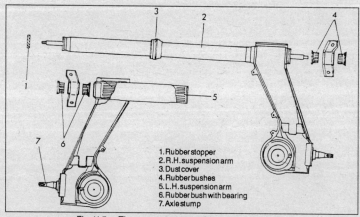

1. Rubber stopper
2. R.H. suspension arm
3. Dust cover
4. Rubber bushes
5. L.H. suspension arm
6. Rubber bush with bearing
7. Axle stump

Fig. 11.5. — The component parts of the suspension arms.

- Thoroughly clean the suspension arm. Coat the outside of the bushes and the inside of the L.H. suspension arm with M.P. grease. The bush with the flange is fitted to the outside.

- Drive inner bush into the arm tube to its stop, with special tools MB990779 and MB990780.

- Drive the outer bush into position until the bush flange rests against the arm. Use MB9900780 (mandrel) to drive in the bush should cover the complete outer face of the bush to prevent damage.

- Coat the outside of the right-hand suspension arm with M.P. grease and fit the rubber stopper. If the dust cover has been replaced, push the new cover up to the stopper on the arm before applying grease to the arm.

- Clamp the left-hand suspension arm into a vice, using soft-metal jaws, and slowly push the right-hand arm into the left-hand arm. Wipe away excessive grease.

- Refer to Section 11.3 to fit the stabiliser bar, as it must be fitted at this stage.

123

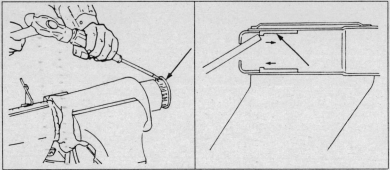

Fig. 11.6. — Removal of the outer suspension arm bush (arrow) from the left-hand suspension arm. Use soft-metal jaws to clamp the arm into a vice.

Fig. 11.7. — Removal of the inner bush from the inside of the left-hand suspension arm.

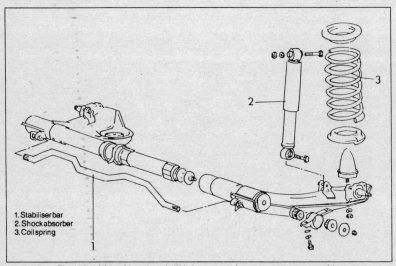

1. Stabiliser bar
2. Shock absorber
3. Coil spring

Fig. 11.8. — View of the rear axle with the suspension components on one side.

- If necessary press new bushes into the arm mountings and fit the two mountings over the arm ends, as shown in Fig. 11.9. Note that the mountings are offset and must be fitted as shown in the illustration. Place the washer with the serration against the bush. Fit a new self-locking nut to 8 - 10 kgm (58 - 72 ft.lb.) when the mountings are in the original installation position.
- Fill the inside of the dust cover and the lip with M.P. grease and attach the cover with a new retaining clamp.

11.1.3.   Installation of Rear Suspension

The installation of the rear suspension is a reversal of the removal procedure. Refit the two spring seats on each side in accordance with the marks made during removal. When the

124

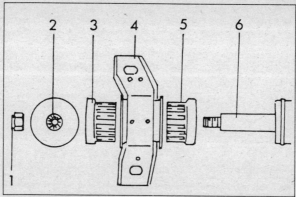

Fig. 11.9. — The correct installation of the bushes and suspension arm mounting brackets.

1. Self-locking nut
2. Washer with serration
3. Outer rubber bush

4. Suspension arm mounting
5. Inner rubber bush
6. Mounting spigot

wheels are resting on the ground (i.e. ramps), tighten the nuts at the ends of the suspension arms to 8 - 10 kgm (58 - 72 ft.lb.) and the lower shock absorber mountings to 6.5 - 8.0 kgm (47 - 58 ft.lb.). Refit the brake assemblies and adjust and bleed the brakes.

11.2.   Rear Hubs and Rear Wheel Bearings

11.2.1   Wheel Hubs — Removal and Installation

- Slacken the wheel nuts, support the rear end of the vehicle on chassis stands and remove the rear wheels.
- Remove the hub grease cap with a screwdriver and clean the outside of the axle stump with a rag.
- Withdraw the hub nut split pin, remove the nut lock and unscrew the wheel bearing nut. Remove the washer.
- Remove the brake drum together with the hub from the axle stump. Sometimes it is necessary to use a puller to remove the brake drum. This can be attached to the wheel studs.

If the wheel bearings are to be replaced, read section 11.2.2. The following text describes the installation and adjustment of the wheel hub. Check the condition of the oil seal at the inside of the hub and replace if oil leaks can be seen.

- Push the wheel hub/brake drum over the axle stump and tap in position with a rubber or plastic mallet. Grease the outer wheel bearing and drive the bearing into the drum.
- Using a torque wrench with a suitable socket, tighten the wheel bearing nut to 2.0 kgm (14.5 ft.lb.), whilst the brake drum is turned to and fro to settle-in the bearings.
- Fully slacken the nut and again tighten with the torque wrench, but this time to 0.5 kgm (3.6 ft.lb.).
- Place the nut lock over the hub and check if the split pin can be inserted. If this is not the case, unscrew the nut by 15° (¼ of a flat of the nut), but not more.
- Apply the handbrake lever several times to bring the brake shoes against the brake drum faces.

11.2.2. Wheel Bearing Replacement

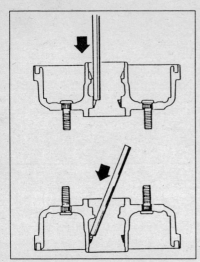

Fig. 11.10. — Removal of the wheel bearing outer races from opposite sides of the brake drum.

The replacement of the wheel bearings is not difficult. Note that wheel bearings are made by several manufacturers and only bearings of the same make should be fitted.

Remove the oil seal from the inside of the brake drum with a screwdriver and lift out the bearing. Using a suitable drift, drive the outer bearing races from the inside of the hub. First drive out one race, turn over the drum and drive out the other race (Fig. 11.10). Cut-outs inside the hub enable the drift to be applied. Drive the new bearing races into the hub from opposite sides until fully home. Always replace the bearing races — never replace the inner cages (the part with the bearing rollers) and leave the old outer races in the hub.

Fill the cavity inside the hub with wheel bearing grease, but leave enough space to insert the axle stump. Also coat the bearing rollers with the same grease. Insert the rear bearing and squarely drive in the oil seal. Remove excessive grease. The lip of the oil seal should also be filled with grease.

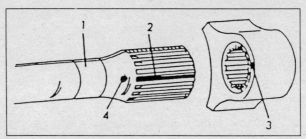

Fig. 11.11. — When fitting the stabiliser bar (1), align the white line (2) with the punch mark (3) or the punch mark (4) with the punch mark (3).

11.3. Rear Stabiliser Bar

The stabiliser bar can only be removed after one of the suspension arms has been removed. Mark the ends of the stabiliser where they engage with the suspension arms before removal to retain the position of the stabiliser splines for installation. Fig. 11.11 shows how a stabiliser bar is marked. The punch mark (3) is marked into the stabiliser bar bracket and the stabiliser bar end should be marked with a punch mark at position (4) in line with mark (3). The L.H. side of the stabiliser bar is marked with a colour band (1). A white line in the serrations (2) gives a guide line to fit the bar to the stabiliser bar bracket, if a new bar is fitted. Otherwise align marks (3) and (4).

When assembling the rear suspension, fit the stabiliser bar before the two halves of the suspension arms are assembled together.

126

12.   STEERING

12.0.   Technical Data

Type: . . . . Rack and pinion steering with safety steering column and tilt mechanism. Some models with power steering

Steering wheel diameter: . . . . 386.0 mm (15.2 in.)
Max. free play at steering wheel:
  Manual steering: . . . . 0 - 30 mm (0 - 1.18 in.)
  Power steering: . . . . 10 mm (0.4 in.) or less
Max. run-out of steering shaft: . . . . 2.0 mm (0.08 in.)
Power-assisted Steering:
  Drive belt deflection:
  Petrol models: . . . . 6 - 9 mm (0.24 - 0.35 in.)
  Diesel model: . . . . 7 - 10 mm (0.3 - 0.4 in.)
Recommended steering fluid: . . . . Automatic transmission fluid Dexron or Dexron II
Capacity: . . . . 960 c.c. (1.7 lm. pts.)

Wheel alignment data: . . . . See Section 10.0
Steering Lock Angles:
  Inner wheel: . . . . 37° 45' ± 1°
  Outer wheel: . . . . 30° 40'

A rack and pinion steering is fitted. The steering column is of the safety-type and will collapse in the case of a frontal collision. The fitted tilt mechanism allows an adjustment range of 3° each in four steps in order to permit selection of the most suitable driving position. A power-assisted steering can be fitted.

12.1.   Steering Column — Removal and Installation

Fig. 12.2 shows an exploded view of the steering column assembly. The column can be removed in the numbered order.

- Remove the horn push. To do this, grip the centre steering wheel padding as shown in Fig. 12.1 and pull it off.

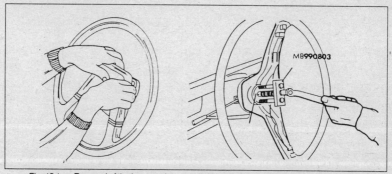

Fig. 12.1. — Removal of the horn push button (left) and withdrawal of the steering wheel (right).

- Unscrew the steering wheel nut and mark the steering wheel hub and the end of the steering column shaft with a centre punch. Remove the steering wheel with steering

127

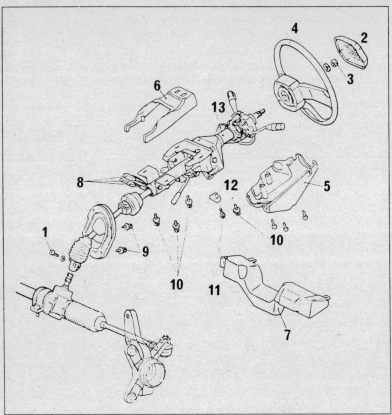

Fig. 12.2. — Details for the removal and installation of the steering column. Remove in the numbered order shown, refit in reverse order.

1 Universal joint bolt	8 Cable connector
2 Horn pad	9 Dust cover bolts
3 Steering wheel nut	10 Tilt bracket bolts
4 Steering wheel	11 Special screw
5 Lower steering column cover	12 Special washer
6 Upper steering column cover	13 Steering column
7 Lap heater duct	

wheel puller MB990803, as shown in Fig. 12.1. Two threaded bores in the steering wheel hub enable the puller to be screwed in. Do not use a hammer to remove the steering wheel, doing so may damage the steering column collapsible mechanism.

● Unscrew the lower steering column cover.

● Remove the upper steering column cover and disconnect the cable connectors from the cable harness. Remove the steering column cover with the steering fully lowered.

● Remove the lap heater

● Slacken the clamp bolt securing the upper steering universal joint to the steering shaft and drive out the bolt.

- Remove the steering column shaft from below the dashboard and withdraw the steering column shaft from the intermediate shaft. Special bolts are used to attach the column bracket and a multi-spline bit must be used to remove them (Part No. MB 990826). Lift the steering column out of the vehicle. Lower the steering column assembly towards the floor by removing the bolts which secure the lower bracket and the tilt bracket.
- To remove the intermediate shaft, unscrew the clamp bolt for the lower universal joint at the steering pinion (Fig. 12.3) and the four screws securing the colum cover assembly to the floor panel and remove the shaft together with the cover out of the vehicle.

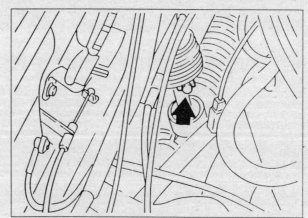

Fig. 12.3 — The arrow shows the clamp bolt for the lower universal joint (inside the engine compartment).

The two universal joint of the intermediate shaft cannot be repaired and the complete shaft must be replaced if one or both of the universal joints are damaged or if stiffness is felt in the joints.

The tilt steering column should not be dismantled.

Replace the steering lock as follows:

Using a hacksaw, cut a slot into the end of the sheared-off steering lock bolt and unscrew the bolt with a screwdriver. The upper steering column bracket can be removed in the same manner, if it is to be replaced (one bolt).

The installation of the steering column is a reversal of the removal procedure. Tighten the upper steering column bracket finger-tight to the dashboard underside. Tighten the universal joint bolt to 3.0 - 3.5 kgm (21 - 25 ft.lb.). Align the steering column correctly before all attachment bolts are tightened.

Fit the steering wheel over the steering column shaft, aligning the centre punch marks and tighten the steering wheel nut to 3.5 - 4.5 kgm (25 - 32 ft.lb.). Operate the steering lock to check its function. If satisfied, tighten the steering lock bolt until the head breaks off.

12.2. Steering Unit

12.2.1. Removal and Installation

- Support the front of the vehicle on chassis stands and remove the two wheels.
- From the engine compartment remove the clamp bolt securing the lower steering universal joint to the steering pinion (Fig. 12.3).

129

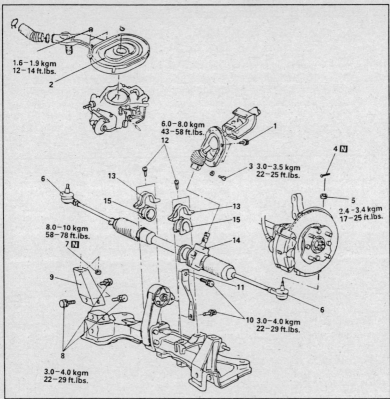

1.6 – 1.9 kgm
12 – 14 ft.lbs.

6.0 – 8.0 kgm
43 – 58 ft.lbs.

3 3.0 – 3.5 kgm
22 – 25 ft.lbs.

2.4 – 3.4 kgm
17 – 25 ft.lbs.

8.0 – 10 kgm
58 – 78 ft.lbs.

10 3.0 – 4.0 kgm
22 – 29 ft.lbs.

3.0 – 4.0 kgm
22 – 29 ft.lbs.

Fig. 12.4. — Details for the removal and installation of the manual steering. Remove the parts in the order shown; refit in reverse order. The items marked with "N" must always be replaced.

1 Dust cover bolts	9 Sub-member
2 Air cleaner, diesel	10 Mounting bolts
3 Universal joint bolt	11 Rear roll stopper stay
4 Split pins	12 Steering mounting bolts
5 Track rod ball joint nuts	13 Steering mounting clamps
6 Track rod ball joints	14 Steering unit
7 Mounting nuts	15 Mounting rubbers
8 Mounting bolts	

- Remove the air cleaner.
- Remove the split pin from the castellated nut on the steering track rod, unscrew the nut and separate the ball joint connection with a suitable extractor (Fig. 12.5).
- Remove the sub-member from the crossmember on the R.H. side of the vehicle.
- Unscrew the undercover from the front of the vehicle (if fitted).
- Remove the bolts securing the steering on the left-hand and right-hand sides to the chassis and withdraw it sideways. A socket with extension and ratchet is required to remove the bolts from the inside of the engine compartment. When taking off the rubber bushes note their fitted position to ensure that they are refitted in their original position.

130

The installation of the steering is a reversal of the removal procedure. The following points should be noted:

● Rotate the rubber bushes on the steering rack tube to the position found during removal

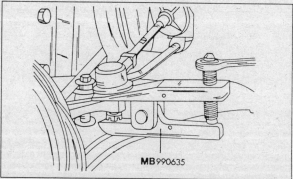

Fig. 12.5—Separating a track rod ball joint.

before fitting the clamps. The projections of the mounting rubbers must fit into the holes of the housing bracket and housing clamps respectively.

● Tighten the steering mounting bolts to no more than 6.0-8.0 kgm (43-58 ft. lb.). The rack tube could be crushed if any higher torques are applied.

● Tighten the track rod joint castellated nuts to 2.4-3.4 kgm (17-23 ft. lb.). Insert the split pins. Tighten the nuts slightly further if the pin cannot be entered.

● Measure the toe-in setting and adjust if necessary as described in Section 10.5.1. Make sure that the steering rubber gaiters cannot rotate whilst adjusting the toe-in.

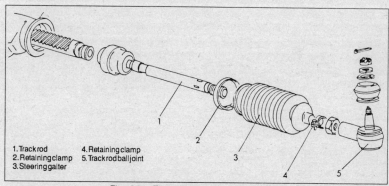

1. Track rod   4. Retaining clamp
2. Retaining clamp 5. Track rod ball joint
3. Steering gaiter

Fig. 12.6. — The component parts of a track rod.

12.2.2.   Stooring   Ovorhaul

It is technically possible to overhaul a steering box, but in most cases it is far better to fit a new or re-conditioned steering box (if obtainable), mainly if rack housing and steering rack have suffered wear. If the steering track rods need replacement, remove the steering from the vehicle as already described and replace the rods as follows:

131

- Thoroughly clean the outside of the steering box and clamp the steering into a vice, using soft-metal jaws. Take care not to crash the rack tube. Referring to Fig. 12.6, remove the clamp band (2), securing the rubber boot (3) and pull back the rubber boot.
- Using a chisel remove the peening of the track rod ball joint opposite the rack housing. Move the rack all the way towards the rack housing and clamp the toothed part of the rack into a vice, again using soft-metal jaws. With a large open-ended spanner unscrew the ball joint housing from the steering rack (Fig. 12.7). Unscrew the track rod from the rack.

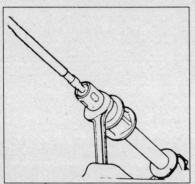

Fig. 12.7. — Removal of the track rod ball joint end from the steering rack.

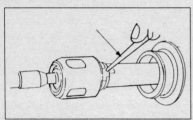

Fig. 12.8. — Peening the ball joint housing to the steering rack.

- Fit the new track rod and tighten the ball joint housing to 7.0 - 10.0 kgm (50 - 72 ft.lb.). Use a small drift as shown in Fig. 12.8 and peen the ball joint housing into the steering rack to secure it in position.
- Fit the steering rubber gaiter with the retaining clamp. Slacken the outer retaining clamp and slacken the track rod ball joint end locknut. Rotate the track rod until a dimension of 182.5 - 184.5 mm (7.2 - 7.3 in.) is obtained between the inner face of the locknut and the end of the rubber gaiter. Make sure that the gaiter is located properly in its groove before the measurement is carried out.

12.3 Replacing a Steering Gaiter

Steering rubber gaiters can be replaced after separating the track rod ball joint from the steering lever. Slacken the track rod end locknut and unscrew the end piece, at the same time counting the number of turns. Remove the gaiter.

Clean out old grease, re-grease the steering rack and refit the gaiter. Screw the track rod end to its original position and tighten the locknut. Check and adjust the toe-in after installation.

12.4. Power-assisted Steering

12.4.1. Removal and Installation

- Jack up the front end of the vehicle and place on chassis stands. Remove the front wheel.
- Remove the air cleaner.
- From the inside of the vehicle remove the clamp bolt securing the lower universal joint to the steering pinion (see Fig. 12.3).
- Drain the steering fluid. To do this, disconnect the return hose from the fluid reservoir and allow the fluid to drain into a container.
- Unscrew the union nut securing the two pipes to the steering unit and withdraw the pipes. Fig. 12.10 shows where the pipes are connected. Mark them in accordance with their connections and plug the ends of the pipe to prevent ingress of dirt.

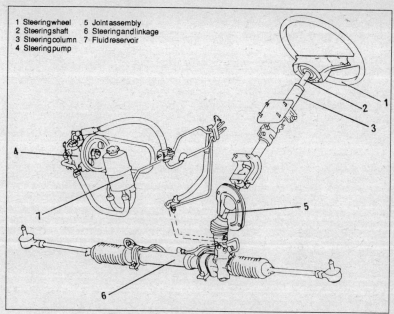

1 Steering wheel   5 Joint assembly
2 Steering shaft   6 Steering and linkage
3 Steering column   7 Fluid reservoir
4 Steering pump

Fig. 12.9. — View of the power-assisted steering.

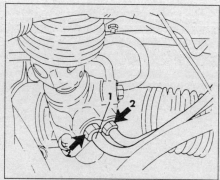

Fig. 12.10. — The connections of the return pipe (1) and the pressure feed pipe (2) on the steering.

- Remove the split pin out of the track rod ball joint nut and using a suitable extractor, as shown in Fig. 12.5, separate the ball joint from the steering lever (on both sides of the vehicle).
- On one side of the steering remove a bolt and a clamp, securing two pipes to the steering mounting clamp. Carefully pull the pipes to one side.
- Remove the support stay for the rear engine roll stopper.
- Remove the sub-member on the R.H. side of the vehicle from the crossmember.
- Remove the undercover (if fitted).
- Remove the steering box mounting bolts on the L.H. and R.H. sides and remove the steering sideways out of the vehicle. A socket with extension and ratchet is required to remove the bolts from the inside of the engine compartment. Note the fitted position of the rubber bearings to ensure their installation in the correct position.

The installation of the steering is a reversal of the removal procedure. Refer to Section 12.2.1 for any points to be noted. The same applies to the power-assisted steering. After installation fill and bleed the steering system as described in Section 12.4.3. Check the system for leaks.

133

12.4.2. Changing the Steering Fluid

Jack up the front end of the vehicle. Disconnect the return hose at the bottom of the fluid container and drain the fluid into a container.

Withdraw the centre H.T. cable out of the distributor and crank the engine with the starter motor, at the same time turning the steering wheel from lock to lock. This will eject all remaining fluid from the system. Re-connect the return hose and secure with the clamp. Re-connect the H.T. lead.

Fill the reservoir to the bottom of the filter and then bleed the system as described in the next section.

12.4.3. Bleeding the Steering System

Remove the centre H.T. lead out of the ignition distributor and ask a second person to operate the starter motor. At the same time turn the steering wheel 5 or 6 times from lock to lock. If the reservoir has just been filled, top-up with the recommended fluid, as the level will sink rapidly. The level should not drop below the filter.

Re-connect the H.T. lead and start the engine. Move the steering wheel from one lock to the other, until no more air bubbles can be seen in the reservoir. **Do not hold the wheel at full lock to either side.**

Check that the fluid level changes only slightly as the wheel is turned. If the fluid level changes considerably, repeat the bleeding operation. If the fluid level rises suudenly when the engine is stopped, there is still air in the system. Noise from the steering pump and control valve may also indicate air in the system. Air in the system will shorten the life of the pump and other parts.

12.4.4. Adjusting the Steering Pump Belt Tension

The tension of the steering pump drive belt is checked at the position shown by the arrow in Fig. 12.11. The belt should deflect between 6 and 9 mm (0.24 and 0.35 in.) in the case of a petrol engine or 7 - 10 mm (0.3 - 0.4 in.) in the case of a diesel engine. If this is not the case, slacken the two pump mounting bolts in Fig. 12.12 and move the pump in its mounting bracket. Tighten the bolts and re-check the tension.

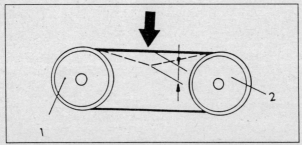

Fig. 12.11. — Check the steering pump belt tension between the pump pulley (1) and the water pump pulley (2).

12.4.5. Steering Pump — Removal and Installation

Disconnect the pressure and the suction hoses from the pump and drain the fluid into a suitable container. Remove the mounting bolts in Fig. 12.11, push the pump towards the inside and remove the drive belt. Fully remove the pump mounting bolts and the bolts securing the pump bracket to the engine mounting and take off the pump.

The installation is a reversal of the removal procedure. Ensure that the hoses are not twisted or in contact with any other component. Refill the system and bleed as described.

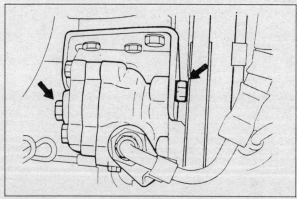

Fig. 12.12. — Adjusting the tension of the power steering drive belt.

12.5.   Steering — Tightening Torques

Mechanical Steering:
Steering Column and Steering Shaft:
Steering wheel nut: . . . . 3.5 - 4.5 kgm (25 - 33 ft.lb.)
Steering column brackets: . . . . 1.0 kgm (7 ft.lb.)
Mounting of tilt mechanism: . . . . 1.0 kgm (7 ft.lb.)
Lock bolt of tilt adjustment: . . . . 0.6 - 0.8 kgm (4 - 6 ft.lb.)
Steering column mounting, upper bracket: . . . . 0.6 - 0.8 kgm (6 - 9 ft.lb.)
Universal joint clamp bolts: . . . . 3.0 - 3.5 kgm (22 - 25 ft.lb.)
Steering Box:
Track rod to steering lever: . . . . 2.4 - 3.4 kgm (17 - 25 ft.lb.)
Track rod locknuts: . . . . 5.0 - 5.5 kgm (36 - 40 ft.lb.)
Steering mounting bolts: . . . . 6.0 - 8.0 kgm (43 - 58 ft.lb.)
Track rod to steering rack: . . . . 8.0 - 10.0 kgm (58 - 72 ft.lb.)
Sub-member to crossmember: . . . . 3.0 - 4.0 kgm (22 - 29 ft.lb.)
Sub-member to sub-frame: . . . . 8.0 - 10.0 kgm (58 - 72 ft.lb.)

Power-assisted Steering:
Steering column: . . . . As mechanical steering
Track rods: . . . . As mechanical steering
Steering mounting: . . . . As mechanical steering
Track rod to steering rack: . . . . As mechanical steering
Sub-member: . . . . As mechanical steering
Pressure and return hoses: . . . . 1.2 - 1.8 kgm (8.5 - 13 ft.lb.)
Pressure hose to steering pump: . . . . 4.0 - 5.0 kgm (29 - 36 ft.lb.)
Steering pump pulley nut: . . . . 2.7 - 4.1 kgm (20 - 30 ft.lb.)
Fluid reservoir: . . . . 0.8 - 1.2 kgm (6 - 9 ft.lb.)
Steering pump to mounting bracket: . . . . 2.5 - 3.3 kgm (18 - 24 ft.lb.)
Pump bracket to engine mounting bracket (small bolts): . . . . 2.0 2.7 kgm (14 20 ft.lb.)
Pump bracket to engine mounting bracket (large bolts): . . . . 2.7 - 4.1 kgm (20 - 30 ft.lb.)
Bolt for belt adjustment: . . . . 2.5 - 3.3 kgm (18 - 24 ft.lb.)
Heat protector to steering pump: . . . . 0.8 - 1.2 kgm (6 - 9 ft.lb.)
Hoses to steering: . . . . 1.2 - 1.8 kgm (9 - 13 ft.lb.)
Engine mounting bracket: . . . . 5.0 - 7.0 kgm (36 - 51 ft.lb.)
Tube clamp to mounting clamp: . . . . 0.8 - 1.2 kgm (6 - 9 ft.lb.)

13. BRAKES

13.0. Technical Data

Type: .... Disc brakes at the front and self-adjusting drum brakes with leading and trailing shoes at the rear. With brake servo unit. Handbrake operating on rear wheels. Dual-line brake system with brake proportioning valve.

Master brake cylinder dia.: .... 23.81 mm (0.94 in.)
Handbrake adjustment: .... 5 - 7 notches of handbrake lever

Front Disc Brakes
Type: AD54
Disc Brake Diameter: .... 242.0 mm (9.53 in.))))
Brake Disc Thickness: .... 16.4 mm (0.65 in.)
Max. run-out of discs: .... 0.15 mm (0.006 in.)
Brake Pad Thickness: .... 10.5 mm (0.41 in.)
Pad material wear limit: .... 2.0 mm (0.08 in.)
Brake Cylinder Diameter: .... 54.00 mm (2.12 in.)
Clearance adjustent: .... Automatic

Rear Brakes
Drum diameter: .... 203.0 mm (8.0 in.)
    Max. diameter: .... 205.0 mm (8.1 in.)
Brake lining thickness:
    Standard: .... 4.3 mm (0.17 in.)
    Min. lining thickness: .... 1.0 mm (0.04 in.)
Brake Cylinder Diameter: .... 20.64 mm (0.81 in.)
Brake adjustment: .... Automatic

All models are fitted with a dual-line brake system. Front wheels are fitted with disc brakes (ventilated); rear brakes with drum brakes. All brake assemblies are self-adjusting. A brake pressure proportioning valve is fitted to the system to control the braking pressure to the wheels.

A mechanical handbrake system operates the rear brakes via cables. A brake servo unit is standard equipment.

13.1. Front Disc Brakes

13.1.1. Replacing the Brake Pads

Refer to Fig. 13.1 for the following operations.:

- Jack up the front end of the vehicle and support on stands. Remove the front wheels.
- Remove the bolt (2) at the inside of the steering knuckle and swing the brake cylinder upwards. Tie the cylinder in position with a piece of wire, as shown in Fig. 13.2. The bolt is coated with special grease which must not be removed. Take care not to allow dust or grit onto the bolt.
- Remove the inner shim (11), the outer shim (15) and the brake pads (12) from the caliper mounting bracket. Always remove the pads on both sides when they are to be replaced.
- Remove the spring clips (13) and (14).

Fig. 13.2 shows the exposed brake pads on the R.H. side. Do not depress the brake pedal after the caliper has been removed from the bracket.

Replace the brake pads as a set if the thickness of the pad material is less than 2.0 mm (0.08 in.). Never replace one brake pad only or attempt to exchange brake pads from the inside to

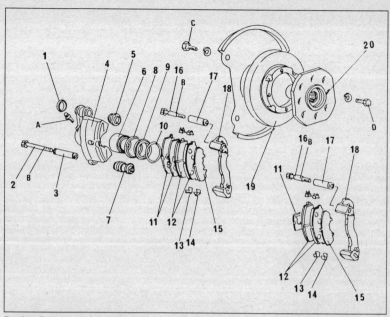

Fig. 13.1. — Exploded view of a brake caliper. The brake pad parts, shown on the R.H. side, are fitted to the Space Wagon. The letters refer to the tightening torques.

1 Cover	7 Lock pin boot	14 Brake pad clip
2 Guide bolt lock pin)	8 Piston seal	15 Anti-squeak shim
3 Sleeve	9 Piston boot	16 Guide pin
4 Caliper body	10 Boot retaining ring	17 Sleeve
5 Guide pin boot	11 Inner shim	18 Caliper bracket
6 Piston	12 Brake pad assembly	19 Brake disc
	13 Brake pad clip	20 Wheel hub

A = 0.7-0.9 kgm
B = 2.2-3.2 kgm
C = 8-10 kgm
D = 4-5 kgm

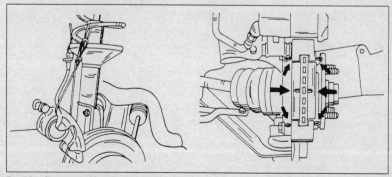

Fig. 13.2. — After removal of the caliper, tie it up with a piece of wire as shown on the left. The brake pads will be exposed as on the right. Remove the parts shown by the arrows.

the outside or vice versa or from one side to the other. Clean the caliper with brake fluid or methylated spirits — never petrol. Check the cylinder seals for signs of leakage.

Brake pad repair kits contain the two brake pads, anti-squeal shims and new spring clips. All

137

parts must be used during assembly.

Check the brake disc for grooves, caused for example by worn brake pads. Measure the disc thickness. Replace the disc if the thickness is less than given in Section 14.0.).

The installation of the brake caliper is a reversal of the removal procedure. Again refer to Section 13.1.1 for further details. The bolt at the bottom of the caliper is tightened to 2.2-3.2 kgm (16 -23 ft.lb.).

13.1.2.   Brake Caliper — Removal and Overhaul

- Slacken the brake hose hexagon on the caliper as long as it is till fitted. Remove the brake hose from the brake pipe connection on the spring strut. To do this, undo the union nut, drive out the spring plate and withdraw the brake hose from the bracket. Plug the open end of the brake pipe to prevent entry of dirt.
- Remove the two brake caliper mounting bracket bolts and lift off the complete brake caliper assembly. Remove the brake pads as described in Section 13.1.1.
- Remove the retaining ring (10) for the rubber dust seal with a screwdriver and remove the seal (9).
- To remove the piston apply an air line to the brake hose connecting bore. Place a rag underneath the piston to prevent damage during ejection. Keep the hands away from the area below the piston. Do not use excessive air pressure.
- Remove the piston seal (8) from the inside of the cylinder bore. Take care not to scratch the surface.

The brake disc can be unscrewed from the wheel hub if necessary.

Thoroughly clean all parts in methylated spirits or brake fluid. Check the inside of the caliper bore for grooves or other damage. Replace the cylinder assembly if wear is excessive. Slight blemishes can be removed with smooth sandpaper. The gliding face of the piston is specially treated and cannot be smoothed with sandpaper. Always replace the cylinder seal and the rubber dust seal.

Before assembly coat all internal parts of the cylinder with clean brake fluid or brake paste. Various repair kits are available to overhaul a caliper and all contain lubrication grease.

Assemble the caliper as follows:

- Coat a new cylinder seal with rubber grease provided in the repair kit and install the seal into the cylinder groove without twisting it (Fig. 13.3).

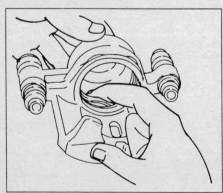

- Coat the inside of the cylinder bore with clean brake fluid.
- Push the piston carefully into its bore without tilting it. Coat the groove for the location of the rubber dust seal with orange-coloured grease and fit the seal into the piston and the caliper cylinder. Secure the seal with the retaining ring.
- Fit the brake caliper to the mounting bracket. Coat the inside of the rubber bushes for glide sleeves and sleeve bolts with orange-coloured grease. Tighten the bolts to 2.2 -3.2 kgm (16 - 23 ft.lb.).

Fig. 13.3. — Fitting the cylinder seal.

138

The installation of the brake caliper is a reversal of the removal procedure. Tighten the bolts to 8.0 - 10.0 kgm (58 - 72 ft.lb.) and bleed the brake system as described in Section 13.4.

13.1.3. Brake Discs

The removal of a brake disc is carried out together with the front wheel hub and these operations have already been described in Section 9.3. Mark the position of the disc in relation to the hub and unscrew the brake disc from the hub. Check the brake disc as follows:

- Measure the thickness of the brake disc. Replace the disc if the thickness is less than specified in Section 13.0. The thickness tolerance must not exceed 0.07 mm (0.003 in.).
- To check a brake disc for distortion, refit it to the hub and fit the hub. Apply a dial gauge to the outer edge of the disc, as shown in Fig. 13.4 and slowly rotate the disc. Observe the needle deflection, indicating the run-out of the disc. This should not exceed 0.15 mm (0.006 in.). Replace the disc if otherwise.

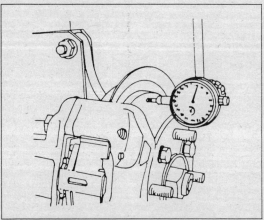

Fig. 13.4. — Checking a brake disc for run-out.

When refitting the disc to the hub tighten the mounting bolts to 5.0 - 6.0 kgm (36 - 43 ft.lb.).

13.2. Rear Drum Brakes

Fig. 13.5 shows an exploded view of the brake system and should be referred to in case of difficulties.

- Jack up the rear end of the vehicle and support on chassis stands. Remove the rear wheels.
- Remove the brake drums as described in Section 11.2.1.
- Using a pair of pliers or a screwdriver, remove the two springs shown in Fig. 13.6.
- Place the forefinger over one of the brake shoe hold-down pins (from the rear of the brake back plate) and grip the spring seat from the front with a pair of pliers. Turn the spring seat by 90° until the head of the pin (7) can be guided through the elongated hole in the spring seat. Remove both spring seats and the spring (13). Remove the second hold-down pin in the same manner.

139

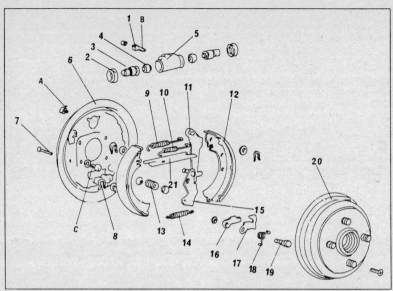

Fig. 13.5. — Exploded view of the rear brake. The letters refer to the tightening torques.

1 Bleeder screw	7 Hold-down pin	13 Spring	19 Pivot pin
2 Rubber dust cap	8 Retaining "U" clip	14 Lower return spring	20 Brake drum
3 Wheel cylinder piston	9 Upper return spring	15 Adjuster lever	21 Handbrake strut
4 Piston cup	10 Handbrake strut spring	16 Toothed latch	A = 9.8 - 1.2 kgm
5 Wheel cylinder body	11 Handbrake lever	17 Stopper lever	B = 0.7 - 0.9 kgm
6 Brake back plate	12 Brake shoe	18 Return spring	C = 5 - 6 kgm

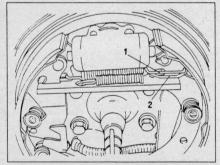

Fig. 13.6. — The position of the return springs between brake shoes (1) and between brake shoe and handbrake strut (2).

• Remove the leading brake shoe together with the strut (21). Tilt the trailing show towards the bottom and disconnect the handbrake cable; To do this, compress the spring, until the handbrake cable end can be disengaged from the hook of the handbrake operating lever (see Fig. 13.7). If the handbrake cable is to be removed, remove the retaining snap ring on the brake backplate, as shown in Fig. 13.8.

• Thoroughly clean all parts. Brake shoes must be replaced if the material thickness is down to 1.0 mm (0.04 in.). Always replace brake shoes as a set and never interchange them from one side to the other to compensate for wear. Check that there are no signs of leaks on the rubber dust caps of the wheel brake cylinders. If this is the case, overhaul the cylinders as described in Section 13.2.2. or fit a new cylinder.

If necessary remove the levers from the brake shoes. To do this, open the respective "U" clip and take off the lever and washer. Use a new clip during installation. Press the ends of the clip together, with a pair of pliers, to secure the lever to the pivot pin.

140

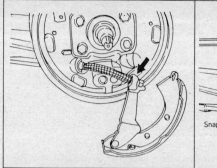
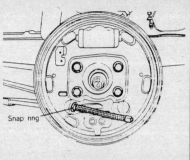

Fig. 13.7. — The arrow shows where the handbrake cable is connected to the handbrake lever.

Fig. 13.8. — The snap ring secures the handbrake cable to the outside of the brake backplate.

Measure the inside diameter of each brake drum. The maximum permissible diameter is 205.0 mm (8.1 in.) and a drum must be replaced, if this dimension is reached.

The installation of the brake shoes is a reversal of the removal procedure. Coat the contacting areas for the brake shoes on the brake back plate with a little brake paste. The return springs must not be stretched during installation. Move the adjuster lever (1) in Fig. 13.9 into the position shown, before the two springs in Fig. 13.6 are fitted.

Fig. 13.9. — Position the adjuster lever (1) into the position shown before fitting the spring.

Refit the brake drum with the hub as described in Section 11.5 and adjust the rear wheel bearings. After installation of the drums depress the brake pedal a few times to bring the self-adjusting mechanism into operation. If necessary adjust the handbrake as described in Section 13.5.2.

13.2.2. Wheel Brake Cylinders — Overhaul

● Remove the brake shoes from the brake backplate as described in Section 13.2.1. Slacken the union nut at the rear of the brake backplate, withdraw the pipe and plug up the open end of the pipe to prevent entry of dirt. Unscrew the wheel brake cylinder from the plate.

● Remove the two rubber dust caps from the cylinder body and push the pistons through the bore. Using the fingers only, remove the piston cups from the pistons. Check the pistons and the inside of the cylinder bore for corrosion or seizure. A cylinder should be replaced if such damage is visible.

● Coat the piston cups and pistons with clean brake fluid and fit the cups to the pistons, with the lips facing towards the inside. Only use the fingers and make sure that the cups are seated properly in the piston grooves.

● Wet the inside of the cylinder bore with clean brake fluid and insert the two pistons without turning over the sealing lips. Fit the rubber dust caps. Coat the face of the cylinder with sealing compound and refit to the brake back plate in reverse order to the removal procedure. Bleed the brake system after installation as described in Section 13.4.

13.3. Master Brake Cylinder

13.3.1. Removal and Installation

The attachment of the master brake cylinder is different for petrol and diesel models. The fluid reservoir is fitted directly onto the cylinder body in the case of petrol models, but is mounted separately in the case of the diesel model. The connection between the fluid reservoir and the cylinder is by means of two hoses. Figs. 13.10 and 13.11 should be referred to when the master cylinder is to be removed.

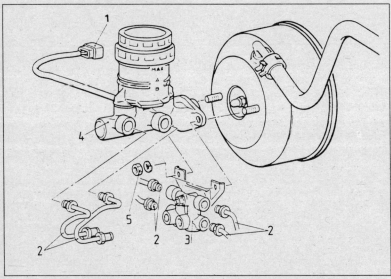

Fig. 13.10. — Details for the removal and installation of the master cylinder (petrol model).

1 Fluid level sensor plug	4 Master brake cylinder
2 Brake pipes	5 Securing nut, 0.8 - 1.2 kgm
3 6-way connector	

● Remove the level sensor harness connector and unscrew the union nuts securing the brake pipes to the cylinder connections. Plug the open ends of the pipes to prevent entry of dirt.

● In the case of the diesel model, disconnect the two reservoir hoses from the master cylinder connections. If this operation is carried out quickly, there is no need to drain the reservoir. Tie the hoses with the ends upwards to prevent the brake fluid from running out.

● Remove the nuts securing the master brake cylinder to the front face of the brake servo unit. Take off the 6-way connector from the master cylinder and carefully lift out the cylinder without spilling brake fluid over painted areas of the vehicle.

● If necessary remove the fluid reservoir of a diesel model in accordance with Fig. 13.11.

The installation of the cylinder is a reversal of the removal procedure. Refer to Figs. 13.10 or 13.11 for details. Tighten the brake pipe union nuts to 1.3 - 1.7 kgm (9 - 12 ft.lb.). Fill the reservoir to the correct level with clean brake fluid. The brake system must be bled of air after installation (refer to Section 13.4). If the fluid reservoir of a diesel model has been removed, refer to Fig. 13.11. The bolts for the mounting brackets are tightened to 0.8 - 1.2 kgm (6 - 9 ft.lb.). Push the connecting hoses well over the two connectors before tightening the clamps.

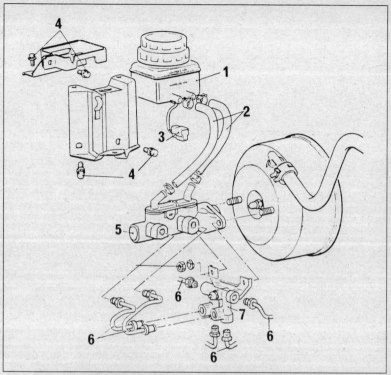

Fig. 13.11.—Details for the removal and installation of the master cylinder (diesel model).

1	Fluid reservoir	5	Master cylinder
2	Connecting hoses	6	Brake pipes
3	Fluid level sensor plug	7	6-way connector
4	Bolts, 0.8 - 1.2 kgm	8	Nut, 0.8 - 1.2 kgm

13.3.2. Overhauling the Master Cylinder

Refer to Fig. 13.12 for an exploded view of the master cylinder as it is fitted to the petrol model. Any differences of a cylinder, fitted to diesel models, can be seen in Fig. 13.14:

- Clamp the cylinder into a vice, using soft-metal jaws and with a screwdriver push the pistons into the cylinder bore. Unscrew the stop bolt (5). Increase or decrease the pressure onto the piston as necessary to remove the screw without force.
- Remove the snap ring from the end of the bore. Push the piston to the inside to release the tension of the spring.
- Remove the internal parts from the cylinder. Sticking pistons must be removed with compressed air. Using the fingers only, remove the piston cups from the two pistons.
- If further dismantling is required, remove the two plugs (13) from the cylinder and shake out the check valves. Mark the two valves for position as they must not be interchanged.

Thoroughly clean all parts in brake fluid or methylated spirits. If cylinder bore and pistons are in acceptable position, measure the bore diameter and the outer diameter of the piston. If the

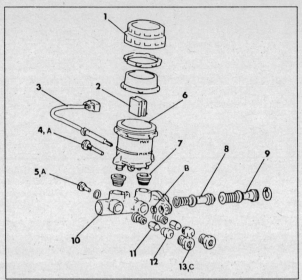

Fig. 13.12.—Exploded view of the master cylinder. The letters refer to the tightening torques.

1. Cap	9. Primary piston
2. Float	10. Cylinder body
3. Fluid level sensor plug	11. Check valve
4. Reservoir stop	12. Pipe seat
5. Piston stop screw	13. Check valve plug
6. Fluid reservoir	A = 0.15-0.3 kgm (1.1-2.2 ft.lb.)
7. Sealing washer	B = 0.8-1.2 kgm (6-9 ft.lb.)
8. Intermediate piston	C = 2.5-3.5 kgm (18-25 ft.lb.)

difference between the two dimensions, i.e. the running clearance of the pistons, exceeds 0.15 mm (0.006 in.), replace the complete cylinder.

Soak new piston cups in clean brake fluid and fit to the pistons, again using the fingers only. Assemble the cylinder in accordance with the exploded view. When fitting the secondary piston, clamp the cylinder into a vice, push the piston towards the inside with a screwdriver and insert the stop screw (5) without excessive force. Release the screwdriver and check that the piston is held in position. Make sure the snap ring is in the groove of the cylinder bore.

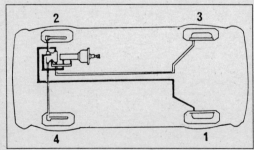

Fig. 13.13. — Brake bleeding sequence

13.4. Bleeding the Brake System

Bleeding of the brake system should be carried out at any time that any part of the system has been disconnected, for whatever reason. If only one brake circuits has been opened, it may be enough to bleed only this circuit. Otherwise commence the bleeding on the L.H. rear wheel and then follow in the

144

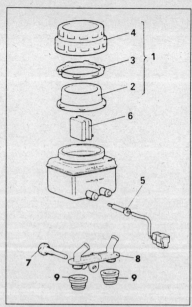

Fig. 13.14. — The fluid reservoir and connection to the master cylinder (diesel model).

1 Reservoir cap
2 Diaphragm
3 Slide ring
4 Reservoir cap
5 Fluid level sensor
6 Float
7 Securing bolt
8 Connector
9 Rubber grommets

order shown in Fig. 13.13.

The procedure given below should be followed and it should be noted that an assistant will be required, unless a so-called "one-man" bleeding kit is available.

Always use clean fresh brake fluid of the recommended specification and never re-use fluid bled from the system. Be ready to top up the reservoir with fluid as the operations proceed. If the level is allowed to fall below the minimum the operations will have to be re-started.

Obtain a length of plastic tube, preferably clear, and a clean container. Put in an inch or two of brake fluid into the container and then go to the first bleed point. Take off the dust cap and attach the tube to the screw, immersing the other end of the tube into the fluid in the container (Fig. 13.15).

Open the bleed screw about three quarters of a turn and have your assistant depress the brake pedal firmly to its full extent while you keep the end of the tube well below the fluid level in the container. Watch the bubbles emerging from the tube and repeat the operation until no more are seen. Depress the brake pedal once more, hold it down and tighten the bleed screw firmly.

Check the fluid level, go to the next point and repeat the operations in the same way. Install all dust caps, depress the brake pedal several times and finally top up the reservoir.

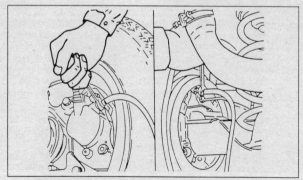

Fig. 13.15. — Bleeding a front wheel (left) and a rear wheel (right).

13.5.   Adjusting the Brakes
13.5.1.   Front and Rear Brakes

Front and rear brakes are self-adjusting and no regular adjustment is necessary. To bring the

145

rear brake shoes nearer to the brake drum faces, operate the foot brake and the handbrake several times. This will actuate the adjusting mechanism.

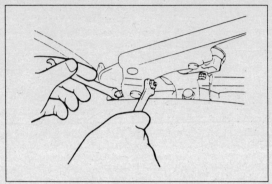

Fig. 13.16. — Adjusting the handbrake.

13.5.2.   Adjusting the Handbrake

If the handbrake lever can be pulled by more than 5 to 7 notches, remove the handbrake cover and tighten the nut on the adjuster rod, as shown in Fig. 13.16, until there is no more slack in the cables. Lift and release the lever to check the number of notches and depress the brake pedal with the engine running several times to actuate the automatic adjusting mechanism on the rear brake assemblies.

Raise the rear of the vehicle, and with the handbrake lever released, check that the rear wheels rotate freely.

13.5.3.   Adjusting the Brake Pedal

As the free play at the tip of the brake pedal is governed by the brake servo unit push rod, there is no need to adjust the free clearance on the pedal. This play must only be checked and adjusted if the brake servo unit has been replaced.

To adjust the brake pedal height, slacken the brake light switch locknut and unscrew the switch until it no longer touches the pedal. Slacken the push rod locknut and with a pair of pliers, rotate the push rod into the required direction until the height is between 176 - 181 mm (6.9 - 7.1 in.). Tighten the locknut. Check that the free play at the pedal tip is between 10 and 15 mm (0.4 - 0.6 in.).

Screw the brake light switch back in position until the clearance between the switch plunger and the contacting pad is between 0.5 - 1.0 mm (0.02 - 0.04 in.). Tighten the locknut.

13.6.   Brake Servo Unit

It is not recommended that the owner should attempt to repair the servo unit. This is best left to your dealer who has special tools to deal with renovating. Remember that a failure of the servo unit to act will not affect the efficiency of the braking system but, of course, additional effort will be required for the same braking distance to be maintained.

ATTENTION! *If you coast downhill, for whatever reason, with a vehicle equipped with a brake servo unit, remember that the vacuum in the unit will be used up after a few applications of the brake pedal and the brake system will from then onwards operate without power-*

assistance. Be prepared for this.

The servo unit is removed by removing the master cylinder (Section 13.3.1), taking off the vacuum hose and removing the servo unit attachment nuts from the mounting studs (from within the vehicle). Disconnect the brake servo push rod at the clevis fork.

13.7.   Brakes — Tightening Torques

Master Brake Cylinder:
   Piston stop screw: .... 0.15 - 0.3 kgm (1 - 2 ft.lb.)
   Cylinder to brake servo: .... 0.8 - 1.2 kgm (6 - 9 ft.lb.)
   Check valve plugs: .... 2.5 - 3.5 kgm (18 - 25 ft.lb.)
Brake servo to pedal bracket: .... 0.8 - 1.2 kgm (6 - 9 ft.lb.)
Brake pipe union nuts: .... 1.3 - 1.7 kgm (9.5 - 12 ft.lb.)
Front Brake Caliper:
   Bleeder screws: .... 0.7 - 0.9 kgm (5 - 7 ft.lb.)
   Brake disc to hub: .... 5.0 - 6.0 kgm (36 - 43 ft.lb.)
   Brake caliper to mounting bracket: .... 2.2 - 3.2 kgm (16 - 23 ft.lb.)
   Brake caliper mounting bracket to steering knuckle: .... 8 - 10 kgm (58 - 72 ft.lb.)
Rear Brake Assembly:
   Bleeder screw: .... 0.7 - 0.9 kgm (5 - 7 ft.lb.)
   Wheel cylinder to backplate: .... 0.8 - 1.2 kgm (6 - 9 ft.lb.)
   Backplate to rear axle: .... 5 - 6 kgm (36 - 43 ft.lb.)

---

14.   ELECTRICAL EQUIPMENT

14.0.   Technical Data

Battery
Capacity:
   Petrol model: .... 60 Ah (N50Z)
   Diesel model: .... 70 Ah ((N70)
Spec. Gravity:
   Fully charged: .... 1.260 -1.280
   Half charged: .... 1.160 - 1.200
   Fully discharged: 1.100
Charging Current:
   60 Ah battery: .... 6.0 amps
   70 Ah battery: .... 7.0 amps
Quick Charging:
   60 Ah battery: .... 60 amps
   70 Ah battery: .... 58.5 amps
Freezing Point:
   Fully charged: .... -60° C
   Half charged: .... —22° C
   Fully discharged: .... —8° C

Starter Motor
Number of pinion teeth: 8
Test Values without Load:
   Voltage: .... 11.5 volts
   Current: .... 60 amps or less
   Speed: .... 6500 rpm

Armature Shaft Diameter:
Front: . . . . 11.0 mm (0.433 in.)
Rear: . . . . 14.2 mm (0.56 in.)
Shaft running clearance, front and rear: . . . . 0.03-0.10 mm (0.0012-0.004 in.)
Commutator diameter: . . . . 38.7 mm (1.524 in.)
Min. diameter: . . . . 37.7 mm (1.484 in.)
Mica Undercut:
Standard: . . . . 0.4-0.6 mm (0.016-0.024 in.)
Wear limit: . . . . 0.2 mm (0.008 in.)
Brush Length:
New: . . . . 17.0 mm (0.67 in.)
Wear limit: . . . . 11.5 mm (0.45 in.)
Brush spring tension: . . . . 1.5 kgm (3.3 lbs.)
Pinion clearance: . . . . 0.5-2.0 mm (0.02-0.08 in.)

Alternator
Make: . . . . Mitsubishi
Voltage: . . . . 12 volts
Output at Engine Speed of 1200 rpm:
Petrol engine . . . . 45.5 amps
Diesel engine: . . . . 38.5 amps
Regulating voltage: . . . . 14.1-14.7 volts
Slip ring diameter: . . . . 33.0 mm (1.3 in.)
Min. diameter: . . . . 32.2 mm (1.268 in.)
Brush length: . . . . 18.0 mm (0.71 in.)
Min. length: . . . . 8.0 mm (0.31 in.)

All models covered in this workshop manual operate with an electrical system of 12 volts with negative earth return. The battery is located in the engine compartment.

A pre-engaged starter motor is used to start the engine. The starter switch is part of the ignition switch and during operation energises a solenoid switch, mounted on the drive end bracket of the starter motor.

The alternator is driven via a "V" belt from the crankshaft pulley. An electronic regulator, built into the alternator controls the charging current.

14.1.   Battery

The 12 volts battery consists of six cells, made-up of positive and negative plates, surrounded by a sulfuric acid solution. The battery provides the current to start the engine, for the ignition system, the lighting of the vehicle and other current consumers.

The following maintenance operations should be carried out at regular intervals to extend the life of the battery and to always keep it at its peak performance.

- Check the battery level once a week. If the battery case is translucent, the level can be seen through the case. Otherwise the filler plugs will have to be removed for inspection. If the electrolyte is below the separator plates, add distilled water. Do not over-fill the battery and wipe away any spilled water before replacing the filler plugs. Tap water must not be used to top-up the battery.

- If frequent topping-up is necessary, it may be that the battery is over-charged by the alternator and the latter should be checked accordingly. A cracked battery case can also be the cause.

- The battery cables should always be firmly clamped and the battery terminals must be free of corrosion to ensure good electrical conduct. Corroded areas can be cleaned with a soda solution and a wire brush. A thin coating of petroleum jelly should be smeared on battery posts before cables are re-connected.

- Check the gravity of the electrolyte in each cell using a hydrometer. This is an indication of the charge condition of the battery. All cells should give the same reading (Section 14.0)

148

and if there is a great variation in one cell, then either the electrolyte in the cell is weak due to being topped-up with distilled water or that cell is defective. In this case, a new battery must be fitted.

14.2.   The Alternator

14.2.1.   Routine Precautions

The alternator contains polarity-sensitive components and the precautions below **must** be observed to avoid damage.

- Check the battery polarity **before** connecting the terminals. Immediate damage will result to the silicon diodes from a wrong connection — even if only momentarily.
- Never disconnect the battery or alternator terminals **whilst the engine is running.**
- Never allow the alternator to be rotated by the engine unless **ALL** connections are made.
- Disconnect the alternator multi-pin connector **before** using electric welding equipment anywhere on the vehicle.
- Disconnect the battery leads if a rapid battery charger is to be used.
- If an auxiliary battery is used to start the engine, take care that the polarity is correct. **Do not** disconnect the cables from the vehicle battery.

14.2.2.   Checking a fitted Alternator

The charging warning light in the instrument panel must be extinguished during normal operation of the engine. If the light comes on whilst the engine is running check the alternator. The first check is on the drive belt as this may have snapped. Then check all electrical connections on the alternator. All further inspection work must be carried out on the removed alternator.

14.2.3.   Removal and Installation

The mounting of the alternator is different for petrol and diesel models. The main difference is the connection of a vacuum hose on the diesel engine. Figs. 14.1 and 14.2 show details of the attachments for the two engine types.

- Disconnect the battery earth cable. Disconnect the alternator cables by withdrawing the plug at the rear end of the alternator.
- On the diesel engine disconnect the vacuum hose and the oil hose.
- Remove the adjuster bolt and the nut and slacken the other mounting point. Swing the adjuster upwards, press the alternator towards the inside and remove the "V" belt. On later models remove the adjusting mechanism.
- Remove the long bolt at the bottom of the alternator after removing the self-locking nut and lift out the alternator.

The installation of the alternator is a reversal of the removal procedure. Place the "V" belt into the pulley grooves and push the alternator towards the outside. Provisionally tighten all mounting bolts and adjust the belt tension as described in Section 4.3.2.

14.2.4.   Dismantling the Alternator

- Remove the rotor shaft nut and withdraw the pulley with the fan and the spacer ring from the shaft. To counterhold the pulley, place an old "V" belt into the groove and clamp the pulley into a vice. Remove the Woodruff key from the shaft.
- Remove the three through bolts and separate the rear bracket from the front bracket by inserting a screwdriver between the front bracket and the stator. If the screwdriver is in-

149

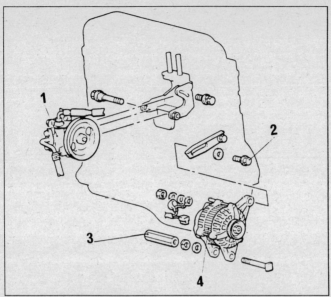

Fig. 14.1. — Details for the removal and installation of the alternator.
1 Power steering pump   3 Sleeve nut, 2.0-2.5 kgm
2 Bolt, 1.2-1.5 kgm   4 Alternator

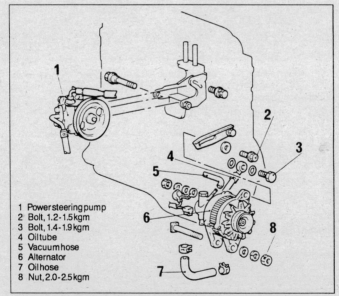

1 Power steering pump
2 Bolt, 1.2-1.5 kgm
3 Bolt, 1.4-1.9 kgm
4 Oil tube
5 Vacuum hose
6 Alternator
7 Oil hose
8 Nut, 2.0-2.5 kgm

Fig. 14.2. — Details for the removal and installation of the alternator of a diesel engine.

serted too deep, the stator windings may be damaged.
- Place the front bracket with the rotor under a press and press out the rotor. Hold the rotor from below, as it will drop out as soon as it is free.
- To remove the front bearing, unscrew the bearing retaining plate and knock the bearing out of the bracket, using a suitable drift. Remove the internal parts.
- Remove the stator, rectifier, brush holder, etc. as an assembly from the rear bracket. To separate the stator and the rectifier, unsolder the stator coil lead wire from the rectifier.

14.2.5. Inspection of Parts

The following text assumes that checking equipment, mainly an ohmmeter, is available.

Brushes and Brush Holders: Check the brushes for good contact on the slip rings. Check the brushes for freedom of movement in their holders and if necessary clean them with a little petrol or use a smooth file to flatten the sides.

Use an ohmmeter and hold one of the test prongs to the insulated brush and the other to the brush holder. The resistance must be "Zero", even if the brushes are moved in their holders. To check the insulation of the brushes, apply the ohmmeter to each brush in turn. The resistance must be "infinitive". Brushes are normally marked with a wear line and brushes must be replaced if worn to this line.

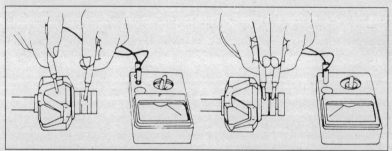

Fig. 14.3. — Checking the rotor windings for continuity (L.H. view) and checking the rotor windings for earth connections (R.H. view).

Rotor: Clean the outside of the slip rings with fine-grade sandpaper if dirty. A badly worn slip ring or a slip-ring beyond the min. diameter must be replaced.

Check the circuit between the field winding and the slip ring, as shown in Fig. 14.3. If there is no continuity, it means that the winding is open. Replace the rotor assembly.

Check for continuity between the slip ring and the stator core as shown in Fig. 14.3. If there is continuity, it means that the winding or slip ring is earthed and must be replaced.

Stator: In case of a short circuit the damaged area will be overheated and perhaps melted and no further tests are necessary. Otherwise check the stator windings for continuity by connecting the instrument as shown in Fig. 14.4. to the ends of the stator windings, i.e. one prong to the stator winding end and the other to the stator core. If there is a reading, replace the stator, as the windings are connected to earth.

To check the stator windings for continuity between the leads of the stator windings, hold the prongs of the instrument in turn to two of the lead ends. If there is no continuity, replace the stator as the windings are interrupted (Fig. 14.4.).

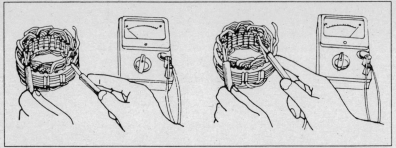

Fig. 14.4. — Checking the stator windings for continuity (L.H. view) and checking the stator windings for connection to earth.

Rectifier Assembly: An exact test of the diodes is only possible with special test equipment. A quick check can be carried out as follows:

Place one of the test prongs to the diode connection and the other one to the diode metal cap. Then reverse the connections. Current must flow in one direction only. If current flows in both directions, there is a short circuit in the diode.

14.2.5.   Assembly

The assembly of the alternator is a reversal of the dismantling procedure. When soldering the leads to the rectifier assembly, proceed as quickly as possible to avoid overheating of the diodes. The best way is to use a pair of pointed pliers and grip the diode pin. This will act as a heat sink. Tighten the pulley nut whilst counterholding the pulley with an old "V" belt.

14.3.   Starter Motor

14.3.1.   Removal and Installation

Disconnect the battery cable and remove the air cleaner. Mark the cables on the solenoid switch and disconnect them. Remove the starter motor mounting bolts from the flywheel housing and remove the unit.

The installation of the starter motor is a reversal of the removal procedure.

14.3.2.   Dismantling the Starter Motor

Refer to Fig. 14.3.:

- Disconnect the link between the solenoid switch and the starter motor terminal, remove the two switch securing screws and withdraw the switch.
- Remove the two through bolts from the rear of the starter motor and withdraw the drive end bracket together with the armature from the starter motor yoke.
- Remove the engagement lever and withdraw the armature from the drive end bracket. Note the fitted position of the lever, the spring and the spring seat to facilitate the assembly later on.
- Remove two screws from the rear cover and lift off the cover.
- Withdraw the brushes from their holders and remove the brush holder.
- Push down the stop ring on the armature shaft with a suitable mandrel and expose the wire clip. Pry out the clip from the groove and pull off the starter motor pinion (Fig. 14.6).

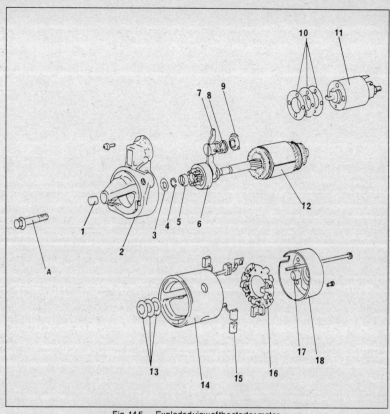

Fig. 14.5. — Exploded view of the starter motor.

1. Front bearing bush
2. Drive end bracket
3. Washer
4. Retaining ring
5. Stop ring
6. Free-wheel clutch
7. Engagement lever
8. Spring
9. Spring seat
10. Plain washers
11. Solenoid switch
12. Armature
13. Washers
14. Starter motor yoke
15. Carbon brush
16. Brush carrier
17. Rear bearing bush
18. Commutator end bracket

Make sure that the shaft is not burred or scored. Use an oil stone or a smooth file to remove any burrs.

14.3.3. Inspection of Parts

Brush Mechanism: The brushes must have a length of more than 11.5 mm (0.453 in.). Check if the brushes can be moved freely in their holders by pulling on their flexible leads. If necessary clean the sides of the brushes with petrol or take off some material with a smooth file. If necessary replace the brushes by unsoldering the old brushes and soldering new brushes into place.

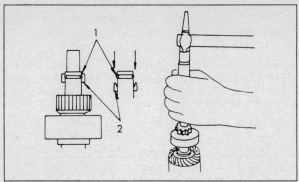

Fig. 14.6. — Removal of the starter motor pinion. Knock back the stop ring (2) and take off the wire clip (1).

Check the brush spring tension with a spring scale, applied at right-angle to the fitted spring. The reading on the spring scale should be between 1.4 - 1.6 kg (3 - 3.6 lb.).

Commutator: A good commutator must have a smooth surface, free of grooves, pits or burnt spots. Clean the commutator with a cloth moistened in petrol. If necessary, use a piece of fine-grade sandpaper to clean-off the commutator surface. Do not use emery cloth.

If the commutator is heavily scored it may be re-machined on a high-speed lathe. Have this carried out at your dealer as a minimum commutator diameter of 37.7 mm (1.4842 in.) must be observed. Undercut the commutator mica segments if necessary, with a short length of ground-down hacksaw blade. A depth of 0.4 - 0.6 mm (0.016 - 0.024 in.) should be obtained. Polish the commutator with fine-grade sandpaper after machining to obtain a smooth surface.

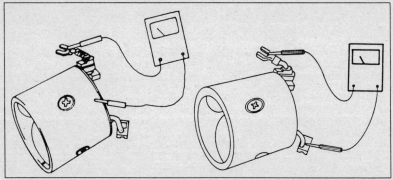

Fig. 14.7. — Checking the field coils for connection to earth (L.H. view) and for open circuit (R.H. view).

Field Coils: Field coils can be checked with an ammeter and a 12 volts battery, connected between the field coil terminals and a good earthing point, as shown in Fig. 14.7 (L.H. view). If the ammeter shows a reading, the coils are shorted to earth and the field coil assembly must be replaced.

To check the field coils for open circuit, connect an ammeter between the the two brushes as shown in Fig. 14.7 (R.H. view). No reading indicates an interruption in the circuit and the field coil assembly must be replaced. A new starter motor yoke can also be fitted.

154

Armature: An armature testing instrument, a so-called growler is necessary to check the armature. If this instrument is not available, substitute the armature with one known to be in good condition. Never attempt to straighten a bent armature shaft or re-machine the armature core.

Bearings: Bearings which are worn to the extend that they allow side clearance of the armature shaft must be replaced. Measure the outside diameter of the armature shaft and the inside diameter of the shaft bushes. If the difference between the two dimensions exceeds 0.10 mm (0.004 in.), replace the bushes. Press out the old bushes and press in new bushes. Ream out the bushes to obtain a shaft running clearance of 0.03-0.10 mm (0.001-0.004 in.).

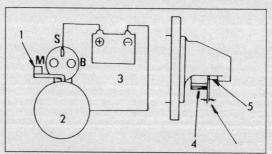

Fig. 14.8. — Testing circuit to check the pinion clearance.

1. Terminal M
2. Starter motor yoke
3. 12 volts battery
4. Starter motor pinion
5. Stop ring

Starter Motor Drive: Check the condition of the starter motor pinion teeth. The pinion must be easily screwed up and down its helical thread. The freewheel clutch must turn in one direction and lock in the other. If necessary replace the complete drive, against one with the same number of pinion teeth.

Solenoid Switch: The solenoid switch cannot be repaired. To check the solenoid coils, connect a 12 volts battery with terminals "S" and "M" (see Fig. 14.8). If the pinion moves out, then the pull-in coil is in good condition. Repeat the same test, but this time connect the battery to the terminal "S" and the solenoid housing. The pinion should move out and remain out when the cable is disconnected from the "M" terminal. If this is the case, the hold-in coil is in order.

Connect the battery between the "M" terminal and the switch body. Pull the pinion out and release. If the pinion quickly returns to its original position, everything is in order. Otherwise replace the solenoid switch.

NOTE: The "S" terminal is the upper terminal; the "M" terminal is the one on the left-hand side of the solenoid switch, as seen from the front of the starter motor.

14.3.4. Assembling the Starter Motor

The assembly of the starter motor is a reversal of the dismantling procedure. Slightly grease the thread of the armature shaft and the pivot bearing for the engagement lever. Lubricate the bearings and pinion with oil.

After assembly connect a 12 volts battery in accordance with Fig. 15.6. to measure the clearance between the pinion end face and the stop ring. If this clearance is not within 0.5 - 2.0 mm (0.02 - 0.08 in.), adjust by adding or removing shims between the solenoid switch and the drive end bracket.

14.4. Fuses

The fuse box is located below the dashboard. The capacity of each fuse and the protected circuit is printed on the fuse box cover. A separate fuse is used for the tail lights.

Before replacing a fuse, check the fuse holder for corrosion. Never try to repair a burnt-out fuse by bridging the fuse holder with aluminium foil. Before inserting a new fuse make sure you have located the reason for the electrical fault.

Various fusible links are fitted to the system. These links are of different colour (green for headlamps und cooling fan motor, brown for electric window operation, red for ignition) and must be replaced with a fusible link of the same colour. The fuse will melt if a pre-determined current is present. Never cover the fusible link with vinyl tape.

14.5. Wiring Diagram Cable Colours

The cables are covered with coloured insulating sleeves. The wiring diagram list these colours with abbreviations. In general the following colours denote the given circuits:

Starter/ignition system	BW = black/white
Charging circuit	W = white
Lighting system	R = red
Flasher indicators	G = green
Instruments	Y = yellow
Other consumers	L = blue
Earth connections	B = black

14.6. Headlamps

14.6.1. Removal and Installation

The component parts of a headlamp are shown in Fig. 14.9. The headlamp bulbs are replaced from the inside of the engine compartment. Remove a headlamp bulb as follows:

● Disconnect the battery negative cable and from the rear of the headlamp reflector withdraw the connector plug. Remove the bulb holder and replace the bulb. Never touch the glass of a new bulb with the fingers only, use a tissue to hold it whilst fitting it into the holder.

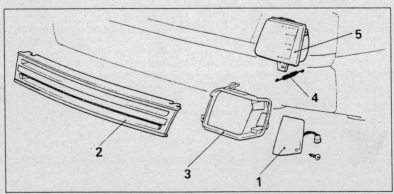

Fig. 14.10. — Details for the removal and installation of the headlamps.

1 Side lamp	4 Spring
2 Radiator grille	5 Headlamp
3 Headlamp bezel	

Replace a headlamp as follows:

- Referring to Fig. 14.10, unscrew the position lamp from the side of the headlamp.
- Remove the radiator grille and the headlamp bezel by referring to Fig. 14.11. To do this, remove caps (1) and unscrew the two screws (2). Take out the grille and remove the clips (4). Remove the bezel.

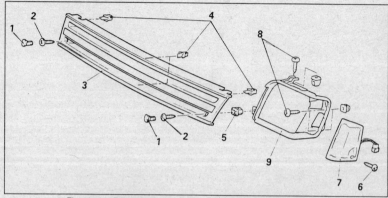

Fig. 14.11.—Details for the removal and installation of the radiator grille.

1 Protective caps	6 Self-tapping screws
2 Self-tapping screws	7 Front combination lamp
3 Radiator grille	8 Self-tapping screws
4 Radiator grille clips	9 Headlamp bezel
5 Screw grommets	

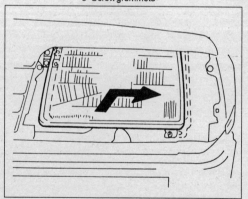

Fig. 14.12.—Remove the headlamps in accordance with the direction of the arrow.

- From the rear of the headlamp reflector, disconnect the cable connector plug.
- Whilst pushing the headlamp unit towards the inside from the front, slide it out towards the side. This movement is shown in Fig. 14.12.
- From the inside of the engine compartment, disconnect the spring, securing the headlamp unit to the bodywork. A pair of pointed pliers can be used for this operation. Remove the headlamp unit from the front of the vehicle.

The installation of the headlamp is a reversal of the removal procedure. The spring is first connected to the headlamp support panel and then to the headlamp unit.

14.6.2. Adjusting the Headlamps

The adjustment of the headlamps should only be carried out with an optical instrument. If an

157

emergency adjustment is necessary, drive the vehicle in front of a wall or the garage door and mark the area in accordance with Fig. 14.13. The vertical adjusting screw, i.e. the up-and-down adjusting screw, is situated below the headlamp; the horizontal adjusting screw, i.e. the left-to-right adjusting screw, is located at the inside of each headlamp.

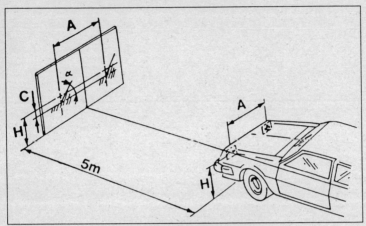

Fig. 14.13. — Headlamp adjusting diagram.
H   Height to headlamp centre points
A   Dimension between headlamp centre points
C   50.00 mm (2 in.)
a   15°

Inflate the tyres to the correct pressure and draw the vertical lines through the respective headlamp centres and a horizontal line through the respective headlamp centre. Start the engine and run with 2000 rpm.

Adjust the lower beam (dipped headlamps) in accordance with the diagram in Fig. 14.13.

DIESEL ENGINE SUPPLEMENT

15. DIESEL ENGINE

15.0. Main Features

Engine Identification: 4D65
Number and arrangement of cylinders: . . . . 4, in-line
Arrangement of camshaft: . . . . In cylinder head (OHC)
Camshaft drive: . . . . Toothed timing belt

Engine Capacity: . . . . :. 1795 ccm
Cylinder Bore: . . . . 80.6 mm (3.17 in.)
Piston stroke: . . . . 88.0 mm (3.46 in.)
Compression ratio: . . . . 21.5 : 1

Max. Performance: . . . . 82 BHP at 4500 rpm
Max. Torque: . . . . 16.8 kgm (121 ft.lb.) at 2250 rpm

Compression Pressures at 250 rpm: . . . . 27.0 kg/sq.cm. (384 psi.)
Firing order: . . . . 1 — 3 — 4 — 2
Valve Clearances (warm): . . . . 0.25 mm (0.010 in.), all valves
Injection timing: . . . . 7° after T.D.C. at idling speed
Idle speed: . . . . 750 rpm
Oil pump type: . . . . Gear-type pump
Oil sump capacity: . . . . See Section 0.3

15.1 Engine — Removal and Installation

NOTE: The air conditioning system must be discharged if one is fitted. This is not a job for the unexperienced and advice should be sought before the operation is attempted.

The engine is removed together with the transmission. Read section 0.5 before jacking up the front of the vehicle for operations to be carried out from underneath. The illustrations on the following pages show the location of the individual items referred to in the following text.

Referring to Fig. 15.2:

- Open the bonnet. Mark the outline of the bonnet panel (using a pencil) and unscrew the bonnet from the hinges. This will give greater freedom of movement and will prevent damage to the bonnet paint work. Lift off the bonnet and store it in a safe place.

- Drain the cooling system. A drain plug (3) is fitted to the bottom of the radiator.

- Disconnect the battery and complete remove the battery (5). Also remove the battery carrier (6). One bolt is fitted from the top, one from the side.

- Drain the fluid from the power steering system as described in the relevant section.

- Disconnect the inlet and the outlet hoses for the heating system at the bulkhead side after

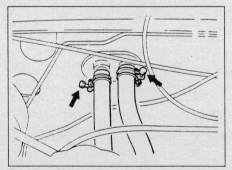

Fig. 15.1. — Disconnect the two heater hoses at the connections shown.

slackening of the hose clamps (Fig. 15.1). Tight hoses can be removed by turning them

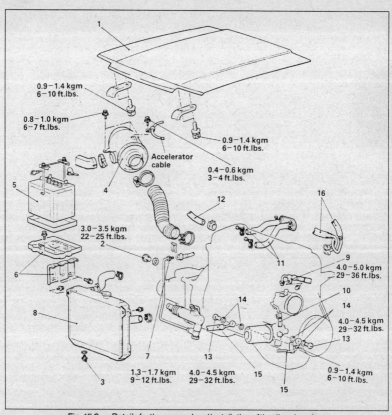

Fig. 15.2. — Details for the removal and installation of the diesel engine.

1 Engine bonnet	7 Clutch pipe and hose	13 Eye bolts
2 Transmission drain plug	8 Radiator	14 Gaskets
3 Radiator drain plug	9 Power steering hose	15 Engine oil cooler tubes
4 Air cleaner assembly	10 Power steering hose	16 Air conditioner hoses
5 Battery	11 Heater hoses	
6 Battery tray	12 Brake servo unit hose	

to and fro—not by pulling them off.

- Remove the air cleaner (4) after disconnecting the hose at the side and the large hose at the end and lift off the engine. Remove the large induction hose. Immediately cover the suction opening to prevent entry of foreign matter.
- Disconnect the vacuum hose (12) from the brake servo unit connection.
- Remove the eye bolts (13) and take off the two gaskets (14).
- Disconnect the hoses from the upper and lower radiator connections after slackening the hose clamps, remove the radiator mounting bolts and lift out the radiator.
- Unscrew the nunion nut (7) securing the clutch fluid pipe to the fluid hose. Drive out the spring clip securing the hose to the bracket and withdraw the hose.
- Disconnect he engine oil cooler hoses (15) and, if fitted the hoses for the air conditioning system. Refer to the note on page 160 before carrying out the last operation.

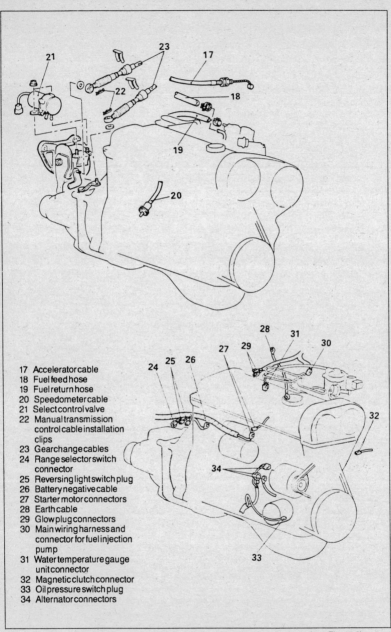

17 Accelerator cable
18 Fuel feed hose
19 Fuel return hose
20 Speedometer cable
21 Select control valve
22 Manual transmission
   control cable installation
   clips
23 Gearchange cables
24 Range selector switch
   connector
25 Reversing light switch plug
26 Battery negative cable
27 Starter motor connectors
28 Earth cable
29 Glow plug connectors
30 Main wiring harness and
   connector for fuel injection
   pump
31 Water temperature gauge
   unit connector
32 Magnetic clutch connector
33 Oil pressure switch plug
34 Alternator connectors

Fig. 15.3. — Details for the removal and installation of the diesel engine (cont. from Fig. 15.2).

Refer to Fig. 15.3 for the following operations:

- Disconnect the accelerator cable (17) from the injection pump and place it to one side.
- Disconnect the fuel feed hose (18) and the return hose (19) from the side of the injection pump. Slacken the hose clamps sufficiently for the hoses to be pulled off.
- Unscrew the knurled nut securing the speedometer drive cable (20) at the transmission end and withdraw the cable.
- Refer to Fig. 15.4 and remove the selector control valve for the transmission from the transmission mounting.
- Remove the two securing clips (22) from the ends of the gearchange cables (23), remove the two spring plates and disconnect the cables from the transmission. Remove the two washers from the levers.

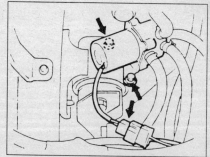

- Pull the two plugs from the range selector switch (24) and the reversing light switch (25). Unscrew the battery negative cable (26) from the engine and free the earth cable (28).
- Pull the connector plug (27) from the starter motor terminal and unscrew the second cable from the solenoid switch.

Fig. 15.4. — The arrows show where the selector control valve is secured to the transmission mounting.

- Disconnect the glow plug cable harness (29) from their connectors.
- Pull off the plug (30) at the rear of the injection pump after removing the plug clamp screw.
- Disconnect the plug (31) from the sensor for the temperature gauge.
- Disconnect the plug (32) from its terminal if an air conditioning system is fitted.
- Disconnect the plug (33) from the oil pressure switch.
- Disconnect one plug and unscrew the remaining cable connection (34) from the rear of the alternator.

Jack up the front end of the vehicle (refer to Section 0.5) and carry out the following operations from underneath the vehicle, referring to Fig. 15.5 for details:

- Disconnect the front exhaust pipe (38) from the exhaust manifold. Use a piece of wire to suspend the exhaust system from the bottom of the vehicle. The mounting nut (37) must be removed to free the pipe. Take off the gasket (39) and immediately discard it, as it must be replaced.
- Disconnect the drive shafts from the L.H. and R.H. sides of the vehicle as described in Section 9 under the relevant heading. The strut bar and stabiliser bar connections on the two suspension arms must be removed in order to withdraw the drive shafts. The two snap rings on the shaft ends can be removed immediately as they must be replaced. Cover the openings in the transmission by placing a piece of plastic over them and taping it in position. This will prevent dirt from entering the transmission.
- Suspend the engine and transmission on a chain or rope and slightly lift the unit until just under tension. Remove the engine and transmission mountings as follows, referring to Section 1.1.2 for detailed information:

— Remove the nut securing the L.H. engine mounting without removing the bolt.
— Remove the covering inside the R.H. wing apron and unscrew the bolt and nut (40) securing the transmission mounting to the mounting bracket. Slowly lift or lower the power unit until the transmission mounting and the mounting bracket are separated and unscrew the mounting (41) from the front side member on the L.H. side.

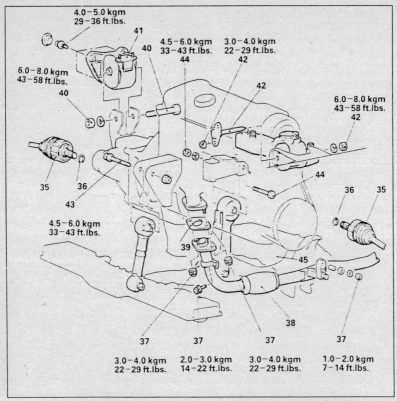

4.0−5.0 kgm
29−36 ft.lbs.

41

40

4.5−6.0 kgm
33−43 ft.lbs.
44

3.0−4.0 kgm
22−29 ft.lbs.
42

6.0−8.0 kgm
43−58 ft.lbs.
40

42

6.0−8.0 kgm
43−58 ft.lbs.
42

40

35   36

43

4.5−6.0 kgm
33−43 ft.lbs.

39

44

36   35

45

38

37   37   37   37

3.0−4.0 kgm
22−29 ft.lbs.

2.0−3.0 kgm
14−22 ft.lbs.

3.0−4.0 kgm
22−29 ft.lbs.

1.0−2.0 kgm
7−14 ft.lbs.

Fig. 15.5. — Details for the removal and installation of the diesel engine (continued).

35 Driveshafts
36 Circlips
37 Exhaust pipe bolt and nuts
38 Front exhaust pipe
39 Gasket
40 Bolt and nut, mounting

41 Transmission mounting
42 Mounting bolt and nuts
43 Mounting bolt, engine damper
44 Bolt and nut, roll stopper bracket
45 Engine and transmission assembly

— Slowly lift the power unit so that the weight of the engine and transmission assembly is not resting on the mounting, and then hold it in that position.

— Remove the mounting nuts and bolts for the L.H. mounting, the engine damper and the roll stopper bracket. Fig. 15.6 shows where the items referred to are attached.

— Push the transmission downwards and at the same time lift the assembly out of the engine com-

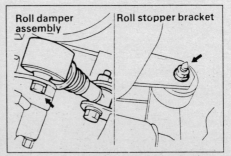

Fig. 15.6. — Engine damper and roll stopper bracket.

partment. Continuously check that none of the connections, cables, etc. can get caught in the engine compartment or are still connected.

- The transmission can be separated from the engine after removal. To do this, remove the starter motor and the bolts securing the transmission to the engine. Withdraw the transmission, but do not allow the weight of the transmission to rest on the main drive shaft (clutch shaft), as this will damage the clutch driven plate or bend the shaft.

To install the power unit, lift the assembly into the vehicle and attach all power unit mountings finger-tight. Fully lower the power unit and tighten all nuts and bolts to the tightening torques given in Section 15.6.
Before installation of the engine, check the following items for wear or deterioration and replace them if necessary with the engine removed:

- Check all engine mountings. Rubber mountings with cracks or other deterioration must be replaced.
- Check the condition of the throttle cable and replace if necessary.
- Check fuel hoses, heater hoses and coolant hoses for damage, cuts, etc. Damage is mainly possible underneath the hose clips, sometimes not visible without moving the clip up or down.

Note the additional points during installation:

- Place a thick rag over the rear of the cylinder head cover to prevent the engine from touching the engine compartment bulkhead when the power unit is lowered into position.
- Connect the transmission with the engine and refit the starter motor. Again take care not to rest the weight of the transmission on the clutch shaft. The clutch driven plate must be correctly centred.
- Lower the engine and transmission into the engine compartment and fit the engine and transmission mountings. Tighten all mountings when the power unit is free of tension.
- Always replace the gasket between exhaust manifold and exhaust pipe.
- After installation fill the transmission with the correct quantity of the specified oil, fill the engine with engine oil and fill the cooling system with anti-freeze. Refill the clutch hydraulic system and bleed the system as described in Section 6.6.2. If a power steering is fitted, fill the system and bleed it, as described in the relevant section.

15.1.1. REMOVAL AND INSTALLATION OF ENGINE MOUNTINGS

The instructions in Section 1.1.2 on page 12 apply to petrol end diesel engines and should be referred to. Fig. 15.5 shows the engine mountings for the diesel engine.

15.2. Dismantling the Engine

The normal order of removal of parts for a complete engine strip-down is given below but this may, of course, be modified if only partial dismantling is required. Proceed as follows:

- Drain the engine oil.
- Remove all engine ancilliary parts. If in doubt, refer to specific sections for removal details of a certain component.
- Remove the clutch. To do this, counterhold the flywheel ring gear by means of a strong screwdriver. Mark the relation of the clutch to the flywheel with a centre punch (punch at opposite points into clutch and flywheel) and evenly and slowly unscrew the clutch

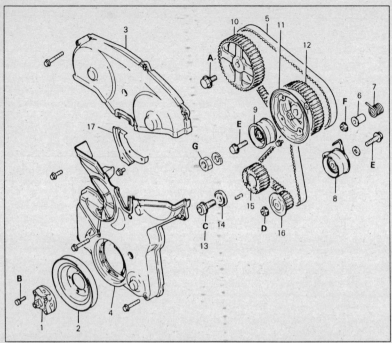

Fig. 15.7. — Sequence for the removal of the timing drive component parts. Follow the numerical sequence to remove. Installation is carried out in reverse order. The letters refer to the tightening torques.

1 Cranking adaptor	7 Tensioner spring	13 Crankshaft sprocket bolt
2 Crankshaft pulley	8 Tensioner	14 Special washer
3 Upper timing belt cover	9 Idler wheel	15 Crankshaft sprocket
4 Lower timing belt cover	10 Camshaft sprocket	16 Oil pump sprocket
5 Timing belt	11 Flange	A = 8-10 kgm (58-72 ft.lb.)
7 Tensioner spring	12 Injection pump sprocket	B = 2-3 kgm (15-21 ft.lb.)
C = 11-13 kgm (80-94 ft.lb.)	D = 3.4-4.0 kgm (25-28 ft.lb.)	E = 4.3-5.5 kgm (32-39 ft.lb.)
F = 2-2.7 kgm (15-19 ft.lb.)	G = 6-7 kgm (44-50 ft.lb.)	

securing bolts.

● Slacken the alternator securing bolts and take off the drive belt. The alternator can now be removed completely. Also remove the tensioning link from the cylinder block.

● Remove the V-belt for the power steering pump. To do this, refer to Section 12.4.4.

● Remove the cooling fan and the fan clutch from the front of the engine and the water pump pulley.

● Refer to Fig. 15.7 and remove the upper timing belt cover (3).

● Remove two bolts and take off the cylinder head cover and remove the gasket.

● Counterhold the crankshaft against rotation and slacken the four crankshaft pulley bolts. Remove the cranking adaptor (1) and the crankshaft pulley (2).

● Unscrew the lower timing cover (4) and remove the gaskets.

● Rotate the engine until the piston of the No. 1 cylinder is at T.D.C. position on the compression stroke. To do this, rotate the crankshaft until the timing marks on the camshaft sprocket and the mark on the injection pump bracket are aligned as shown in Fig. 15.8. To check the

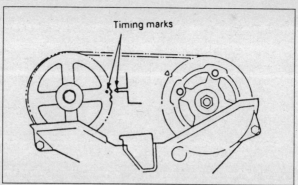

Fig. 15.8. — Align the two timing marks as shown to set the piston of No. 1 cylinder at top dead centre position.

correct position move the two rocker arms of the first cylinder. Both should have slight play. If this is not the case, rotate the engine a further revolution.

- Using a felt pen or chalk, mark a line across the timing belt to identify its fitted position.
- Remove the camshaft wheel securing bolt and withdraw the wheel together with the timing belt from the camshaft. Crankshaft and camshaft should not be rotated when the belt has been removed and the the the cylinder head is still in position.
- Remove the timing belt tensioner (8) from the cylinder block. Undo the nut, marked "F" in Fig. 15.7 and take off the spacer (6) and the spring (7). Then unscrew the bolt marked "E" and take off the idler wheel (9) for the timing belt.
- From the front of the injection pump sprocket unscrew the flange (11) and then remove the pump gearwheel (12). Note that a puller is used to withdraw the gearwheel, as described in the section covering the fuel injection system. Do not attempt to hammer the wheel off the shaft, as this could damage the injection pump.
- Unscrew the rocker shaft from the cylinder head. Further details can be found in the section covering the cylinder head. Unscrew the camshaft bearing cap bolts and lift out the camshaft.
- Remove the camshaft oil seal from its location.
- Hold the flywheel ring gear with a strong screwdriver and remove the crankshaft timing gear bolt. Use two tyre levers, inserted under the pulley at opposite points, and push the timing wheel off the crankshaft.

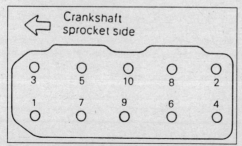

Fig. 15.9. — Sequence for the removal of the cylinder head bolts.

- Referring to Fig. 15.9 remove the cylinder head bolts in the order of the numbered sequence shown. A special Allen key (Part No. MD 998051) must be used to undo the bolts.

- The cylinder head is located by two dowels and must be lifted straight up. Use a rubber or plastic mallet to free a sticking head. Never attempt to wedge the blade of a screwdriver between the sealing faces in order to separate the head. Take off

167

the cylinder head gasket and immediately clean all gasket faces.

- Remove the oil pump drive gear. Before removing the nut, first remove the nut on the L.H. side of the cylinder block and insert a screwdriver into the exposed plug opening, as shown in Fig. 15.10 to retain the left-hand balance shaft in its position. The screwdriver shaft should have a diameter of 8 mm (0.31 in.) and a length of 60 mm (2.5 in.).

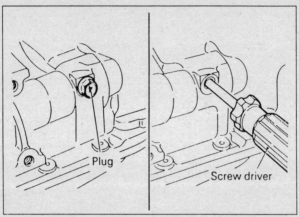

Fig. 15.10. — Preventing the rotation of the balance shaft (silent shaft).

- Slacken the bolt securing the balance shaft (also known as silent shaft) timing gearwheel until it can be removed by hand. Remove the belt tensioner (referred to as belt tensioner "B") and the second timing belt (Fig. 15.11).

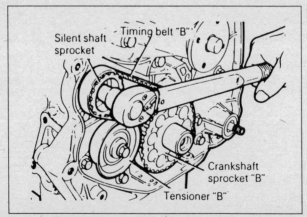

Fig. 15.11. — Removal of the second timing belt together with the associated parts.

- Remove the balance shaft timing wheel and also the second crankshaft timing wheel. Use two tyre levers if the wheels have a tight fit.
- Unscrew the oil sump and remove the oil suction strainer.
- Insert a screwdriver through the hole in Fig. 15.10 to counterhold the balance shaft and

remove the bolt securing the driven wheel of the oil pump.

- Remove the front housing together with the balance shaft. A screwdriver can be inserted into the notch at the side of the housing to prise it off. Take care not to damage the sealing faces.
- Withdraw the oil pump gearwheel and the L.H. shaft from the housing and the R.H. shaft from the cylinder block.
- Turn the cylinder block so that the bottom end is at the top or, on a bench, rest the block on the cylinder head face. Rotate the crankshaft until two of the connecting rods are at bottom dead centre. Unscrew the two big end bearing cap nuts and carefully tap the cap with a hammer until it can be removed. Take off the bearing shell and immediately insert it into the removed cap.
- Using a hammer handle push the connecting rod with the piston towards the top of the cylinder bore. If a carbon ring has formed at the top of the bore, preventing an easy removal, use a scraper and remove the carbon without damaging the bore. A number is stamped into the side of the connecting rod and this should always face towards the crankshaft pulley side. Mark the connecting rod and the piston with the cylinder No. Attach the removed bearing cap and the shell to the connecting rod and remove the other connecting rod and piston in the same manner.
- Rotate the crankshaft until the other two big end bearing caps are at bottom dead centre and remove the two connecting rod and piston assemblies as described above. Make sure that each assembly is marked with the cylinder number.
- Block the flywheel by inserting a strong screwdriver into the teeth of the ring gear and remove the flywheel bolts. Remove the flywheel, using a rubber or plastic mallet if necessary. Take care not to drop the flywheel. Remove the rear oil seal retainer from the cylinder block and unscrew the rear oil seal flange. Take off the gasket. Remove the oil seal from the flange with a suitable drift.
- Slacken the crankshaft main bearing cap bolts, commencing at the outsides and working towards the centre. Remove the caps one after the other, using a rubber mallet if they stick to the block. The caps are numbered and each cap has an arrow, facing towards the front of the engine (Fig. 15.12). The bearing shells must be kept with the caps.

Fig. 15.12. — Removal of crankshaft main bearing caps. The bearing number (1) and an arrow (2) is cast into each bearing cap.

- Carefully lift out the crankshaft.
- Remove the remaining main bearing shells from the crankcase and keep them together with the other shell and bearing cap of each bearing. Use a piece of string or wire and tie the parts together.

15.2.1.   PISTONS AND CONNECTING RODS — DISMANTLING

The piston pin has a floating fit in the piston and the connecting rod small end. Wire clips are used to retain the piston pins in position. No special tools are required to separate the pistons and connecting rods. Remove the wire clips from both sides of the piston and drive out the piston pin with a suitable mandrel.

Remove the piston rings with a pair of piston ring pliers (Fig. 1.14). Take care not to break the rings if any other tool is used.

15.2.2.   VALVES AND ROCKER SHAFTS — DISMANTLING

The removal of the valves requires the use of a valve spring compressor. Compress the valve spring until the two valve cotter halves can be removed with a pair of pointed pliers from around the valve stem.

Remove the parts from each valve and keep each valve in its correct order of installation. Also keep the parts of each valve in a small cardboard box or plastic bag.

15.3.   Assembling the Engine

Refer to the sections commencing at 15.4 for details of the assembly procedure for individual parts and units. Follow the general instructions already given for the petrol engines, commencing on page 17.

15.4.   Overhaul of the Engine

15.4.0.   CYLINDER HEAD AND VALVES

The cylinder head is made of light-alloy. Valve guides and valve seat inserts are pressed into the cylinder head. The arrangements of the inlet valves, exhaust valves for the diesel engine are shown in Fig. 15.13 in an exploded view.

The individual components of the valve and timing mechanisms should be checked for wear or damage and parts must be repaired or overhauled as necessary.

15.4.0.0.   Technical Data

Cylinder head material: . . . . Light-alloy with pressed in valve guides and valve
                                                               seat inserts
Max. distortion of cylinder head surface: . . . . . . Less than 0.10 mm (0.004 in.) Do not re-face

Valves
Valve seat angle:. . . . . .45°, all valves
Correction angles: . . . . .30° and 65°, all valves

Valve Stem Diameters:
   Inlet valves, without turbo charger: . . . . .7.96 - 7.975 mm (0.3134 - 0.3140 in.)
   Inlet valves, with turbo charger: . . . . .7.930 - 7.950 mm (0.3122 - 0.3130 in.)
   Exhaust valves (all engines): . . . . .7.930 - 7.950 mm (0.3122 - 0.3130 in.)
Valve Seat Width:. . . . . .0.9 - 1.3 mm (0.035 - 0.051 in.)
Valve Stem Running Clearance in Guides:
   Inlet valves — Without turbo charger: . . . . .0.03 - 0.06 mm (0.0012 - 0.0024 in.)
             — With turbo charger:. . . . . .0.05 - 0.09 mm (0.002 - 0.0035 in.)
      Wear limit: . . . . .0.10 mm (0.004 in.)
   Exhaust valves: . . . . .0.05 - 0.09 mm (0.002 - 0.0035 in.)
      Wear limit: . . . . .0.15 mm (0.006 in.)

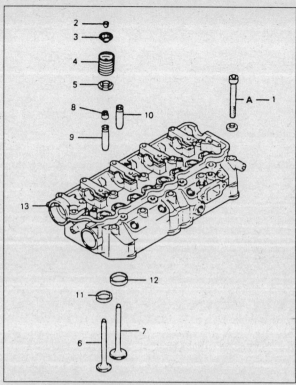

Fig. 15.13. — Exploded view of the cylinder head.

1 Cylinder head bolt
2 Valve cotter halves
3 Valve spring cup
4 Valve spring
5 Spring seat
6 Inlet valve
7 Exhaust valve
8 Valve stem seal
9 Inlet valve guide
10 Exhaust valve guide
11 Inlet valve seat
12 Exhaust valve seat insert
13 Cylinder head

Thickness of Valve Head Edge: .... 1.5mm (0.06 in.), all valves
   Wear limit — Inlet and exhaust valves: .... 0.7mm (0.028 in.)

Valve Guides
Valve Guide Length:
   Inlet valve guides: .... 56.0 mm (2.20 in.)
   Exhaust valve guides: .... 58.0 mm (2.28 in.)
Valve Guide Outer Diameters:
   Nominal diameter: .... 13.06 - 13.07 mm (0.5142 - 0.5146 in.)
   Oversizes: .... 0.05, 0.25 and 0.50 mm
Valve Guide Inner Diameter: .... 8.00 - 8.018 mm (0.3150 - 0.3157 in.)
Fitting temperature: .... Room temperature

Valve Springs
Free length: .... 49.1 mm (1.934 in.)
   Min. free height: .... 48.1 mm (1.895 in.)

Length under Load of 27.6 kg (6.6 lbs.): .... 40.4 mm (1.591 in.)
Max. distortion of valve spring at upper end,
    spring placed vertical on surface plate: .... 1.5 mm (0.06 in.)
Spring Arrangement during installation: .... Colour code must be at the top

Valve Clearances (engine cold):
    Inlet valves: .... 0.15 mm (0.006 in.)
    Exhaust valves: .... 0.15 mm (0.006 in.)

Camshaft
Camshaft end float: .... 0.10 - 0.20 mm (0.004 - 0.008 in.)
Cam Height:
    Inlet and exhaust cams: .... 40.00 mm (1.5748 in.)
    Wear limit: .... 39.50 mm (1.5551 in.)
Bearing journal diameter: .... 29.935 - 29.950 mm (1.1785 - 1.1791 in.)
Bearing running clearance: .... 0.05 - 0.09 mm (0.002 - 0.0035 in.)
Max. run-out of shaft: .... 0.10 mm (0.004 in.)

Rocker Shafts
Rocker shaft diameter: .... 18.878 - 18.898 mm (0.7432 - 0.7440 in.)
Running clearance of shaft: .... 0.01 - 0.05 mm (0.0004 - 0.002 in.)

15.4.0.1.   Inpection of Parts

Valve Springs: Check the valve springs for free length and load. Replace springs which do not conform to the values given in Section 15.4.0.0. All relevant operations are described in Section 1.4.0.1 and this section should be referred to.

As for the petrol engines, valve springs are identified by a colour spot at one end and when fitting the springs, this spot must always be at the top, with the close coiled end to the head.

Valve Guides: Remove the valve stem seals, fitted over each valve guide, with a pair of pliers as shown in Fig. 1.19 and throw away the seals. Never re-use them.

Valve guides and valve stems should first be inspected for visible wear as described in Section 1.4.0.2 on page 22.

To replace the valve guides, press out the old guides from the rocker shaft side as shown in Fig. 1.20, using the mandrel shown or any mandrel that will fit inside the guide bore. There is no need to heat the cylinder head as described on page 23, as the guides are pressed in at room temperature. Press the new guides into the cylinder head from the upper face. Fig. 1.20 shows the operation on the petrol engines. Similar tools are used for the diesel engine.

As for the petrol engines, valve guides are available in three oversizes, i.e. 0.05, 0.25 and 0.50 mm (0.002, 0.01 and 0.02 in.) and are marked with "5", "25" and "50" to identify them. The locating bores in the cylinder head must be reamed out to take the new guides.

Inlet valve guides and exhaust valve guides are of different length. Exhaust valve guides are longer and care must be taken to press the correct guides into the cylinder head.

NOTE: Valve guides to be removed and replaced at room temperature of 20° C. Valve seats must be re-ground, irrespective of their condition, if the valve guides have been replaced.

Valve Seats: Check the valve seats as described on page 23 in Section 1.4.0.3. Extended wear can only be rectified by fitting new valve seat inserts. In this case the cylinder head should be taken to a dealer to have the new seat inserts fitted. New valve seat inserts are available in oversizes of 0.3 or 0.6 mm (0.012 and 0.024 in.) and the cylinder head locating bores must be machined to the size in question to take the new inserts. Only precision machinery can carry out this operation.

A re-cut valve seat must be lapped. Use a suction tool to grind-in the new valve. Use fine lapping compound and work the seat until an uninterrupted ring is visible around the face of the

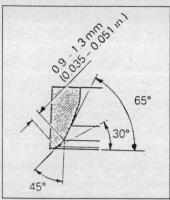

Fig. 15.14. — The valve seat angles of the diesel engine.

0.9 - 1.3 mm (0.035 - 0.051 in.)

65°

30°

45°

after grinding-in the valve, clean the cylinder head, and even more important the inside of the valve guide bores thoroughly. Any lapping paste left inside the cylinder head will accelerate the wear of the new parts.

Measure the width of the valve seats with a caliper. Inlet and exhaust valve seats should have a width of 0.9-1.3 mm (0.035-0.05 in). Fig. 15.14 shows the cutter angles used to re-cut the valve seats and also shows where the seat width is measured.

Valves: Valves with bent or pitted stems should be replaced. Grinding or straightening of the valve stems is not permissible. A maximum of 0.5 mm (0.02 in.), however, can be taken off the ends of valve stems if the contacting area for the rocker levers needs attention. This should be carried out in a grinding machine with a proper chuck to ensure a straight face at the end of the stem. If stems ends are badly worn, check the rocker levers as described in the next section as these may also have suffered. Slight blemishes on the valve head faces can be removed by grinding-in the valves as described in Section 1.4.0.3. Deeper grooves or other damage can be rectified in a valve grinding machine. The valve head thickness must not be smaller than 0.7 mm (0.027 in.) after grinding the valves to their original seat angle. Also measure the stem diameter and compare the results with the "Technical Data" in Section 15.4.0.0. Reject any valves which do not conform to the minimum values.

Check the running clearance of each valve stem in the valve guide bores as described in Section 1.4.0.2 on page 22, and decide if it is necessary to replace the guides before any further inspection work is carried out on the valves.

15.4.0.2   Rocker Shafts and Rocker Levers

Fig. 15.15 shows the cylinder head together with the camshaft. To remove any of the parts, follow the numerical order of the illustration. Check the rocker shafts and rockers for wear, pitting and other visible damage. Measure the outside diameter of the rocker shaft and the inside diameter of the rockers. The difference between the two dimensions should not exceed 0.01 - 0.05 mm (0.004 - 0.002 in.) and is the running clearance for rocker levers.

If the running clearance is exceeded it is not always certain that shaft and rocker levers must be replaced. Check the shaft for grooves at the areas where the rocker levers are operating. Deep grooves at these areas indicate wear of the shaft. If on the other hand the shaft has no visible ridges it may only be the rocker lever that needs replacing.

A maximum of 0.5 mm (0.02 in.) can be ground of the rocker lever ends where they contact the valve stems. Badly pitted rocker lever ends make the adjustment of the valves difficult and only a smooth surface should be visible.

If after grinding to the thickness given there is no improvement, replace the rocker lever in question.

The following points should be noted when dealing with the rocker shaft assembly, when the cylinder head is dismantled into the parts shown in Fig. 15.15:

● Fit the camshaft as described later on and tighten the six camshaft bearing cap bolts finger-tight.

● Assemble the rocker arms and the rocker shaft springs to the rocker shaft.

● Fit the rocker shaft assembly over the bearing caps and fit the bolts.

● Tigthten the camshaft bearing bolts and the rocker shaft bolts to the torque given in

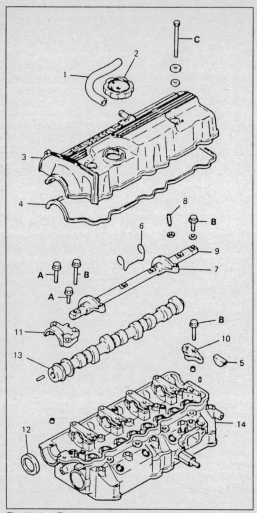

1 Breather hose
2 Oil filler cap
3 Rocker cover
4 Rocker cover gasket
5 Semi-circular seal
6 Rocker arm spring
7 Rocker arm
8 Adjusting screw
9 Rocker shaft
10 Rocker shaft pedestal
11 Camshaft bearing cap
12 Camshaft oil seal
13 Camshaft
14 Cylinder head
A = 1.9-21. kgm (14-15 ft.l.b)
B = 2.8-3.2 kgm (21-23 ft.lb.)
C = 0.5-0.7 kgm (3.7-5.0 ft.lb.)

Fig. 15.15. — The component parts fitted to the upper parts of the cylinder head.

the Fig. 15.15. After the installation hook the rocker shaft spring to the depression of the bearing cap. Make sure that all four rocker arm springs are properly in position.

Fit a new camshaft oil seal into the front of the cylinder head until the outer face is flush with the head. Apply sealing compound to the the centre groove of the semi-circular packing and fit the seal in position. The remaining operations are carried out in reverse order to the removal procedure. The installation of the timing gear is described in Section 15.4.4. The valve clearances must be adjusted as described in later on before the cylinder head cover is fitted in position. Note that the valve clearances must be adjusted on a cold engine.

Cylinder Head Thoroughly clean the cylinder head face of old gasket material and check the surface for distortion. To do this, place a steel ruler over the cylinder head face in the directions shown in Fig. 1.32 and with a feeler gauge measure the gap between the ruler and the head sur. Measure along the different directions shown. The cylinder head surface must not be re-ground. Distortion means the replacement of the cylinder head.

15.4.0.3. Cylinder Head — Assembly and Installation

Refer to Fig. 15.13 when assembling the cylinder head:

- Place the valve spring seats over the valve guides and fit the valve stem oil seals. To avoid oil leaks, a special tool, as shown in Fig. 16.16 should be used for this operation. Place the seals over each guide and carefully tap down with the hollow tool. Never attempt to use the old valve stem seals.

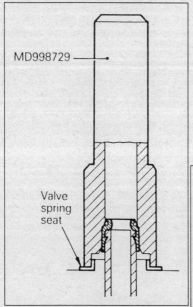

MD998729

Valve spring seat

- Coat the valve stems with thin engine oil and insert into the correct valve guide. Take care not to damage the valve stem seal when the valve is inserted. Make absolutely sure that the valve is inserted into the guide where it has been lapped into the valve seat.

- Fit the valve springs (correct side up), place the upper spring retainer (cup) over the valve and using a valve compressor, as shown in Fig. 1.34 compress the valves springs until the two valve cotter halves can be inserted into the groove of the valve stem. Remove the

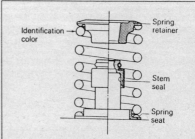

Identification color

Spring retainer

Stem seal

Spring seat

Fig. 15.16. — Fitting a valve stem oil seal.   Fig. 15.17. — The correct installation of a valve spring

valve compressor and check that the cotters have engaged in their groove by tapping the ends of the valve stems slightly with a hammer. Place a rag over each valve stem end to prevent the cotter halves from flying out.

The installation of the cylinder head is carried out as follows:

- Thoroughly clean the sealing faces of cylinder head and cylinder block and place a new cylinder head gasket in dry condition over the cylinder block. Under no circumstances use sealing compound.
- Tighten the cylinder head bolts in the reverse order to Fig. 15.9 in several stages to a tightening torque of 10.5 - 11.5 kgm (76 - 83 ft.lb.). Use the special cylinder head wrench available for this purpose. These values apply to a cold engine. The cylinder head bolts

of a warm engine are tightened to 11.5 - 12.5 kgm (83 - 90 ft. lb.).

- Place a new inlet manifold gasket in position and fit the inlet manifold together with the carburettors and tighten the nuts to 1.5 - 2.0 kgm (11 - 15 ft. lb.).
- Fit a new exhaust manifold gasket, place the manifold in position and tighten the manifold nuts to 1.5 - 2.0 kgm (11 - 15 ft. lb.).
- All other operations are carried out in reverse order to the removal procedures.

15.4.0.4.   Adjusting the Valve Clearances

Valve clearances must be adjusted with the engine cold. The values are 0.15 mm (0.006 in.) for the inlet and exhaust valves.

The clearances are adjusted as shown in Fig. 1.38, using a ring spanner and a screwdriver. Check each clearance in the order given below with a feeler gauge. Insert the gauge of correct thickness between the end of the valve stem and the adjusting screw. The other end of the rocker lever must be resting against the heel of the cam, i e. the valve must be fully closed. To check if the correct valve is being dealt with, grip the end of the lever with thumb and forefinger and check if a small clearance can be felt.

Adjust the clearances as follows:

- Rotate the engine until both valves of the No. 1 cylinder are closed, i.e. both rocker levers must have a slight play as described above. The timing mark in the camshaft sprocket must be opposite the timing mark on the injection pump bracket.
- Adjust these two valves and in the same engine position the other valves shown in Fig. 15.18.

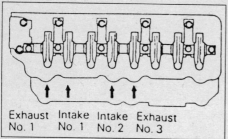

Exhaust Intake   Intake   Exhaust
No. 1   No. 1   No. 2   No. 3

Fig. 15.18. — Location of the valves to be adjusted when the piston of No. 1 cylinder is at top dead centre.

- Slacken the locknut for the valve adjusting screw with a ring spanner and turn the adjusting screw with a screwdriver. Turn the screw in a clockwise direction to reduce the valve clearance or in an anticlockwise direction to increase the clearance.
- Tighten the locknut without rotating the adjusting screw. Recheck the clearance as before after the locknut is tight.
- Rotate the engine by one complete turn and check that both valves of No. 4 cylinder are closed.

In this position adjust all valves marked with the arrows in Fig. 15.19 as described.

- After adjusting the valves fit the rocker cover with a new gasket. Check the oil level and if necessary correct. Check the idle speed and adjust if necessary.

15.4.0.5.   Checking Cylinder Compression

Refer to Section 1.4.0.10., but the note the compression pressures given in Section 15.0.

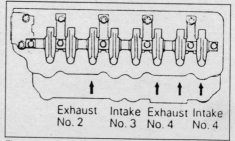

Exhaust Intake   Exhaust Intake
No. 2   No. 3   No. 4   No. 4

Fig. 15.19. — Adjust the valves shown by the arrows when the piston of No. 4 cylinder is at top dead centre position. Always make sure that each valve is fully closed.

15.4.1.   PISTONS AND CONNECTING RODS
15.4.1.0.   Technical Data

Pistons
Material and construction: . . . . Special alloy, solid skirt
Piston pin fit: . . . . Fully floating

Piston Diameter: . . . . 80.56 - 80.59 mm (3.1716 - 3.1728 in.)
Max. ovality of bores: . . . . Less than 0.02 mm (0.0008 in.)
Max. taper of bores: . . . . 0.02 mm (0.0008 in.)
Piston running clearance: . . . . 0.03 - 0.05 mm (0.0012 - 0.0020 in.)
Oversize pistons available: . . . . 0.25, 0.50, 0.75 and 1.0 mm

Side Clearance of Rings in Grooves:
  No. 1 ring: . . . . 0.07 - 0.09 mm (0.0028 - 0.0035 in.)
    Wear limit: . . . . 0.10 mm (0.004 in.)
  No. 2 ring:
    Without turbo charger: . . . . 0.02 - 0.06 mm (0.0008 - 0.0024 in.)
    With turbo charger: . . . . 0.11 - 0.13 mm (0.0043 - 0.0051 in.)
    Wear limit: . . . . 0.12 mm (0.003 in.)
  Oil control ring: . . . . 0.02 - 0.07 mm (0.0008 - 0.0028 in.)
  Piston ring oversizes: . . . . As for pistons

Piston Ring Gaps:
  No. 1 rings: . . . . 0.35 - 0.50 mm (0.014 - 0.020 in.)
  No. 2 rings: . . . . 0.25 - 0.40 mm (0.01 - 0.016 in.)
    Wear limit: . . . . 0.8 mm (0.03 in.)
  Oil control rings: . . . . 0.25 - 0.45 mm (0.01 - 0.018 in.)
    Wear limit: . . . . 0.8 mm (0.031 in.)

Piston Groove Width:
  No. 1 Ring: . . . . 2.11 - 2.13 mm (0.0831 - 0.0839 in.)
  No. 2 Ring:
    Without Turbo Charger: . . . . 2.01 - 2.03 mm (0.0791 - 0.0799 in.)
    With Turbo Charger: . . . . 2.10 - 2.12 mm (0.0827 - 0.0835 in.)
  Oil Control Ring: . . . . 4.01 - 4.04 mm (0.1579 - 0.1589 in.)

Piston pin diameter: . . . . 24.994 - 25.000 mm (0.9840 - 0.9843 in.)

Connecting Rods:
Length between centres: . . . . 150.0 mm (5.91 in.)
Max. bend or twist of connecting rods: . . . . 0.03 mm (0.0012 in.) per 100 mm (3.94 in.) of length
Big end end float: . . . . 0.10 - 0.25 mm (0.004 - 0.001 in.)
  Wear limit: . . . . 0.40 mm (0.016 in.)

15.4.1.1.   General

The general instructions given on page 33 also apply to the diesel engine, but remove the
piston pins as described in Section 15.2.1 on page 170. Carry out all inspections described
on pages 33 to 36, noting the standard and wear limit values in Section 15.4.1.0.

15.4.1.2.   Fitting Pistons and Connecting Rods

Refer to Fig. 1.44 for the following operations, but note that two wire clips are used to retain
the piston pin. If parts are re-used, make sure to fit them into their original position. If cylinder
bores have been re-bored, fit the new piston into the relevant cylinder bore.

● Arrange the connecting rods with the number in the shank facing towards the front of the
   engine.

- Fit the oil control ring to the piston, using a pair of piston pin pliers.
- Fit the centre piston ring (compression ring) and the upper compression ring with a pair of piston ring pliers, with the size mark and the maker's mark facing towards the piston crown. Note that the two compression rings are not identical, although of the same size.
- Arrange the piston ring gaps in accordance with Fig. 15.20 on the circumference of the piston skirt. Make sure the "Front" mark points to the front of the engine.
- A piston ring compressor is required to fit the pistons to the cylinder bores. Place the compressor around the piston rings (without disturbing their position) and push the piston rings into their grooves. If a compressor is not available, lay a piece of this metal around the pistons rings. Never try to fit pistons without compressing the piston rings.
- Insert the corrrect connecting rod into the cylinder bore, check that the arrow in the piston faces towards the front and guide the connecting rod, with the bearing shell inserted, into the cylinder bore. The lug in the bearing shell must be engaged into the cut-out of the connecting rod. The remaining installation is carried out as described on page 37 to 38. Tighten the connecting rod nuts to 5.0 kgm (36 ft.lb.).

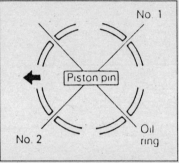

Fig. 15.20. — Correct arrangement of the piston ring gaps.

15.4.2. CRANKSHAFT AND BEARINGS

15.4.2.0. Technical Data

Number of bearings: 5
Main journal diameter: . . . . 57.000 mm (2.24 in.)
Crankpin journal diameter: . . . . 45.000 (1.77 in.)
Max. permissible out-of-round: . . . . .0.005 mm (0.0002 in.)
Crankshaft end float:
   Nominal: . . . . 0.05 - 0.18 mm (0.002 - 0.0071 in.)
   Wear limit: . . . . .0.30 mm (0.012 in.)
Crankshaft thrust taken at: . . . . Centre main bearing
Main bearing running clearance: . . . . 0.02 - 0.05 mm (0.0008 - 0.0002 in.)
   Wear limit: . . . . .0.10 mm (0.004 in.)
Big end bearing running clearance: . . . . 0.02 - 0.05 mm (0.0004 - 0.002 in.)
   Wear limit: . . . . .0.10 mm (0.004 in.)

15.4.2.1. Crankshaft — Overhaul Instructions

The crankshaft fitted to the diesel engine is of the same construction as the one fitted to the petrol engines. Refer to the sections covering the inspections, crankpins, main bearing journals, main bearing running clearance, installation of crankshaft, the checking of the cylinder block and the flywheel, commencing on page 38. All illustrations also apply to the diesel engine.

15.4.3. CAMSHAFT AND TIMING DRIVE

15.4.3.0. Technical Data

Camshaft drive: . . . . Toothed belt

End float of camshaft: . . . . 0.10-0.20 mm (0.004-0.008 in.)
Cam Heights: . . . . See Section 15.4.0.0.
Bearing journal diameter: . . . . See Section 16.4.0.0.
Bearing running clearance: . . . . 0.05-0.09 mm (0.002-0.0035 in.)
Max. run-out of shaft: . . . . 0.10 mm (0.004 in.)

Valve Timing
Inlet valves open: . . . . 20° before T.D.C.
Inlet valves close: . . . . 48° after B.D.C.
Exhaust valves open: . . . . 54° before B.D.C.
Exhaust valves close: . . . . 22° after T.D.C.

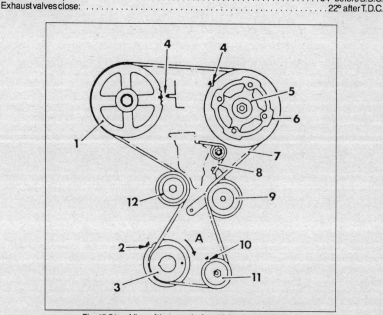

Fig. 15.21. — View of the camshaft and injection pump drive.

1 Camshaft sprocket	7 Timing belt
2 Timing mark	8 Tensioner spring
3 Crankshaft sprocket	9 Belt tensioner
4 Timing marks	10 Timing mark (crankshaft)
5 Injection pump sprocket	11 Oil pump sprocket
6 Flange	12 Idler wheel

15.4.3.1.   Short Description

The camshaft and timing drive of the diesel engine are shown in Fig. 15.21. The camshaft is mounted in five bearings and driven by a toothed belt. The belt also drives the injection pump gear and the oil pump (this in turn driving one of the balance shafts) and is kept under tension by a belt tensioner, fitted to the centre of its run. The opposite side of the belt is routed over an idler wheel. A second belt, having its own belt tensioner, drives the second balance shaft. Fig. 15.7 shows the component parts of the camshaft timing drive. Fig. 15.22 shows the drive for the second balance shaft.

The removal of the camshaft can be carried out by referring to Fig. 15.15. If the engine is fitted to the vehicle, slacken the camshaft sprocket bolt and then rotate the crankshaft until the

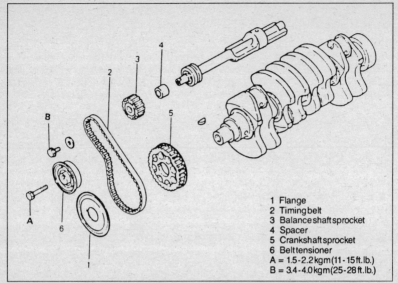

1 Flange
2 Timing belt
3 Balance shaft sprocket
4 Spacer
5 Crankshaft sprocket
6 Belt tensioner
A = 1.5-2.2 kgm (11-15 ft.lb.)
B = 3.4-4.0 kgm (25-28 ft.lb.)

Fig. 15.22. — The drive parts for the balance shaft. The letters refer to the tightening torques.

two timing marks are aligned as shown in Fig. 15.8. Fully remove the camshaft sprocket bolt and remove the sprocket together with the timing belt. If no further work is to be carried out, rest the camshaft sprocket with the timing belt on the lower timing belt cover. Time. Take care not to drop the half-moon shaped sealing rubber in the cylinder head. The camshaft oil seal must be replaced.

15.4.4.2. Inspection of Parts

Refer to Section 1.4.4.3 on page 45. The same instructions also apply to the diesel engine. The camshaft end float is checked in a different manner. Measure the width of the camshaft bearing and then deducted from the width of the camshaft bearing journal. The difference is the camshaft end float. It it, however, possible to check the camshaft end float with a dial gauge as described for the 1.8 litre engine on page 45.

15.4.3.3. Fitting the Camshaft

- Coat the camshaft bearing journals and the cams with engine oil and also the bearing faces in cylinder head and bearing caps.
- Place the camshaft into the cylinder head and rotate a few times to settle the shaft into the bearings.
- Install the bearing caps in according with their number identification. No. 1 and No. 5 cap have no identification number. The other three have their numer stamped into the position shown in Fig. 15.23.

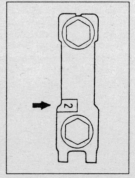

Fig. 15.23. — Bearing cap No.

180

- Fit the bearing cap bolts finger-tight and then fit the assembled rocker shaft in position over the bearing caps. Fit the bolts. Tighten the camshaft bearing cap bolts and the rocker shaft pedestal bolts to the torque values given in Fig. 15.15.
- Fit the camshaft oil seal, using a suitable piece of tube without damaging the seal. Drive the seal in position until the outer face is flush with the camshaft bearing cap.
- Fit the camshaft sprocket together with the timing belt over the dowel pin in the end of the camshaft and fit the bolt. Tighten the bolt to 8 - 10 kgm (58 - 72 ft.lb.). If the engine was completely dismantled, fit the remaining parts of the timing gear as described in the following section.

15.4.4. ADJUSTING THE VALVE TIMING

The component parts of the timing mechanism can be replaced when the engine is in the vehicle, as described during the dismantling of the engine. Also refer to the illustrations in this section for particulars.

The component parts of the timing mechanism are shown in Figs. 15.7 and 15.22.

The following description assumes that the components of the timing mechanism are completely removed, as this is the case during an engine overhaul or during replacement of parts.

- Fit the balance shaft timing gear (3) in Fig. 15.22 and provisionally fit the bolt.
- Place the crankshaft timing wheel (5) over the end of the crankshaft. Align the timing marks of all timing wheels as shown in Fig. 15.24.

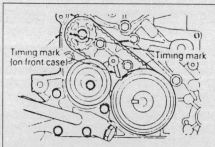

Fig. 15.24. — Details of fitting the timing gearwheel for the balance shaft.

- Place the timing belt over the two drive wheel so that the tensioner side is tight.
- Fit the belt tensioner. The centre point of the tensioner pulley must be located at the left- hand side of the mounting bolt. The pulley flange must be directed towards the front of the engine. Fig. 15.25 shows the tensioner pulley in fitted position.
- Refer to Fig. 15.26 and move the belt tensioner into the direction of the arrow, whilst lifting it with a finger, to give sufficient tension to the tension side of the timing belt. In this position tighten the bolt to secure the tensioner. Prevent the shaft from turning when the bolt is tightened.
- Check that the timing marks on the sprocket and on the front housing are still aligned, as shown in Fig. 15.24 and push with the forefinger against the timing belt at the point shown by the arrow in Fig. 16.25. With the tensioner tightened as described, it must be possible to deflect the belt by 5 to 7 mm

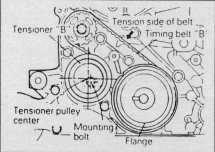

Fig. 15.25. — Fitting the tensioner for the small timing belt. Note where the tension side of the belt is located.

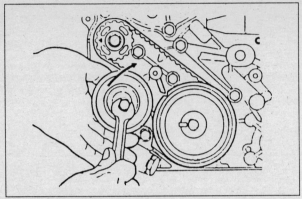

Fig. 15.26. — Tensioning the small toothed belt. Push the tensioner into the direction of the arrow whilst tightening the tensioner bolt.

- Fit the oil pump drive wheel and tighten the nut to 5.0 - 6.0 kgm (36 - 43 ft.lb.). Insert a screwdriver into the opening on the left-hand side of the cylinder block as shown in Fig. 15.10. If the screwdriver blade (approx. 8 mm /0.3 in diameter) can be inserted by approx. 60 mm (2.4 in.), the alignment is correct. If it can be inserted only by 25 mm (1 in.), rotate the oil pump drive wheel by one revolution and again align the timing marks. Keep the screwdriver in position until the timing belt has been fitted.

The timing belt can now be fitted as follows:

- Fit the tensioner pulley in the lowest position into the injection pump bracket slot.
- Remove the glow plugs.
- Slacken the locknuts of all valve clearance adjusting screws and unscrew each screw until its end projects by 0 - 2 mm (0 - 0.08 in.).
- Rotate the engine until the piston of No. 1 cylinder is at top dead centre in the firing stroke. Refer to Fig. 16.21 and align all timing marks in accordance.
- Place the timing belt in position, but each time the belt is fitted over one of the timing wheels, make sure there is no slack between the sprockets or between the sprocket and the pulley. The belt should be installed first over the crankshaft timing wheel, then over the idler wheel, then over the camshaft sprocket, over the injection pump sprocket and finally over the oil pump drive wheel. Rotate the crankshaft by half a tooth of the camshaft pulley in reverse direction. This will reduce any slackness in the belt. Finally place the belt over the tensioner pulley.
- Remove the screwdriver inserted into the cylinder block.
- Slacken the tensioner mounting bolt by ¼ to ⅓ of a turn and allow the spring tension to move the tensioner against the belt.
- Turn the crankshaft anti-clockwise by 3 teeth of the camshaft sprocket from the timing

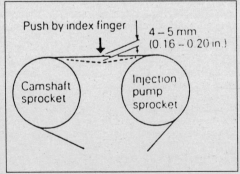

Push by index finger

4 - 5 mm
(0.16 - 0.20 in.)

Camshaft sprocket

Injection pump sprocket

Fig. 15.27. — Checking the timing belt tension.

mark and hold the sprocket in this position. Check at all sprockets that the teeth of the belt have engaged properly. Turn the crankshaft once more in clockwise direction until the timing mark on the camshaft sprocket is aligned as shown in Fig. 15.8.

- Refer to Fig. 16.27 to check the timing belt tension. Use the thumb or index finger and press against the centre of the belt as shown in the illustration. The belt should deflect by the amount shown. If this is not the case, re-tension the belt.
- Re-check that all timing marks are in line, rotate the crankshaft by one revolution in normal direction of rotation and check the timing marks once more. Never turn the crankshaft against the normal direction of rotation.
- Carry out all other operations in reverse order to the removal procedures.

15.4.5.   Balance Shafts

Two balance shafts are fitted to this engine, one at the top of the R.H. side of the cylinder block and the other one at the bottom L.H. side of the block. The shafts are driven by means of two belt wheels, one by the large toothed belt and the other one by a smaller toothed belt. Figs. 15.7 and 15.22 show the layout of the two timing belts.

The front housing, which must be removed to take out the shafts, contains the oil pump and the oil relief valve. An oil suction strainer is fitted to the bottom of the housing. The oil pump is fitted inside the front housing. Fig. 15.28 shows the component parts of the housing together with the drive shafts.

The R.H. shaft rotates in the same direction as the crankshaft; the L.H. shaft rotates in opposite direction. Both shafts are rotating with twice the speed of the crankshaft.

The shafts are running in bearings at the front end rear. The front end of the L.H. shaft is located in the front housing. The R.H. shaft is located at front and rear in a bearing bush, fitted to the cylinder block. The rear end of the L.H. shaft has a similar location. The removal of the shafts has already been described during the dismantling of the engine.

Before fitting the shafts check the front housing for cracks or other damage. Check the bearing bore for the L.H. shaft in the housing. If worn, replace the front housing.

If the engine has been overhauled, replace the oil seals for crankshaft, R.H. balance shaft and oil pump. Otherwise replace the oil seals if the sealing lips are no longer in good condition.

Measure the outside diameter of the bearing journals and the inside diameter of the bearing bores in the cylinder block. If the difference between the two dimensions is excessive the bushes in the block must be replaced. This is a job for a specialist shop as the new bushes must be line-reamed.

Fit the balance shafts by referring to Fig. 15.28, but note some of the points to be observed:

- Insert the two oil pump gears from the front into the front housing, aligning the marks in a similar manner as shown in Fig. 1.66 for the petrol engine. The two alignment marks must be opposite each other. Fit the pump cover and tighten the screws.
- Insert the L.H. shaft into the driven pump gear. Provisionally fit and tighten the screw.
- Lubricate the bearing journals of the R.H. shaft with engine oil and insert into the cylinder block. Wrap masking tape around the end of the crankshaft and place the front housing gasket in position.
- Insert the L.H. shaft into the cylinder block at the same time place the housing over the cylinder block. Insert a screwdriver into the block, as shown in Fig. 15.10) to lock the shaft in position and tighten the shaft bolt.
- Fit the oil suction pipe with a new gasket and tighten the nuts to 1.5 - 2.2 kgm (11 - 16 ft.lb.).
- Coat the oil sump with sealing compound at the points shown in Fig. 1.70 and fit a new

183

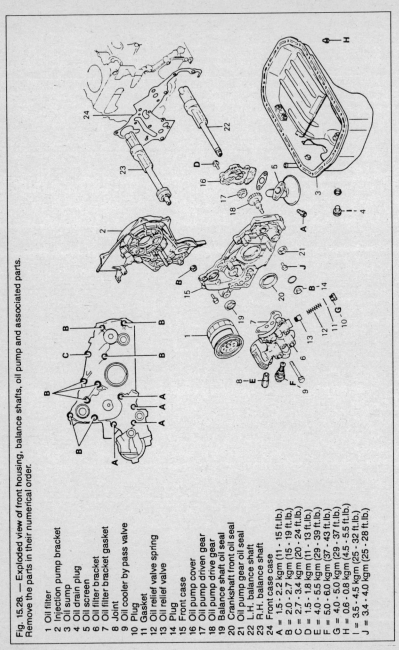

Fig. 15.28. — Exploded view of front housing, balance shafts, oil pump and associated parts.
Remove the parts in their numerical order.

 1 Oil filter
 2 Injection pump bracket
 3 Oil sump
 4 Oil drain plug
 5 Oil screen
 6 Oil filter bracket
 7 Oil filter bracket gasket
 8 Joint
 9 Oil cooler by pass valve
10 Plug
11 Gasket
12 Oil relief valve spring
13 Oil relief valve
14 Plug
15 Front case
16 Oil pump cover
17 Oil pump driven gear
18 Oil pump drive gear
19 Balance shaft oil seal
20 Crankshaft front oil seal
21 Oil pump gear oil seal
22 L.H. balance shaft
23 R.H. balance shaft
24 Front case case

A = 1.5 - 2.2 kgm (11 - 15 ft.lb.)
B = 2.0 - 2.7 kgm (15 - 19 ft.lb.)
C = 2.7 - 3.4 kgm (20 - 24 ft.lb.)
D = 1.5 - 1.8 kgm (11 - 13 ft.lb.)
E = 4.0 - 5.5 kgm (29 - 39 ft.lb.)
F = 5.0 - 6.0 kgm (37 - 43 ft.lb.)
G = 4.0 - 5.0 kgm (29 - 37 ft.lb.)
H = 0.6 - 0.8 kgm (4.5 - 5.5 ft.lb.)
I = 3.5 - 4.5 kgm (25 - 32 ft.lb.)
J = 3.4 - 4.0 kgm (25 - 28 ft.lb.)

15.5. Engine — Tightening Torque Values

Cylinder head bolts:
Engine cold: . . . . 10.5 - 11.5 kgm (76 - 83 ft.lb.)
Engine warm: . . . . 11.5 - 12.5 kgm (83 - 90 ft.lb.)
Camshaft bearing caps:
Bolts for caps and rocker shaft (5): . . . . 2.8 - 3.2 kgm (20 - 23 ft.lb.)
Bolts for caps only (6): . . . . 1.9 - 2.1 kgm (14 - 15 ft.lb.)
Camshaft timing gear bolt: . . . . 8.0 - 10 kgm (58 - 72 ft.lb.)
Injection pump sprocket nut: . . . . 8 - 9 kgm (58 - 65 ft.lb.)
Timing belt idler bolt: . . . . 4.3 - 5.5 kgm (31 - 40 ft.lb.)
Inlet and exhaust manifold: . . . . 1.5 - 2.0 kgm (11 - 14.5 ft.lb.)
Locknut for valve adjusting screws: . . . . 1.2 - 1.7 kgm (8.5 - 12 ft.lb.)
Main bearing cap bolts: . . . . 6.5 - 7.0 kgm (47 - 51 ft.lb.)
Big end bearing cap nuts: . . . . 5.0 - 5.3 kgm (36 - 38 ft.lb.)
Crankshaft pulley bolts: . . . . 2.0 - 3.0 kgm (14 - 22 ft.lb.)
Crankshaft timing gear bolt: . . . . 11 - 13 kgm (80 - 94 ft.lb.)
Oil pump drive gear nut: . . . . 5.0 - 6.0 kgm (36 - 43 ft.lb.)
Belt tensioner nut: . . . . 4.3 - 5.5 kgm (31 - 40 ft.lb.)
Balance shaft timing gear bolt: . . . . 3.5 - 4.0 kgm (25 - 30 ft.lb.)
Front housing bolts:
Mounting bolts (8): . . . . 2.0 - 2.7 kgm (14 - 20 ft.lb.)
One single bolt: . . . . 2.7 - 3.4 kgm (20 - 25 ft.lb.)
Bolt for housing and oil filter bracket: . . . . 1.5 - 2.2 kgm (11 - 16 ft.lb.)
Flywheel bolts: . . . . 13 - 14 kgm (94 - 101 ft.lb.)
Drive plate bolts (automatic): . . . . 13 - 14 kgm (94 - 101 ft.lb.)
Engine mounting bolts: . . . . See Section 1.1.1
Oil pump cover: . . . . 1.5 - 1.7 kgm (11 - 12 ft.lb.)
Oil pressure switch: . . . . 1.5 - 2.1 kgm (11 - 14 ft.lb.)
Oil sump bolts: . . . . 0.6 - 0.7 kgm (4.5 - 5 ft.lb.)
Sump oil drain plug: . . . . 3.5 - 4.5 kgm (25 - 33 ft.lb.)
Injection pump bracket bolts (3): . . . . 3.0 - 4.2 kgm (22 - 30 ft.lb.)
Injection pump mounting bracket nut: . . . . 2.0 - 2.7 kgm (14 - 20 ft.lb.)
Oil pump driven gear bolt (front of balance shaft): . . . . 3.4 - 4.0 kgm (25 - 29 ft.lb.)
Oil pressure relief valve: . . . . 4 - 5 kgm (30 - 36 ft.lb.)
Starter motor bolts: . . . . 2.2 - 3.1 kgm (14.5 - 30 ft.lb.)
Alternator mounting: . . . . 2.0 - 2.4 kgm (14.5 - 15 ft.lb.)
Alternator belt adjusting link: . . . . 2 - 3 kgm (14 - 21 ft.lb.)
Exhaust tube to manifold: . . . . 1.5 - 2.5 kgm (11 - 18 ft.lb.)
Exhaust tube to silencer (clamp): . . . . 1.0 - 1.5 kgm (7 - 11 ft.lb.)
Rear silencer to front silencer: . . . . 2 - 3 kgm (14 - 21 ft.lb.)
Transmission mountings: . . . . See Fig. 1.7
Front engine mounting to engine: . . . . See Fig. 1.7
Roller stopper brackets: . . . . See Fig. 1.7
Clutch bolts: . . . . 1.5 - 2.2 kgm (11 - 18 ft.lb.)
Transmission case to engine: . . . . 4.3 - 5 kgm (31 - 36 ft.lb.)

15.6. Lubrication System

The lubrication system is constructed in similar manner as specified in Section 2.0 for the petrol engines., i.e. a gear-type oil pump, fitted to front housing, driven through toothed belt, with the L.H. balance shaft driven from pump gearwheel. Refer to Section 2., commencing on page 68 for details of removal and installation, pump overhaul, oil filter, oil level and oil pressure switch which are treated in similar manner for this engine.

15.7. Diesel Fuel Injection System

Absolute cleanliness is essential during any repairs or work on the diesel fuel injection system, irrespective of the nature of the work in question. Thoroughly clean union nuts before unscrewing any of the injection pipes.

The fuel injection pump cannot repaired or overhauled and an exchange pump or a new pump must be fitted in case of malfunction or damage.

The adjustment of the injection timing and also the removal and installation of the injection pump requires certain special tools and these operations should not be undertaken if these are not available. The following text describes these operations, in case that the listed special tools can be obtained or hired.

Diesel engines either operate with direct injection or indirect injection. The Mitsubishi diesel engine operates with indirect injection, i.e. the fuel is injected into a pre-chamber in the cylinder head which is in connection with the combustion chamber. The combustion is initiated in the pre-chamber and the resulting pressure increase directs the burning fuel particles into the main combustion chamber, where it is fully burnt.

15.7.0. PRECAUTIONS WHEN WORKING ON DIESEL INJECTION SYSTEMS

Whenever repairs are carried out on a diesel fuel injection system, whatever the extent, observe the greatest cleanliness, apart from the following points:

- Only carry out work on diesel injection systems under the cleanest of conditions. Work in the open air should only be carried out when there is no wind, to prevent dust entering open connections.
- Before removal of any union nut clean all around it with a clean cloth.
- Removed parts must only be deposited on a clean bench or table and must be covered with a sheet of plastic or paper. Never use fluffy shop rags to clean parts.
- All open or partially dismantled parts of the injection system must be fully covered or kept in a cardboard box, if the repair is not carried out immediately.
- Check the parts for cleanliness before installation.
- Never use an air line to clean the exterior of the engine when connections of the injection system are open. With the availability of air compressors which can be plugged into a cigar lighter socket, you may be tempted to use air for cleaning.
- Take care not to allow diesel fuel in contact with rubber hoses or other rubber parts. Immediately clean such a hose if it should happen accidently.

15.7.1 FUEL FILTER

The fuel filter should be replaced in approx. every 20,000 miles, but must be drained of accumulated water, when the fuel filter warning light indicates that excess water is in the filter. To drain the filter, slacken the water drain plug at the bottom of the filter, as shown in Fig. 15.29 and operate the priming pump knob, as shown on the R.H. side of Fig. 15.29, until enough fuel has run out to clear the water.

To replace the filter insert, proceed as follows:

Remove the fuel filler cap to lower the pressure in the tank. Disconnect the electrical leads from the water level sensor connector and the wiring harness connector. Grip the fuel filter with both hand and unscrew the filter element from the filter head.

To remove the complete filter, disconnect the fuel hose and unscrew the two filter securing bolts, shown in Fig. 15.30 by the arrows.

The installation is a reversal of the removal procedure. The fuel system must now be bled of air as follows:

- Slacken the bleeder plug on the side of the fuel filter. Operate the hand pump (priming pump), as shown in Fig. 15.29, until the fuel running out of the bleeder plug hole is free of air bubbles. Catch the draining diesel fuel with a thick rag.

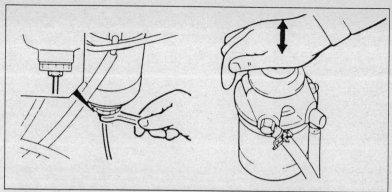

Fig. 15.29. — The L.H. view shows how the water is drained from the filter. Operate the priming pump plunger as shown in the R.H. view until fuel, free of water is running out of the drain plug opening.

- Tighten the bleeder plug, clean off all traces of diesel fuel and continue to operate the pump knob until it feels heavy.

NOTE The fuel system must be bled of air when the tank is empty, when the fuel filter has been replaced or the fuel lines have been disconnected. If air remains in the injection system it will be difficult to start the engine. Therefore, make sure that all has been removed in the manner described.

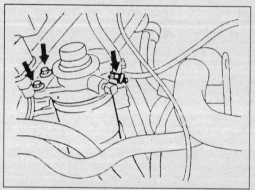

Fig. 15.30. — The arrows show the two securing screws for the fuel filter body and the electrical connector.

15.7.2. INJECTION PUMP — REMOVAL, INSTALLATION, AND TIMING

The timing adjustment of the injection pump requires the use of special tools. The injection pump should, therefore, only be removed if these can be obtained to carry out the job. It should also be remembered that the timing belt must be removed and refitted in order to remove the pump.

- Disconnect the two water hoses from the thermostat housing. Keep the ends of the removed water hoses higher than the cylinder head to prevent coolant flowing out of the hoses.
- Disconnect the battery.
- Remove the upper timing belt cover.
- Disconnect the plug for the electrical connector of the fuel pump.
- Disconnect the union nuts connecting the injector pipes to the injectors and the injection

pump. When slackening the pipes at the pump ends, counterhold the delivery valve holder on the injection pump head with an open-ended spanner to prevent the valve holders from rotating, as shown in Fig. 15.31. Mark the pipes before removing them.

- Disconnect the fuel feed and return hoses from the injection pump. Suitably plug-up the hose ends to prevent entry of dirt. Fuel will squirt out as soon as the union nuts are slack and the necessary care must be taken.

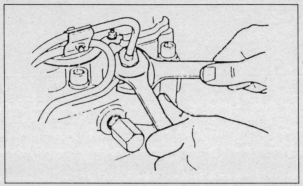

Fig. 15.31. — Slacken the injection pipes on the injection pump by means of two open-ended spanners.

- Disconnect the accelerator cable from the pump.
- Remove the nut and spring washer securing the injection pump sprocket. Take care not to drop the nut and washer into the lower timing belt cover during removal.
- Rotate the engine until the piston of the No. 1 cylinder is at top dead centre in the compression stroke.
- Use a puller, as shown in Fig. 15.32 and remove the pump drive gear from the shaft. Take care not to damage the sprocket or shock-load the pump shaft. Also take care not to place the timing belt under excessive stress, as the sprocket moves off the injection pump shaft. After removal do not rotate the crankshaft and make sure the timing belt cannot slip off the crankshaft or camshaft gearwheel.

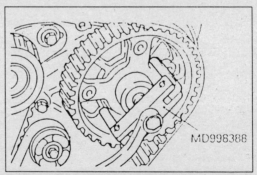

Fig. 15.32. — The injection pump sprocket must be removed with a two-arm puller.

- Remove the pump attachment bolts, nuts and washers and remove the pump. Make sure not to lift the pump on the accelerator lever.

The installation of the pump is a reversal of the removal procedure. Adjust the timing belt tension as described in the relevant section.

The injection pump must now be adjusted as follows, but it must be noted that apart from

188

special tools some knowledge is required to set the pump to the correct timing position. Provided that these conditions are met, proceed as follows:

● If the engine has been rotated in the meantime, reset it to the top dead centre position in the No. 1 cylinder, making sure that the compression stroke has been obtained. The notch in the crankshaft pulley must be opposite the "TDC" mark on the timing indicator, as shown in Fig. 15.33.

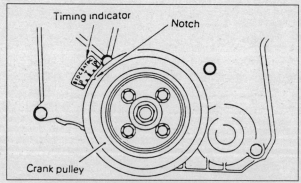

Fig. 15.33. — The top dead centre position of the No. 1 cylinder.

● Slacken, but do not remove the union nuts of the four injection pipes on the injection pump side, using two open-ended spanners, as shown in Fig. 15.31.
● Slacken, but do not remove the two nuts and bolts securing the injection pump.
● Remove the plug in the centre of the four pipes and insert the special tool MD998384 into the plug hole and screw into place. The end of the plunger must protude by 10 mm (0.4 in.) before the tool and a dial gauge is fitted as shown in Fig. 15.34.

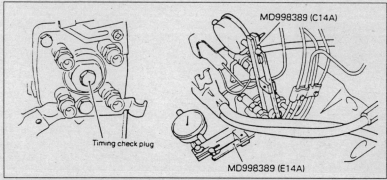

Fig. 15.34. — The location of the plug (left) and the fitted special tool with a dial gauge (right). The lower of the two tools is used for the Space Wagon engine.

● Turn the crankshaft until the notch in the pulley is approx. 30° before the top dead centre in the compression stroke of No. 1 piston. In this position set the dial gauge to zero (Fig. 15.35). Slightly turn the crankshaft backwards and forwards to make sure that the dial gauge cannot deviate from the "Zero" position.

- Turn the crankshaft in normal direction of rotation until the notch in the crankshaft pulley is opposite the 7° after top dead centre mark (Fig. 15.36). In this position read off the dial indicator reading. This should be between 0.97-1.03 mm (0.038-0.041 in.), with 1.0 mm (0.04 in.) the best value when adjustments are necessary.

- If the dial indicator reading is not within the values given, rotate the injection pump to the right or left, in accordance with Fig. 15.37, until the dial indicator shows the above value. Tighten the pump bolts and nuts to 2.0-2.7 kgm (15-19 ft.lb.),

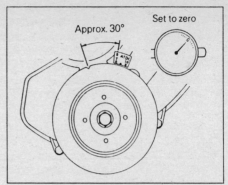

Fig. 15.35. — Adjusting the injection timing. The dial gauge is set to "Zero" when the the notch in the crankshaft is set to 30° before top dead centre of No. 1 piston.

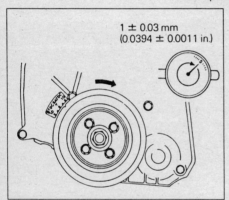

1 ± 0.03 mm
(0.0394 ± 0.0011 in.)

Fig. 15.36. — Rotate the crankshaft in its normal direction of rotation to the 7° mark on the timing scale and check the dial gauge reading.

- Turn the crankshaft once more to the position shown in Fig. 15.35 and repeat the measurement. The correct dial gauge reading should now be obtained.

- Remove the special tool and the dial gauge, fit the plug with a new copper washer.

- Fit the injection pipes with the union nuts and tighten the nuts with two open-ended spanners, as shown in Fig. 15.31. The torque must be estimated not to exceed 2.3-3.7 kgm (17-26 ft.lb.).

- After fitting the injection pipes, bleed the fuel system as described in Section 15.7.1 to eject the air out of the pipes and connections.

15.7.3. INJECTOR HOLDERS AND INJECTORS

15.7.3.0. Removal and Installation

Refer to Fig. 15.38 for details of the parts to be removed. Disconnect the fuel return hose after opening the two clamps. Unscrew the fuel return pipe securing nut. Counterhold the hexagon of the return pipe connection with an open-ended spanner, similar as shown in Fig. 15.31, to prevent it from rotating with the nut.

Remove the fuel return pipe from all injector holders and remove the gaskets. The injectors must be removed with a long 22 mm socket, to reach the hexagon. Remove the gasket from the hole in the cylinder head.

The installation is a reversal of the removal procedure. Always replace the nozzle tip gasket. Tighten the injector holder to 5.0 - 6.0 kgm (36 - 43 ft.lb.).

Refit the fuel return pipe with new gaskets and fit the nuts. Counterhold the hexagon of the connectors and tighten the nuts to 3.0 - 4.0 kgm (22 - 29 ft.lb.). Refit the fuel return hose and

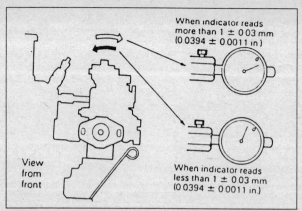

Fig. 15.37. — Rotate the injection pump in the direction shown to set the injection timing.

bleed the fuel system as described in Section 15.7.1 to remove all air out of the fuel injection system (also see Fig. 15.29, right).

NOTE: The injection pressure of the injectors should only be tested in a specialist shop. Never attempt to carry out this operation yourself.

To find a faulty injector, unscrew the union nuts one after the other at the injector connection and start the engine. Run the engine at increased speed. If the engine noise does not change after a certain injection pipe has been disconnected, the faulty injector has been found.

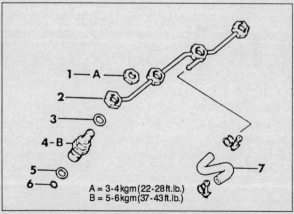

Fig. 15.38. — Removal and installation details for the injectors. The letters refer to the tightening torques.

1 Nut
2 Fuel return pipe
3 Return pipe gasket
4 Injection nozzle
5 Nozzle holder gasket
6 Nozzle tip gasket
7 Fuel return hose

15.7.4. GLOW PLUGS

The glow plugs receive electrical current when the ignition switch is turned to the glow position. The plugs receive a voltage of at least 11.5 volts and are heated within seconds to a an approx. temperature of up to 1100° C. The glow time depends on the temperature of the engine and may be between 25 seconds during very cold temperatures and 2 seconds during the summer months. If the engine is not started immediately, the power supply is interrupted and will be operated once more when the key is turned into the glow position.

Because of the high temperatures it is quite possible that one of the glow plugs burns out. Glow plugs can also be damaged through faulty injectors, wrong injection times and low injection pressure.

The plugs are located in the cylinder head. Remove the nuts from the ends of the plugs and remove the bus bar. Unscrew the plug in question. A socket with extension and ratchet should be used to remove the plugs. Tighten the new plug to 1.5 - 2.0 kgm (11 - 15 ft.lb.).

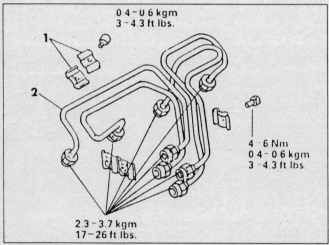

Fig. 15.39. — Removal and installation details for the injection pipes.

15.7.5. INJECTION PIPES

Fig. 15.39 shows the set of injection pipes (2) together with their attachment parts (1) and tightening torques. Always hold the connector of the respective connection when a pipe is slackened or tightened. Use two open-ended spanners as shown in Fig. 15.29. The fuel system must be bled of air as described in Section 15.7.1 after a pipe has been disconnected.

15.7.6. IDLE SPEED ADJUSTMENT

Run the engine to operating temperature and switch off all lights and accessories. The transmission must be in neutral, if an automatic box is fitted.

A good idle speed can only be obtained if the valve clearances and the injection timing are correctly adjusted. A revolution counter must be connected in accordance with the instructions of the manufacturer.

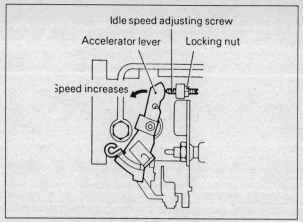

Fig. 15.40.—Idle speed adjusting details.

- Start the engine and read off the idle speed.
- If the speed is not within 800 ± 50 rpm, refer to Fig. 15.40 and slacken the locking nut. Use a screwdriver and turn the idle speed adjusting screw until the correct speed has been obtained. The screw is screwed further into to increase the idle speed, as shown by the arrow.
- Counterhold the adjusting screw against rotation and tighten the locking nut.

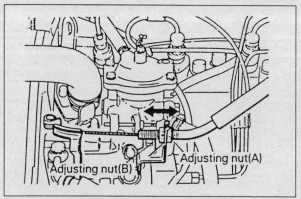

Fig. 15.41.—Throttle cable adjustment.

15.7.7.   THROTTLE CABLE ADJUSTMENT

The engine must be at operating temperature, with the idle speed correctly adjusted, before the throttle cable can be adjusted. The adjusting point is shown in Fig. 15.41 from which can be seen that two nuts are used to move the cable in its bracket. First slacken the two nuts so that the throttle lever is free. Now turn the adjusting nut (A) until the throttle lever just starts to move. From this position turn the nut backwards by ½ of a turn and tighten the nut (B). Operate the accelerator pedal and check that the throttle lever can travel between "fully closed" and "fully open.

15.7.8. AIR CLEANER

Fig. 15.42 shows details of the air cleaner. An air intake hose, attached with two hose clips, is fitted between the air cleaner cover elbow and the air inlet. The removal and installation of the air filter element and/or the complete air cleaner is self-evident from the illustration.

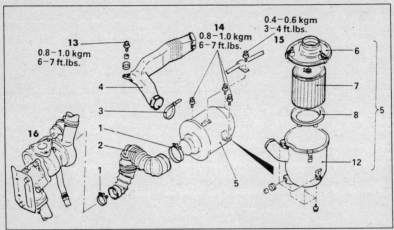

Fig. 15.42 — The diesel engine air cleaner.

1	Hose clamps	9	Air flow sensor
2	Air intake hose	10	"O" sealing ring
3	Hose clamp	11	Crankcase ventilation filter
4	Air duct	12	Air cleaner body
5	Air cleaner assembly	13	Screw, 0.8 - 1.0 kgm
6	Air cleaner cover	14	Screw, 0.8 - 1.0 kgm
7	Air cleaner element	15	Screw, 0.4 - 0.6 kgm
8	Plate assembly	16	Turbo charger

15.7.9. TIGHTENING TORQUES

Injectors and attachments: . . . . See Fig. 15.38
Injection pipes: . . . . See Fig. 15.39
Injection pump securing nuts: . . . . 1.5 - 2.2 kgm (11 - 16 ft.lb.)
Injection pump securing bolts: . . . . 2.0 - 2.7 kgm (15 - 19 ft.lb.)
Injection pump sprocket nut: . . . . 8.0 - 9.0 kgm (58 - 65 ft.lb.)
Timing check plug: . . . . 0.8 - 1.0 kgm (6 - 7.2 ft.lb.)
Pump bracket bolt: . . . . 1.8 - 2.5 kgm (13 - 18 ft.lb.)
Fuel Filter:
    Filter cartridge: . . . . 1.2 - 1.5 kgm (9 - 11 ft.lb.)
    Water level sensor: . . . . 1.2 - 1.5 kgm (9 - 11 ft.lb.)
    Drain and bleeder plugs: . . . . 0.4 - 0.6 kgm (3 - 4 ft.lb.)

15.8. Exhaust System and Turbo Charger System

15.8.0. EXHAUST SYSTEM

Fig. 15.43 shows the exhaust system for the diesel engine model and the petrol models, together with all tightening torques. Removal and installation of the individual parts can be carried out by referring to this illustration. The following points must be noted:

Fig. 15.43. — The component parts for the exhaust system for the petrol model (top) and diesel model (bottom). The letters refer to the tightening torques.

1 Main silencer
2 Hanger bracket
3 Rubber O-ring
4 Suspension bracket
5 Suspension bracket
6 Pipe to manifold nuts, 2 - 3 kgm
7 Front exhaust pipe
8 Gasket
9 Rubber hanger

A = 2 - 3 kgm (14 - 22 ft.lb.)
B = 3 - 4 kgm (22 - 29 ft.lb.)
C = 1 - 2 kgm (7 - 14 ft.lb.)
D = 1 - 1.5 kgm (1 - 11 ft.lb.)
E = 0.5 - 1 kgm (3.5 - 7 ft.lb.)

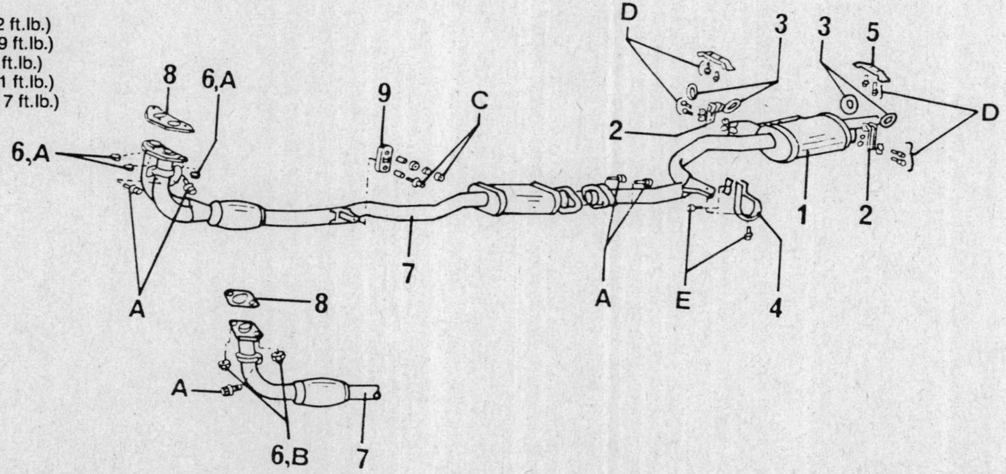

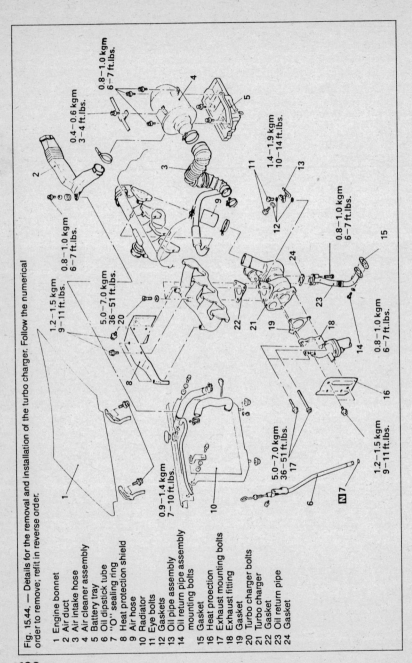

Fig. 15.44. — Details for the removal and installation of the turbo charger. Follow the numerical order to remove; refit in reverse order.

1 Engine bonnet
2 Air duct
3 Air intake hose
4 Air cleaner assembly
5 Battery tray
6 Oil dipstick tube
7 "O" sealing ring
8 Heat protection shield
9 Air hose
10 Radiator
11 Eye bolts
12 Gaskets
13 Oil pipe assembly
14 Oil return pipe assembly mounting bolts
15 Gasket
16 Heat proection
17 Exhaust mounting bolts
18 Exhaust fitting
19 Gasket
20 Turbo charger bolts
21 Turbo charger
22 Gasket
23 Oil return pipe
24 Gasket

196

- Check all rubber parts for damage or deterioration and replace if necessary.
- When fitting the main silencer (1) and the front exhaust pipe (7), temporarily fit the front exhaust pipe and the muffler in that order and tighten the bolts and nuts. Check that the rubber suspension parts are not stretched.
- After installation check the gaps between all parts of the exhaust system and parts of the chassis/vehicle. Start the engine and listen to rattling noises. The same check should be carried out when the vehicle is driven.

15.8.1.   TURBO CHARGER SYSTEM

Fig. 15.43 shows the component parts of the turbo charger system, including the inlet and the exhaust manifold. The removal and installation of the several parts are in general straight forward, but the following points must be noted:

- After disconnecting the connection between the turbo charger assembly (21) and the exhaust fitting (18), slacken the turbo charger mounting bolts (20). Remove the bolts one after the other to avoid dropping of the turbo charger.
- Remove the turbo charger from the engine, taking care not to catch the oil return pipe on the engine.

During installation fill the turbo charger with clean engine through the opening where pipe (13) is to be connected. This will give the turbo charger enough oil for the initial running of the engine.

Wiring Diagram
SPACE WAGON for Europe

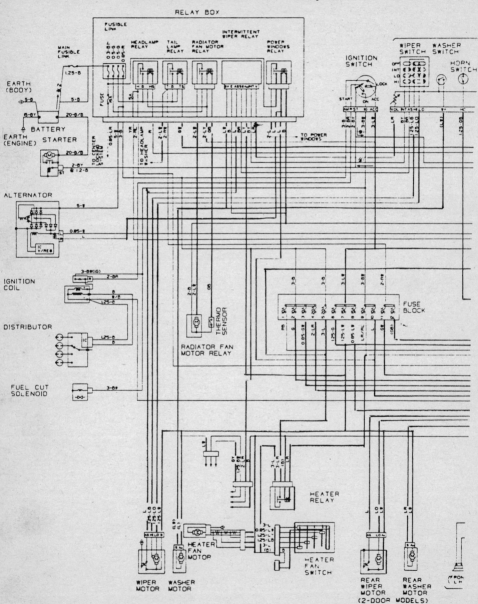

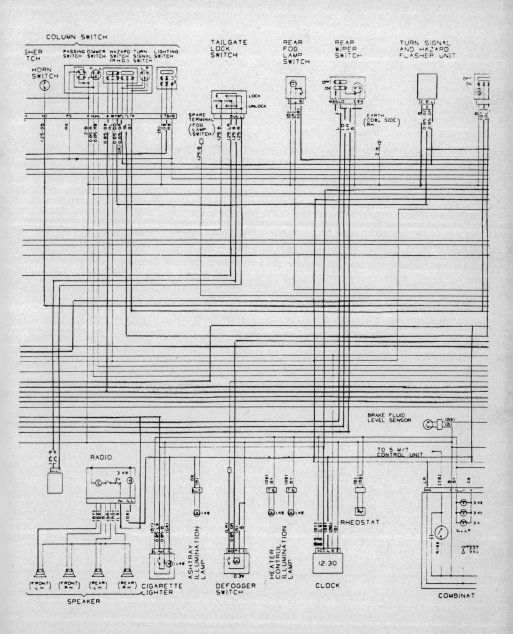

COLUMN SWITCH

SHER TCH

HORN SWITCH

PASSING SWITCH | DIMMER SWITCH | HAZARD SWITCH (R.H.D) | TURN SIGNAL SWITCH | LIGHTING SWITCH

TAILGATE LOCK SWITCH

LOCK
UNLOCK

SPARE TERMINAL (FOG LAMP SWITCH)

REAR FOG LAMP SWITCH

REAR WIPER SWITCH

WASLO

EARTH (COWL SIDE) RM

TURN SIGNAL AND HAZARD FLASHER UNIT

BRAKE FLUID LEVEL SENSOR

TO 5 M/T CONTROL UNIT

RADIO

CIGARETTE LIGHTER

ASHTRAY ILLUMINATION LAMP

DEFOGGER SWITCH

HEATER CONTROL ILLUMINATION LAMP

CLOCK

12·30

RHEOSTAT

COMBINAT

(FRONT LH) | (FRONT RM) | (REAR LH) | (REAR RM)

SPEAKER

199

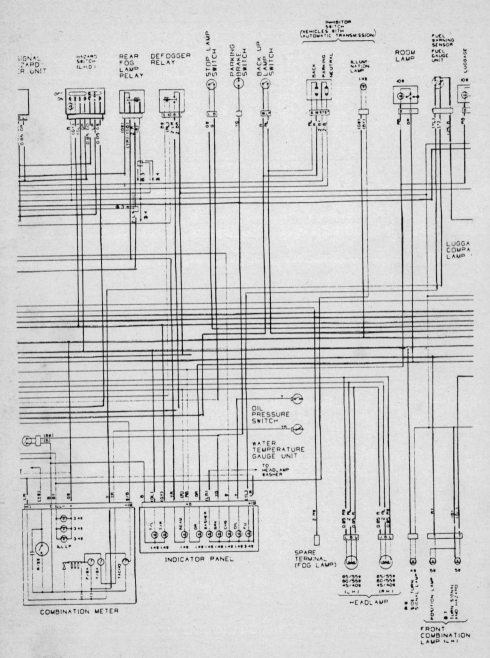

200

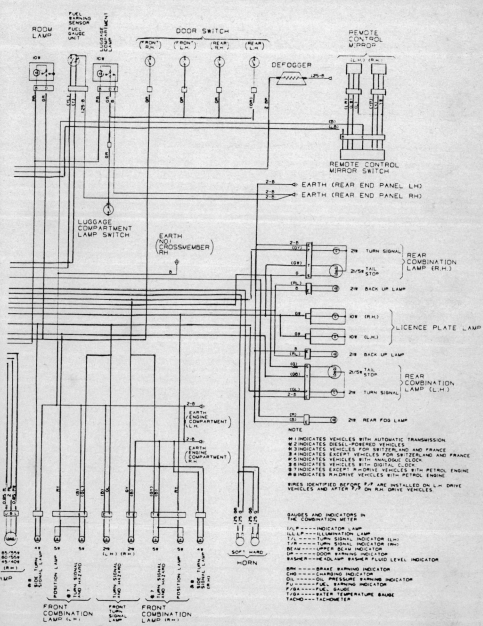

NOTE

✱ 1 INDICATES VEHICLES WITH AUTOMATIC TRANSMISSION.
✱ 2 INDICATES DIESEL-POWERED VEHICLES.
✱ 3 INDICATES VEHICLES FOR SWITZERLAND AND FRANCE
✱ 4 INDICATES EXCEPT VEHICLES FOR SWITZERLAND AND FRANCE
✱ 5 INDICATES VEHICLES WITH ANALOGUE CLOCK.
✱ 6 INDICATES VEHICLES WITH DIGITAL CLOCK.
✱ 7 INDICATES EXCEPT R.H.DRIVE VEHICLES WITH PETROL ENGINE
✱ 8 INDICATES R.H.DRIVE VEHICLES WITH PETROL ENGINE

WIRES IDENTIFIED BEFORE F/F ARE INSTALLED ON L.H. DRIVE
VEHICLES AND AFTER F/F ON R.H. DRIVE VEHICLES.

GAUGES AND INDICATORS IN
THE COMBINATION METER

I/LP----INDICATOR LAMP
I.LLP---ILLUMINATION LAMP
T/L-----TURN SIGNAL INDICATOR (LH)
T/R-----TURN SIGNAL INDICATOR (RH)
BEAM----UPPER BEAM INDICATOR
DR------DOOR WARNING INDICATOR
WASHER--HEADLAMP WASHER FLUID LEVEL INDICATOR

BRK-----BRAKE WARNING INDICATOR
CHG-----CHARGING INDICATOR
OIL-----OIL PRESSURE WARNING INDICATOR
FU------FUEL WARNING INDICATOR
F/GA----FUEL GAUGE
T/GA----WATER TEMPERATURE GAUGE
TACHO---TACHOMETER

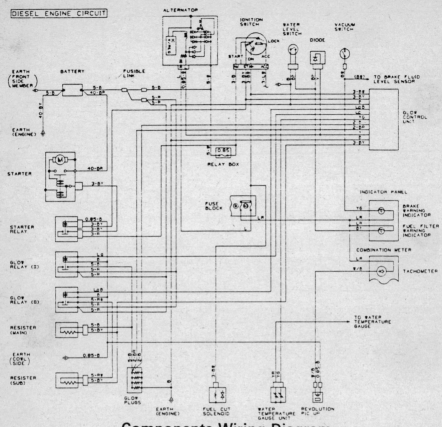

Components Wiring Diagram
SPACE WAGON for Europe

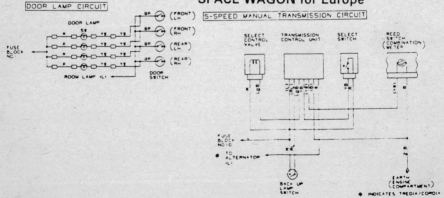

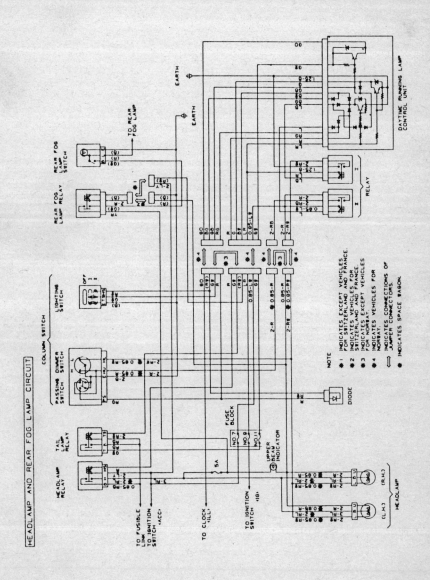

HEADLAMP AND REAR FOG LAMP CIRCUIT

203

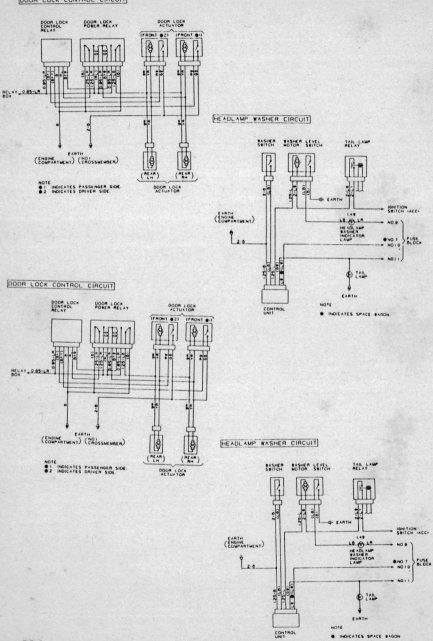

DOOR LOCK CONTROL CIRCUIT

HEADLAMP WASHER CIRCUIT

DOOR LOCK CONTROL CIRCUIT

HEADLAMP WASHER CIRCUIT